WALKING

TO

CAMELOT

LINCOLNSHIRE

Boston

The Wash

Frampton Marsh
River Welland
Surfleet
The Fens
Fosdyke Bridge
Spalding

Baston
Whitwell
Greatford
Oakham
Greatford
Brooke
Stamford
Rutland Water
Peterborough
RUTLAND

Leicester
LEICESTERSHIRE

Hallaton
Market Harborough

Birmingham
Coventry
Great Oxendon

NORTHAMPTONSHIRE

Warwick
Great Brington
WARWICKSHIRE
Flore
Farthingstone
Stratford-upon-Avon
Bedford

Warmington
Edgehill
Chipping Warden
Cotswolds
Banbury

Rollright Stones
Long Compton
Stow-on-the-Wold
Adlestrop
Cheltenham
Lower Slaughter
Leckhampton Hill
Cold Aston
Gloucester
Northleach
Widford
Rendcomb
Chedworth
Oxford

Cherington
Cirencester
*Thames and
Severn Canal*
Avening
OXFORDSHIRE
Tetbury

Severn
Swindon
M25
LONDON
Thames

Castle Combe
Reading

Bristol
Box
Bath
Avoncliff
Bradford-on-Avon
Mells
Beckington

SOMERSET
WILTSHIRE
A303
Glastonbury
Bruton
Alfred's Tower
Castle Cary
Redlynch
Cadbury Castle
South Cadbury
Sandford Orcas
Sherborne
Southampton
Dorset Downs
A31

Evershot
DORSET
Cattistock
Cerne Abbas Giant
Maiden Newton
Abbotsbury
Bournemouth

Chesil Beach
Weymouth
English Channel

Portland Bill

0   20 miles

0   20 kilometres

N
W   E
S

Walking

to

Camelot

*A Pilgrimage through the Heart
of Rural England*

JOHN A. CHERRINGTON

Figure.1
Vancouver / Berkeley

Cataloguing data available from Library and Archives Canada
ISBN 978-1-927958-62-9 (pbk.)
ISBN 978-1-927958-63-6 (ebook)
ISBN 978-1-927958-64-3 (pdf)

Editing by Scott Steedman
Copy editing by Stephanie Fysh
Map by Eric Leinburger
Design by Natalie Olsen
Cover images © giftgruen, johny schorle, morningside, pencake, sure / photocase.com
Printed and bound in Canada by Friesens
Distributed in the U.S. by Publishers Group West

Figure 1 Publishing Inc.
Vancouver BC Canada
www.figure1pub.com

To my wife, Dee.

Walking is a subversive detour, the scenic route

through a half-abandoned landscape of ideas

and experiences.

—— REBECCA SOLNIT——
Wanderlust: A History of Walking

In the days of her childhood the footpath over the meadow had been a hard, well-defined track, much used by men going to their fieldwork, by children going blackberrying . . . and, on Sunday evenings, by pairs of sweethearts who preferred the seclusion of the fields and copses beyond to the more public pathways. The footpath had led to a farmhouse and a couple of cottages, and, to the dwellers in these, it had been not only the way to church and school and market, but also the first stage in every journey. It had led to London, to Queensland and Canada, to the Army depot and the troopship. Wedding and christening parties had footed it merrily, and at least one funeral had passed that way.

—— FLORA THOMPSON ——
Still Glides the Stream

*Karl, John, and Colin
resting at their farm B&B.*

Still round the corner there may wait

A new road or a secret gate

. . .

The road goes ever on and on

Down from the door where it began.

Now far ahead the road has gone,

And I must follow, if I can,

Pursuing it with eager feet,

Until it joins some larger way,

Where many paths and errands meet.

And whither then? I cannot say.

— J.R.R. TOLKIEN —
The Lord of the Rings

INTRODUCTION

FISHING BOATS CRAM the muddy-banked sliver of salt water known as The Haven. An old-fashioned windmill looms in the misty distance. Battered carnival caravans greet us on the town's outskirts, where a few modern-day gypsies tinker in the dusk with gaily painted circus equipment. Pungent aromas of fish, tar, hemp, and cotton candy waft through the air. The pubs are smoke-filled and raucous.

Karl and I are surprised to see groups of leather-jacketed young men and women just hanging about, smoking and drinking, as we trudge by Market Square with our heavy backpacks. We pass a plethora of shops and eateries — including The Russian Restaurant, Baltic Foods, and a few Chinese takeaways. We stop in one doorway and watch as industrious waiters and well-dressed patrons speak in various Eastern European languages. Town centre lies in the shadow of St. Botolph's Church, the city's best-known landmark, known to locals as Boston Stump.

We arrived in Boston, Lincolnshire, by train after a mad dash from Heathrow and with the jet lag that always brings on my flu symptoms but never affects Karl and his cast-iron stomach. We had taken short walks together in the English countryside the year before and been smitten with the walking bug. Now we had come to Boston to walk the Macmillan Way, a 290-mile route running from this ancient port on the North Sea halfway to Scotland all the way through the heart of England to the English Channel.

Karl is lean, short, muscular, half deaf, and tough as nails. He is also seventy-four years old and a proud Canadian of mixed Irish and Dutch ancestry. When he's in one of his lighter moods — usually after a couple of pints — he'll quote poetry and be self-deprecating, with his "wooden shoes, wooden head, and wouldn't listen." At other times, he's a bullheaded, pugnacious former logging camp manager and bantamweight boxer who is afraid of nothing. When visiting Palm Springs recently, he and his wife were attacked at night by a knife-wielding assailant who demanded the keys to their car. Karl walked backwards to a vacant condo, smashed the window with his bare hands, pulled out a shard of broken glass, and chased the young assailant away. You get the picture. The cops were so impressed they even paid for the broken window.

Karl also can keep walking pace with most Olympic athletes. He is a man of intensity, endurance, and integrity. So I made him promise that on this trip he would let me pause now and then to look at historic buildings and take photographs instead of always charging ahead to the next village and getting himself lost or into mischief.

Nowhere else in the world can one walk in literally any direction on footpaths over private land throughout the entire country. Britain has over 140,000 miles of footpaths, green lanes, bridleways, and other public rights-of-way, many of which date from medieval times or earlier. Unlike in North America, roads and paths traditionally travelled by the populace remained in the public domain long after new asphalt routes jammed with motorized transport came to dominate the landscape.

Karl was seeking adventure and wanted to prove to himself that he was still tough enough to complete a long-distance walk. At fifty-four, I was twenty years younger but not in shape, having led a sedentary life as a solicitor in the village of Fort Langley, near Vancouver, British Columbia. I had visited England in past years on driving trips, even taken short walks, but this would be a new challenge. The guidebook promised varying landscapes — beginning in Lincolnshire with fenlands, then on through the rolling hills of Northamptonshire and the enchanting, honey-coloured Cotswolds, then Somerset, with its legendary Castle Camelot in Cadbury, and finally, on into Dorset's rolling hills to emerge at Chesil Beach on the English Channel.

The Macmillan Way was established as a memorial to Douglas Macmillan, who founded the Society for the Prevention and Relief of Cancer in 1911. The charity, now known as Macmillan Cancer Support, helps people cope with cancer and ensures that within the vast labyrinth of Britain's health system, patients receive the best possible care. More than two thousand nurses and three hundred doctors work with the Macmillan charity around the country, making it one of the foremost charities in the nation. Many people walk the Way to raise funds for Macmillan Cancer Support and to raise awareness for both cancer and fitness.

Most long-distance paths in England run east–west or follow the coastline. Macmillan trends in a steady southwest direction. The route passes through few park areas. It is truly a test of private land walking rights. I was intrigued by the challenge of "giving it a go," as the English say — combining my love of history with my passion for rural landscapes. You cannot walk two miles in England without experiencing some cultural or historical artifact, landmark, or memorial. Rolling hills are interspersed with coombs, fens, and meadows. To walk the Way in springtime would be divine, the verdant English countryside alive with hawthorn and honeysuckle blooming down green lanes, with the singing and swooping of swallows, thrushes, larks, and wood pigeons coursing through the fields and woods. And it would be challenging to do it with just a backpack, booking ahead at bed and breakfasts en route. Alas, blisters, bulls, and English rain are also part of the joie de vivre of long-distance walking.

Imagine my surprise when I learned while planning the trip that Macmillan Way also passed through the ancient village of Cherington, where my forebears lived as early as the Domesday Book of 1086. I began to envision this walk as a link to the past, a pilgrimage to places that have played an important part in shaping the life of my ancestors and hence my own. My mother had recently passed away, so it was time for a spell of reflection. Then too, there was Cadbury Camelot, reputed site of King Arthur's legendary hill fort, conveniently en route.

It has always struck me as bizarre that academics and journalists cavalierly separate the world into neat divisions based on economic status, such as "third world" versus "industrialized world." In many ways a villager in Canada has more in common with a villager in the UK, Spain, or even Japan than she does with an urban dweller in Toronto, London, or Madrid. Those who reside in small towns or villages have not severed their connection with the land.

Villages have played a vital role in human history. They represent the first stage in our civilization, when people began to settle down on the land and engage in agriculture. Up to the Industrial Revolution, production in most countries flourished chiefly in a home milieu. That there may be a role for the village today seems manifest, as millions of people around the globe are returning to the cottage-industry concept of working from home — not with a loom or a blacksmith's anvil, but with computers.

The importance of the village was touched on by the travel writer H.V. Morton, who in his *In Search of England* had this to say in 1927: "That village, so often near a Roman road, is sometimes clearly a Saxon hamlet with its great house, its church, and its cottages. There is no question of its death; it is, in fact, a lesson in survival, and a streak of ancient wisdom warns us . . . to keep an eye on the old thatch because we may have to go back there some day, if not for the sake of our bodies, perhaps for the sake of our souls."

Joanna Trollope opines: "For all the drawbacks of rural life and its tough and uncompromising history, the English continue to feel a determined union with the countryside. It is a sense of both belonging and finding salvation there, in a community — preferably consisting of church, pub, farms, cottages, a small school and a Big House. We have, we English, a national village cult; we cherish the myth that out there, among fields and woods, there still survives a timeless natural innocence and lack of corruption."

In a very real sense, villages represent the underlay, the basic fabric of British culture. It is the common footpath, bridleway, and green lane that draw the threads of this fabric together, like some vast spiderweb stretching outward around the country.

The signposts, stiles, lanes, and paths of England have become iconic, and survive within a swirling milieu of fast-paced asphalt and metal modernity. Yet they form an indissoluble link with England's past. Nathaniel Hawthorne once observed: "These by-paths . . . admit the wayfarer into the very heart of rural life, and yet do not burden him with a sense of intrusiveness. He has a right to go whithersoever they lead him; for, with all their shaded privacy, they are as much the property of the public as the dusty high-road itself, and even by an older tenure . . . An American farmer would plough across any such path . . . but here it is protected by law, and still more by the sacredness that inevitably springs up, in this soil, along the well-defined footprints of the centuries."

Walking is the most popular outdoor recreational pursuit in Britain. People can trek on any one of several dozen long-distance footpaths, defined as any route over 31 miles. Some are loop walks, which allow one to park at the village church, walk several hours, devour a ploughman's lunch at a pub en route, and be back at one's car without retracing one's steps. That said, not enough Brits get out and do this, and only a small percentage emerge at all from their stuffy cocoons in the cities. The rich Londoner might buy a quaint cottage in some country village to which he scoots in his Porsche for the weekend, but most urban dwellers prefer to holiday on the Continent, with cheap flight vacations to Spain, Portugal, and other hot spots around the Mediterranean.

Legally speaking, both the common law and the Countryside and Rights of Way Act of 2000 protect the right to walk. What is unique about this vast network of British paths is that most routes pass over private land. There are also "permissive paths," where there is no public right but the owner has agreed to a temporary right of passage; and finally, there is the "right to roam" that is mandated under the 2000 statute, whereby walkers have a conditional right to roam over some portions of uncultivated private land. This right to roam is a partial redress of the elimination of such rights by the Enclosure statutes of the seventeenth and eighteenth centuries, which removed millions of acres of common land from the public domain.

The Ramblers is the largest walkers' rights association in Britain, and indeed the world. It is an activist group that boasts some 123,000 active members and played a vital role in the passage of the 2000 statute. The Ramblers do not hesitate to launch court action to save a path from being closed by a landowner or the highway department, and its credo is that public paths form an invaluable part of the national heritage. There exist some 485 Rambler groups in the country, with 350 affiliated bodies, such as the Footpath Societies.

This book is a celebration of walking — specifically, walking a long-distance path through the heart of the English countryside. Along the way we will examine the topography, flora and fauna, and rural customs of the English heartland, plus meet a fascinating array of historical and contemporary personalities. The perspective is that of a North American, probing the English landscape, history, and character.

The journey awaits us. In the tradition of William Wordsworth, W.H. Hudson, Edward Thomas, and Robert Louis Stevenson, cross-country walking is an escape into another world. One enters Narnia via C.S. Lewis's wardrobe door, the portal to that other dimension. A single stile will suffice as our own portal to escape the present, discover the past, and rediscover the self.

BOSTON IS AN ancient port situated on the Wash, a North Sea bay on England's east coast one hundred miles north of London. It was a wool-exporting town for the Hanseatic League in the thirteenth century and diversified to salt and woven fabrics over succeeding centuries. The port has a strong tradition of religious dissent, as it is here that John Cotton became vicar of St. Botolph's in 1612. His fiery preaching energized church attendance, but his Nonconformist beliefs enraged the Church of England so much that he was soon encouraging parishioners to join the Massachusetts Bay Company and emigrate to America, where he himself fled in 1633, helping to establish Boston's namesake — a true Pilgrim father.

We are too fagged with jet lag to walk much of the town this evening. We find our B&B, which turns out to be a rather sleazy little hotel off the main drag, and crash. I am dimly aware of sounds of revelry from the streets, and wonder if the gypsy carnival runs at night.

Before nodding off, I lie there in a dingy, cramped single bed thinking about the adventure before us. In the news this spring of 2004, Madonna is battling it out at hearings before the Countryside Agency over the planned opening of walking paths on her vast country estate near the Wiltshire–Dorset border — threatening in good old American West style to shoot any trespassers on her land. Another wealthy landowner, Nicholas van Hoogstraten, has been fighting the Ramblers for thirteen years; after numerous court battles, the High Court ordered him to reopen a footpath on his East Sussex estate to the public. He calls the Ramblers "the scum of the earth."

In English literary history, the footpath and stile form a common backdrop in the works of many writers, including Shakespeare, Thomas Hardy, Wordsworth, D.H. Lawrence, and George Eliot. Often the footpath is a haven for lovers to meet for an evening rendezvous at a chosen stile. It is cherished by others as a convenient connecting point to another village. Many landowners, however, view the common footpath as the domain of vagabonds, gypsies, and rogues. In Eliot's *The Mill on the Floss,* Mr. Tulliver blames his lawyer for losing his lawsuit against a "right of . . . thoroughfare on his land for every vagabond who preferred an opportunity of damaging private property to walking like an honest man along the high-road." So van Hoogstraten and Madonna are in a long tradition of landowners wishing to close off their leafy acreages to the public.

I fall asleep and dream of gypsies, trains, and Pilgrims — and, oh yes, of Madonna, standing with a shotgun at a wooden gate, clad only in her wellington boots, guarding her estate.

1

LINCOLNSHIRE LANES

"Beyond the Wild Wood comes the wild world," said the Rat.

"And that's something that doesn't matter, either to you or to me.

I've never been there, and I'm never going; Nor you either,

if you've got any sense at all."

— KENNETH GRAHAME —
The Wind in the Willows

I AWAKE DAZED WITH JET LAG, then smell the gammon sizzling in the breakfast room. I quickly dress and stumble to the appointed table, where Karl sits with his coffee. I am bleary-eyed, stomach still rumbling. Harold, the greasy-haired, middle-aged proprietor, who resembles a wrencher, curtly offers us a full English breakfast: fried tomatoes, mushrooms, eggs, gammon, and the option of sardines. I decline the sardines but am foolish enough to order the main concoction, which is duly presented — only a tad less greasy than the proprietor's hair. All the while, the radio blares loudly, the strident DJ interspersing rap music with bits of an imaginary conversation between Britney Spears and a bimbo hotel receptionist, occasionally throwing in a crude joke and burping loudly.

Harold the Wrencher asks if we've noticed the East Europeans in town. I say we had, and that I understood they came here looking for jobs under relaxed EU labour laws and were helping harvest the vegetable crops of the Lincolnshire lowlands.

"Aha," he says, "that's true, mate, that's true; but we locals are upset because they work for lower wages than our English lads. But time will tell, won't it? At least they're better than the gypsies."

Karl's breakfast consists of half of a cup of coffee. He will snack on trail mix and quaff a pint of Guinness midday if the opportunity arises, but otherwise his only real meal of the day is dinner. He shakes his head reprovingly as I struggle to finish the soggy repast awash on my chipped plate.

"Tomorrow, John, just have toast and coffee instead of that swill. Your stomach will thank you. Now let's get moving."

I can't resist another brief look at St. Botolph's. I discover that the church boasts 7 doors, 12 columns in the nave, 24 steps to the library, 52 windows, and 365 stairs to the top of the "Stump" — well, you get the picture. Obviously, the builders were trying to exhort the populace to repent of their sins in the face of time marching on. I consider it a good omen that St. Botolph, a Saxon monk who died in 680, is known as the English saint of travellers, and that his feast day is celebrated on June 17, the date that Karl and I hope to march onto the sands of Chesil Beach to complete our Macmillan Way journey, some 290 miles away. We also expect to add 60 miles or more by taking a few interesting diversions.

We say goodbye to Boston without further ado and trudge southwest, through some gates and out to the dike area beyond. Immediately we find ourselves immersed in a vast sea of garbage, screeching herring gulls, and giant earthmoving machines that are working to reshape the local landfill, known as Slippery Gowt. We stop at the spot on the Haven inlet where in 1607 William Brewster and his pilgrims congregated to board a sailboat to Holland and thence to America, only to be arrested by the authorities for trying to emigrate without permission. Many of these determined folk were aboard the *Mayflower* when it sailed in 1610.

We both climb nimbly over the first stile. Karl is in an ebullient mood. Thus far the rain has held off, though a brisk wind blows off the North Sea and fleeting clouds scud across the sky like skittish sheep.

It is a sine qua non for civilized walking in Britain that one carry a walking stick. Mine happens to be made of blackthorn, with a gnarled knob grip and sharp nodules sticking out like quills, which nodules I have found occasionally useful in fending off violent dogs and bovines. The Dutch call it a *wandelstok;* the German term is *Spazierstock;* the Scots wield a *kebbie;* the French deem it *une canne.*

The stick has a variety of uses. It supports one when one is fatigued, especially uphill. It clears those early-morning spiderwebs, brushes aside fallen branches, tests the depth of streams, wards off canines and charging cattle, and gives one a sense of balance and well-being. My son-in-law made a walking stick by hollowing out a straight maple branch, in which he placed a fishing line, compass, and jackknife; he even composed a song about it that he calls "The Survival Stick." And there are numerous historical reports of walkers stashing the odd vial of spirits within a hollowed-out stick for when they paused for a nip on a rural footpath or, for that matter, on a London street.

Another rule for planning a long-distance trek in England is to prepare one's feet. Ensure that you build up calluses beforehand, that your boots are well worn in, and that your pack is not too heavy. Otherwise, blisters will develop and you will be miserable. (I learned all this the hard way.) So take preventive measures. Blister spray, which allows one to literally acquire a second layer of skin each morning of the trip, is available in England.

Finally, make sure you wear waterproof clothing and carry a compass, water, a guidebook or Ordnance Survey map, and good binoculars. Not all walking manuals are as thorough as the *Macmillan Way Guide* (which we called simply "the *Guide*"), so the detailed Ordnance map is a must: it shows every little path and stream, even key farmhouses. The binoculars you will need to scope out the next field you are about to enter, because that field may contain a herd of dangerous bovines, including perhaps an ill-tempered bull. And because the path is often ploughed over by the farmer, you will have to assess which route to follow in crossing, taking care not to trespass, while trying to determine which gate or stile on the far side of the vast acreage is on the proper route. Believe me, an African trek with armed guides is much easier and safer. It's a fair bet that more people are killed and injured by bovines in British fields each year than tourists are killed on African safaris. So be careful.

If you are North American, then you also have to know that every day holds one or more *Fawlty Towers* experiences. Paul Theroux has noted that the English think North Americans funny, but it is their own habits which seem wildly out of whack — such as, he notes, paying a licence fee each year to watch the telly, or saying they are sorry when you step on their toes. A few other examples: charging you twopence for a tiny white plastic spoon with which to eat the yogurt you have just purchased at the local grocery; refusing to let you eat before seven o'clock (the French are worse — it's 7:30 or even 8:00 PM); their habit of stopping for a spot of tea every hour without exception; looking puzzled when you enter their village and ask directions to a village two miles away — then remarking that they have never been there; queuing without complaint for service; and coming up with place names like Knockdown, a village close to Bangup Lane, which is not far from Tiddleywink.

The concepts of comfort and customer service in this country are, well, just concepts — not practice. The English still have not come to terms with central heating, and most natives would rather put on a jumper than touch the sacred thermostat. They have a propensity to post the "Closed" sign wherever possible and invent weird hours of operation — castles, manor houses, museums, and shops have erratic opening times, sometimes allowing visitors only two or three designated days a week for just a few hours. Service facilities can be haphazard, even dodgy. I once took the train to Greenwich and, upon alighting, headed for the loo, only to be met with a sign stating that the station toilets were closed on account of the Railway Authority being unable to secure a sewage discharge easement from a neighbouring landowner! Then, of course, there is the matter of driving on the left. (The most hazardous part of travelling in Britain for a North American is walking across a road; one looks the wrong way as one steps off the curb.) But I digress.

That said, the English are immensely tolerant, reticent, self-effacing, slow to anger (except while driving), and all too modest about their country. After years of travel in Britain, the two most common words that come to mind are "sorry" and "closed," often appearing in the same sentence. And the English will give their lives to protect their dogs. They are so politically correct that until recently it was difficult to obtain permission to fly the national flag — the Union Jack — for fear of offending minority groups. Not that the Brits are a flag-waving people; that is reserved for the pageantry of the Queen's Jubilee and other national celebrations. And when it comes to World Cup soccer matches ("football" to Brits), since England, Scotland, Wales, and Northern Ireland all have separate teams, the English fly the Cross of St. George from rooftops and cars until England is inevitably ousted from competition.

THE PACK STILL FEELS heavy. Karl's weighs in at a mere twenty-five pounds, and he just laughs at my grimaces. Our *Guide* cautions us, when striding past Frampton Marsh, "do keep as quiet as possible all along the sea bank, so that disturbance to wildfowl and other birds is kept to a minimum." More than 160 species of birds nest or stop over this area. We see mainly gulls, geese, lapwings, and a few redshanks and avocets. A pair of acrobatic lapwings are putting on a show overhead like the Blue Angels, swooping, diving, and rolling at impossible angles. What a lot of effort to expend just to attract a mate! Speaking of which, we pass by a birdwatching blind from which much giggling emits, though we cannot see inside. The Lincolnshire Wildlife Trust has requested that visitors report "unsuitable behaviour" to police, after several reports were received of people having sexual encounters in the hides. Rachel Shaw of the Trust advises, "There are certain things that happen at nature reserves that really shouldn't."

The Fens are a wild, lonely place, and have formed the setting for many novels, such as Dorothy Sayers's *The Nine Tailors* and Graham Swift's *Waterland*. Though there is a haunting beauty here, it is far from Arcadia. Swift was well aware of the loneliness: "Realism; fatalism; phlegm. To live in the Fens is to receive strong doses of reality. The great flat monotony of reality; the wide empty space of reality. Melancholia and self-murder are not unknown in the Fens. Heavy drinking, madness and sudden acts of violence are not uncommon."

The eeriness of the landscape is brought home to us by squall after squall now slashing us from the North Sea, as those scudding clouds turn violent and black and dense. Lightning flashes through the mist. Thunder cannonades like artillery fire over the vast reaches of marshland, scaring the birds. There is nothing to do but stuff our Tilleys into the packs, shroud our heads in our Gore-Tex hoods, and soldier on. There is no shelter in the Fens, nary a shrub for protection. Then, in midafternoon, the vast gunsmoke clouds miraculously part like the Red Sea and the sun blazes through, casting a bright sheen over the surrounding wetlands.

Local residents walk over the tidal marsh and pick up samphire, a plant with salty, aromatic leaves often pickled and eaten. Huge quantities of marsh samphire used to be harvested and burned for the soda content used in the production of soap and glass. The fenland surrounding us consists of drained shallow water, where dead plants help give rise to new growth in saturated peat, allowing vegetable crops to flourish. In fact, the great drainage schemes of the eighteenth century led to tens of thousands of acres being reclaimed for farming, turning this region into the agricultural hub of central England — and Boston into a major port. In 2003, the Great Fen Project was initiated to restore portions of the Fens to their original state. Certain farms, abandoned or no longer viable, are purchased and then selectively flooded to create nature reserves.

We reach Fosdyke Bridge, a village of some five hundred people on the River Welland. Residents must be especially noise sensitive, as our *Guide* cautions us to "please keep as quiet as possible to limit disturbance to house owners." Why, do they think walkers are so unruly as to shout and curse and play ghetto blasters? In any event, we don't see a soul as we tiptoe through the village. It feels like Sleepy Hollow.

Yet Fosdyke Bridge has a claim to fame. In October of 1216, wicked King John (of Robin Hood fame) was passing through these parts with his retinue of sycophantic servants and lapdogs when he was taken ill. He had reached King's Lynn in Norfolk, but decided to return to Spalding, which is very close to us. For an unknown reason, the king chose to send his baggage train, which included the crown jewels, by a different route, on a causeway bordering the Wash. The baggage train was lost on the way, reportedly engulfed by an incoming tide. The king had no time to ponder this misfortune, as he died a few days later.

In the thirteenth century, the tidal streams and surrounding marshlands were constantly inundated by North Sea waters. Recent satellite imagery and tide-table data have led historians to believe that the king's baggage train likely met its demise at or near Fosdyke Bridge on the River Welland. And so Karl and I find ourselves peering into the inky waters of the river, seeking a glint of light from rubies and diamonds.

Fifteen miles later and with very sore feet, we stagger into Surfleet, and into our booked B&B, which we find to be a dilapidated old inn. Most of the B&Bs en route are farmhouses, but occasionally one has to throw the dice and book an inn. This one is pleasantly situated on the river. We are greeted at the pub entrance by a huge grey bull mastiff, which advances toward us barking furiously, causing me to raise my stick in apprehension.

"He won't bite you, mate," a voice utters. A beefy tattooed bloke in a black T-shirt emerges from within.

The bull mastiff retreats and we are ushered in. The pub is cluttered with dumpy sofas and soft, sagging armchairs, the usual hunting-scene reproductions on the grimy walls, a pool table, and a dark-stained burgundy carpet. One solitary patron stands at the bar staring curiously at our Tilley hats, packs, and sticks. We are escorted by Black Shirt upstairs to our room, where two beds lie in dim light. Black Shirt reveals that he is currently between jobs in the army and navy, just looking after the inn for the owner, who is vacationing in Spain. The toilet is down the hall and shared between us and four other rooms. Have they never heard of ensuites?

Speaking of toilets — wherever you travel in Britain, do not make the mistake of asking to use the washroom. My first encounter at a petrol (gas) station went like this: "Do you have a washroom, please?"

"You want a room to do some washing, sir?"

"Ah, no, I would like to use a bathroom."

"A bathroom, sir? Do you wish to take a bath?"

This was becoming embarrassing. "Ah, no, you see, I really have to go — you know, go! How about a restroom?"

"You wish to take a rest, sir?"

I finally pointed to my groin.

"Ah, sir, perhaps you mean the loo!"

Often a Brit will use the term "toilet" as well, which does not mean precisely the object of one's desire, but rather the room itself. Refined people say "lavatory."

I lie on my back, exhausted but too tired to sleep. Loud music emanates from the pub below. Well, it *is* Friday night and the barkeeper will soon no doubt utter his famous "Time, please, gentlemen," and all will be quiet. Then I hear someone approach the door, which is ajar because the lock fixture is missing. So are the lower two inches of the door itself, which looks like it has been gnawed by a porcupine. I anxiously sit up. There, his slobbering tongue hanging out, is the huge head of the mastiff, who has come to tuck me in. I take a melatonin tablet to finally fall asleep.

Next morning we arise refreshed. Muscles ache in a healthy way, and we are eager to conquer the next fifteen miles to reach the village of Baston. Our goal is to cover twelve to fourteen miles per day, in order to accomplish the entire walk within twenty-six days, with two nights planned for each of Stow-on-the-Wold and Sutton Montis, astride "Cadbury Camelot." Today's entire route parallels the River Glen.

First, though, I have to stop and explore the Surfleet church. I am drawn to it because the fourteenth-century spire leans at an alarming angle and gives the impression of imminent collapse. Inside, I find delightful stained glass windows, an ancient font, and the effigy of a knight. The tranquil village basks in morning sun that dapples the predominantly red-brick buildings. Lilliputian rowboats lie docked adjacent to tiny riverside bungalows that in turn abut a splendid golf course. I half expect Bilbo and his fellow hobbits to emerge and trundle down to the waterside, fishing poles in hand.

We observe numerous pumping stations and prosperous-looking farms. These pumping systems were first installed in the seventeenth century and were originally powered by windmills, but few of the latter remain intact. When J.B. Priestley visited the area in 1933, there were still dozens of working windmills, and he labelled the region "Dutch England." Those that remain in these northern Fens are largely used as tea shops for tourists, offering cakes and muffins made from stone-ground flour. There are ruins of some 135 ancient windmills in Lincolnshire, and we pass one such relic at Glen Mill.

Beyond Glen Mill loom eight modern steel windmills. Sir Bernard Ingham, former press secretary to Margaret Thatcher, claims that wind farms resemble "a cluster of lavatory brushes in the sky." There is an obvious clash here between aesthetics and the drive for cleaner energy consumption.

Near the village of Pinchbeck we cross the River Glen, pass through a hunting gate, and stop at the entrance to Spalding Tropical Forest. Here, in stark contrast to the fenland, the creators of this arboretum have amassed the largest tropical forest in the United Kingdom. Masses of dense jungle foliage, cascading waterfalls, and lush plants with enormous flowers extend over several acres. Karl especially marvels at the hundred species of colourful orchids.

The English have been obsessed since at least the eighteenth century with bringing the world's treasures to their little northern island. Aside from the classical art works and sculptures looted from foreign lands — like Cleopatra's Needle in London, and countless Egyptian exhibits at the British Museum — it is their obsession with flora and fauna that astounds one. Countless estates abound with trees, shrubs, and flowers from around the world. Stourhead combines such floral sampling with Greek temples and follies; Longleat adds exotic wildlife — beware of monkeys riding on your car; and England's finest arboretum, Westonbirt, displays its eclectic floral fare along our Macmillan pathway in Gloucestershire.

A flock of forty-two huge white swans appears around a bend in the river. They try to take off as we approach but are so fat and cumbersome that their legs graze the water and most of them barely make it aloft; several crash on takeoff, like overloaded 747s. This open country is dedicated to the birds: there are bird boxes attached to poles for miles, placed by the Hawk and Owl Trust to attract barn owls. Alas, only a few owls have been spotted, the cozy birdhouses having been seized by squatters — kestrels, doves, jackdaws, and crows.

It is not until noon of our second day that we encounter other hominids on the footpath. An elderly couple, one riding a Shetland pony and the other a large black horse with burrs in his mane, follow us for a mile or so. I hail them, but they turn off and head into the mist at a farm track. The track heads toward the tiny village of Tongue End. Imagine *that* as your mailing address.

Spalding lies three miles south of here and is renowned for its annual tulip parade. Surrounding fields grow huge quantities of tulips and daffodils, with close industry ties to the Netherlands. There is even a Tulip FM radio station. The River Welland bisects the town, which now boasts a population of some 28,700 people. Spalding has been continuously occupied since Roman times, when it was a centre for salt production.

Spalding is one of those places that most people in the United Kingdom have barely heard of, yet it possesses interesting attributes. In addition to its fame as the flower capital of the country, it was the first town in the UK where bar codes were used on products. One of the oldest yew hedges in the country is at Ayscoughfee Hall, birthplace of the Spalding Gentlemen's Society. This archaic-sounding association was in fact a group of intellectuals who came together beginning in 1710 to discuss the important philosophical, scientific, and political questions of the day. The intellectual revolution of the late seventeenth and eighteenth centuries produced the flowering of rationalism and humanism that paved the way for modern parliamentary democracy and the ensuing economic order. Arguments were refined over a glass or two of port in forums such as the Spalding Gentlemen's Society, which boasted Sir Isaac Newton, Alexander Pope, Sir Joseph Banks, and Alfred Lord Tennyson as members. The society is still active today.

Our path winds toward Kates Bridge, an ancient settlement that demarcates the end of the Fens. No, it is not named after some village maiden, but rather a Danish god called Kat or Catta. We stop to admire a cluster of willow trees beneath the bridge. This was at one time the head of navigation on the River Glen. The thriving community declined in the nineteenth century, when railways became the favoured means of transport. Now the hamlet consists of a petrol station, a tractor dealership, five houses, and one farm.

The loose limestone fields are gradually becoming higher and dryer as we approach Baston. This village is thought to be the site of the first major battle between King Arthur's Romano-Britons and the invading Anglo-Saxons, in the late fifth century. Many Saxon graves have been unearthed here.

DIARY: *Images of today's walk — the heavy, burdensome pack (I must dump some clothes, but not any of my books); two Perrier bottles wedged upright into a hollowed-out fence post; the dank smell of the marsh; endless grasses and rushes, with swallows swooping and thrushes singing; stiles and waymarks to which the green Macmillan sticker is affixed; brick cottages; the ubiquitous red telephone booths, inside one of which Karl tried to call home but the line was dead — the first of many broken-down phone booths we would encounter along Macmillan. British Telephone says the phones and booths are too costly to maintain in this day of mobiles. So one by one they fall into disrepair and will soon become anachronistic relics of the countryside.*

We stay the night at Baston's Baskervilles Inn, where each room is named after a character in the Arthur Conan Doyle novel *The Hound of the Baskervilles*. Ours is *Mrs. Oldthorpe,* while next door is *Sherlock Holmes*. Karl and I had not planned on having to share rooms like this, but in rural England, you take what you can get. Until the twentieth century, a traveller at a crowded inn was expected to share not only a room with a perfect stranger, but also the same bed.

We start a regular nightly ritual of washing out our undergarments and socks with detergent in the soap basin. Most B&Bs don't do laundry: you have to plead for heat to be turned on so you can dry off your clothes on the wall register. Karl tells me that one must vigorously rub the socks together after laying them immersed in water for at least an hour. The proprietress allows us only two hours of heat this evening, so I worry whether the clothes will be dry in the morning. A bigger concern is Karl's snoring, for I am rather noise sensitive. I pinch his big toe after half an hour of his walrus outbursts, and he rolls over. Mission accomplished. (My snoring is even worse, but fortunately, Karl is a deep sleeper and half deaf.)

On the trail next morning by the River Glen, we encounter an elderly fisherman in tweed hat and waders with whom we stop to chat. He says he has lived in the area all his life and has watched the demise of the native red squirrel — decimated, he says, by the introduction of the American grey squirrel. But the red squirrel is finally making a comeback. Government and nature groups are targeting key areas where red squirrels are still found, and trapping squirrels — killing the grey ones and releasing the red ones unharmed. (Personally, I think the grey squirrels are just as cute and someone should stand up for their rights too.) Then he complains about the American mink wreaking havoc with the aquatic life in the rivers. Mink are eating the fish and killing off ferrets, water rats, and small otters. We commiserate, then leave him to his fly casting.

"Karl," I muse, "the very first book ever read to me by my mother was *Chatterer the Red Squirrel*, by Thornton Burgess, and I have gone through life believing that Shadow the sly weasel was the Darth Vader threat from which Chatterer was always running. Now I find that it's just a bunch of grey squirrels that have decimated Chatterer and his mates."

"Don't lose any sleep over it. They're all pests and varmints as far as I am concerned, and they do a hell of a lot of damage if they get into your cellar or attic."

The scene as we wend our way along the stream is reminiscent of Kenneth Grahame's *The Wind in the Willows*, with badger setts, willows overhanging the brook, and abundant bracken, marsh, and hedgerow to house myriad wildlife. Here indeed lies a quiet little microcosm of rural Lincolnshire, a world unto itself. Our fisherman friend is well entitled to be protective of this natural habitat.

Near the entrance to a copse of beeches, we discover a dead badger on the side of the path. The creature is much larger than I imagined. Its sharp, angular teeth and long, non-retractable claws are truly fearsome. This animal can do a lot of damage. Badgers are almost never seen in daylight; Grahame notes in his classic that "Badger hates society, and invitations, and dinner, and all that sort of thing." However, badgers have a reputation for wisdom. In T.H. White's *The Once and Future King*, the young King Arthur is turned into a badger by Merlin as part of his education. Arthur meets an old badger who tells him, "I can only teach you two things — to dig, and love your home." The badger is also the house symbol for Hufflepuff in the Harry Potter book series.

Ratty in *The Wind in the Willows* is in fact a water vole, a semi-aquatic rodent which has a rounder nose than a rat, a chubby face, and, unlike the rat, hair covering its tail, ears, and paws. There are believed to be some 220,000 surviving voles in the United Kingdom, and the old fisherman was right — they have been fast declining due to the American mink, a predator. In the comic novel and movie *Cold Comfort Farm*, one of the main characters, Urk, refers to his unrequited love, Elfine Starkadder, as his "little water vole." In Evelyn Waugh's novel *Scoop*, his hero declaims, "Feather-footed through the plashy fens passes the questing vole." And British archaeologist David Miles opines that the vole existed in Britain some 500,000 years ago. In fact, the vole may be the longest surviving original Briton. Such adorable little creatures are therefore much maligned with the "rat" appellation.

The English really are in love with animals. There are countless stories of macho fathers condoning the beating of their sons at boarding school yet breaking down and crying at the sight of an injured sparrow. As Sarah Lyall writes in *The Anglo Files*, "Every British animal has its cheerleaders." And the epitome of evil in English society is someone who mistreats an innocent beast. Near London's Hyde Park this year the government will unveil, at a cost of one million pounds, the Animals in War Memorial, to celebrate the animals who aided the nation in numerous wars. The massive stone sculpture will portray in bas-relief pigeons, dogs, monkeys, horses, donkeys, even glow-worms. Chiselled into the stone is the chilling proclamation "They had no choice."

A mudflat we pass is covered with tracks — the etchings and scratchings of little creatures that resemble a Trafalgar Square–like meeting place. As we leave the brook and follow the path through the copper beech grove into a copse, a furry white creature suddenly rushes out of the bracken and does a merry dance around Karl, at one point even crawling partway up his boot.

"It's just a ferret, and I think he's blind," Karl laughs. "I have read that they are often born blind."

The ferret, however, is known for its ferocious bite, being a member of the weasel family, and I suggest that Karl steer the animal away from us. He takes his walking stick and gently flicks the creature to the side of the path, where it sits pondering the situation.

"Now," I say, "all we need is Mr. Toad, Mole, and Ratty to trundle by, Karl. I can see where Kenneth Grahame received his inspiration."

There is a North American connection here. Sales of *The Wind in the Willows* did not take off until President Theodore

Roosevelt publicly wrote to Grahame in 1909 to tell him that he had "read it and reread it, and [had] come to accept the characters as old friends." So popular is the anthropomorphic genre in England — and the world — that British author William Horwood has written two entrancing sequels to the Kenneth Grahame classic, which continue to captivate children and adults alike. And with his multi-volume Duncton Wood series, Horwood has brought tears to the eyes of millions of readers over the life and plight of English moles. Indeed, I will never kill a mole again — let them have my lawn, they deserve their tunnels and homes. Oh, crikey!

We divert slightly off trail to visit Bowthorpe Park Farm in Manthorpe, where stands the largest living English oak tree by girth, the Bowthorpe Oak. This tree boasts a circumference of some forty feet. Now, next to North America's giant firs and sequoias, you might think this rather short, stubby tree would appear dwarfish. But it has a majesty of its own, and its veined, textured bole and gnarled gnome-like branches remind one of a scene from Mirkwood in *The Hobbit*. The tree is estimated to be over one thousand years old and has made it into the *Guinness Book of Records*. The trunk is hollow; a former farm tenant built a roof and door — the tree held within it thirty-nine people standing or thirteen people tucking into high tea.

There are older trees in Britain, since the estimable yew outlives all other species. The record so far belongs to the Fortingall Yew in Perthshire, estimated to be between three and five thousand years old. Other notable specimens are the Gog and Magog oaks at Glastonbury and the Tolpuddle Martyrs' Tree in Dorset, a sycamore beneath which six poor farm labourers formed the first trade union in Britain, in 1834.

"Not much challenge to a logger, though, Karl."

"Log it, burn it, and pave it, John." But Karl has a twinkle in his eye.

We amble back to the main path. Our next destination is Wilsthorpe. The inhabitants must all be asleep here, together with their dogs. Not a soul stirs. We search for a landmark Roman villa ruin, but it eludes us. The word *village* is derived from the Roman *villa*, as many settlements grew up around the several thousand homesteads built by Roman merchants and soldiers who remained in Britain after Caesar's conquest.

There are so many similar-sounding names in this country that it all makes for great confusion. For example, a few miles to the west lies the village of Woolsthorpe, where you can stop and visit the house where Isaac Newton lived, and even sit on a bench under the apple tree — actually, its progeny — where the great man observed the proverbial apple drop.

Speaking of Isaac Newton, the National Trust has recently begun a program called "Making the Countryside Real," intended to teach city children about rural life, and Woolsthorpe Manor, Newton's home, is the scene for the first field trip — a neat way to combine history with the flavour of the countryside. Polls indicate that urban schoolchildren harbour fears of rural areas.

We stop to catch our breath in the charming stone village of Greatford. It is here that, in 1788, Dr. Francis Willis temporarily "cured" King George III of his madness, in a private asylum he operated at Greatford Hall. Today we might call the king's ailment a severe psychiatric disorder, whereas George just told Dr. Willis, "I am nervous; I am not ill, but I am nervous."

The king was required to undergo the same regimen of fresh air and physical labour assigned to other patients, and so he toiled in the fields, anonymous but set apart from other patients. Upon being cured, the king rewarded Dr. Willis with a pension of one thousand pounds a year for twenty-one years. In 1801, the king suffered a relapse and returned to Greatford for further treatment. After a third and final relapse in 1810, he remained completely mad until his death in 1820.

None of which stopped Dr. Willis from becoming so well known as a psychiatrist that many other wealthy aristocrats travelled to Greatford Hall for treatment. Villagers were amused by the curious sight of these patients working in the fields clad in black coats and wearing powdered wigs, for Dr. Willis believed hard physical labour was vital to the treatment process. Little did they know that one of these labourers was their sovereign.

"It's too bad the good doctor was about thirteen years too late with the cure," I muse. "Then perhaps the American Revolution would have been averted."

"If I had just lost the American colonies to a bunch of backwoodsmen, I think I would have developed a chronic nervous condition too, John."

We trudge through fields laced with shoulder-high rapeseed plants, immersing ourselves in sopping yellow stalks that coat our hair and clothes with yellow, sticky powder. A light rain adds to the clammy experience. The path through the fields has turned into gumbo.

"Not exactly *Field of Dreams* today, Karl."

"Come on, John, it would look just grand on a sunny day."

We finally exit the field, climb over a stile, hit a brief section of tarmac, and abruptly leave the road to enter a lovely green lane about six miles north of the market town of Stamford. Green lanes are ancient drover roads that farmers used for centuries to drive cattle and sheep from Scotland and northern England to the pasturage of the Midlands and then on to London for consumption. The remnants of these roads make for some of the loveliest walking in Britain.

This lane runs along the Lincolnshire–Rutland border. It is dark, with lush growth and high hedgerows — and holds a morbid surprise. About a hundred yards along, I spot a bright object lying in the verge, and stop to investigate. To my shock, I find a pair of red high-heeled shoes beside a heap of fancy clothes — in fact, a complete female wardrobe: a new and expensive-looking pink silk blouse, black skirt, pantyhose, bra, the works. But where's the body? Nobody just randomly dumps a complete set of designer clothes in a dark lane. Gingerly, I reach out with my walking stick and raise the label on the blouse.

Etched in ink on the underside of the label is a phone number, and then this:

Raped me in back of cab
Help! Tiffany.

Karl and I stand stunned.

"My God!" Karl exclaims.

"We have to report this right away to the police, Karl. Stamford is the closest town."

Karl nods and we set out, but we also carefully examine the east side of the lane near the heap of clothes, just to ensure we haven't overlooked a body. I shudder. Stamford is a long six miles from here.

Close to two hours later we push ourselves up a steep hill before the plunge down to Stamford. Scattered rain falls, the drops dribbling like a leaky faucet, just enough to wet the Gore-Tex and turn bridleways into gooey mire. The summit of the hill overlooking Stamford brings us to Cobbs Nook Farm.

Below us, silvery steeples poke up through the swirling mist like beacons for the lonely wayfarer.

On the outskirts of Stamford a passerby informs us that the police station is at the far end of town at the top of another hill. This is testing our endurance — mine, at least. I am just an out-of-shape solicitor, but my seventy-four-year-old companion surges ahead, mouth rigidly set, walking stick propelling him along this last half mile. We don't stop to admire the fine Georgian buildings along the main street.

It's a gruelling grind up the final hill. Pedestrians turn aside on the steep sidewalk to avoid us, scared of these two bedraggled apparitions pounding upward. We arrive out of breath at a nondescript building on the hilltop, to be greeted inside by a burly young cop who has had a bad day. We are sodden; rain drips from our clothes onto the grey tile floor. I show him the location of Tiffany's clothes on my *Macmillan Way Guide* map page, which he promptly photocopies.

"On which side of the lane did you find the clothes, sir?" he asks.

"East side."

"Then I am afraid it is outside of our jurisdiction, sir, because that's the Rutland County side, and I will have to fax this over to the Oakham police and ask them to send out a patrol car to investigate." He sounds almost relieved.

"You will do this right away?"

"Yes, don't worry, but you have to understand — over a hundred thousand teenagers a year run away from home in Britain, and this could be just another poor girl who's ended up victimized by getting involved with unsavoury people, perhaps living the partying nightlife. Half the time the missing teenager is never even reported to the police. Give me the address or phone number we can reach you at this evening in case the Rutland constabulary need to talk with you further."

We advise him of our local B&B, to which we trudge next, passing a shop sign that reads: "Good stabling and loose barrels." Our landlady greets us on the seventh ring of the bell. She is rosy-cheeked, amiable, and all business. She introduces herself as Mabel Trance, but we are to call her Mabel.

"You all right, then?"

She is looking at our dripping clothes and rumpled hair. No, I almost say, we are not all right — we are cold, hungry, and tired, and I feel like Ratty after a wet day in the Wild Wood.

"Yes, er, Mabel, quite all right. Just need to dry out and go for a bite to eat."

But when I advise her that the police may be calling for us that evening, she lets out a squeal. I calm her. "And please, Mabel, I don't want a cooked English breakfast in the morning, but would love some porridge."

That night we dine at an Elizabethan pub close to our B&B. The steak is great; the chips, dry; the wine, superb. Everyone is so polite. Of course, there is that small matter of poor service. I feel like a lout for repeatedly hailing the waitress for condiments like ketchup and vinegar.

Alas, it had been a long and trying day, and surely it is time to have some fun. It so happens that whereas in Britain this is a bank holiday weekend, in Canada it is Victoria Day, in honour of our then longest-reigning queen. (Some Canadians call it the May Two-Four, referring to both the date it traditionally falls upon and Canadian slang for a case of twenty-four beers, copious amounts of which are drunk on this celebratory weekend.) So after downing our first bottle of Shiraz, we commence work on the second bottle and I cause Karl to stand with me, clink glasses, and in loud nasal voices declaim together: "To the Queen!" Whereupon the pub's gibberings cease entirely and all eyes turn upon us disdainfully, as if we are lunatics.

"It's Queen Victoria's birthday this weekend, mates. Is it left to us colonials to celebrate it alone? Why, where is your national pride?"

Karl blanches and tugs at my elbow to sit down. By now the patrons are averting their eyes, obviously regarding me as just so much déclassé foreign trash. I would never have done such a thing in North America and am embarrassed. But dammit, surely it's time for the English to shrug off their hangdog political correctness and celebrate their past with a little chutzpah. They may have much to apologize for, but the English have even more to be proud of — little things, such as empathy and liberty. Karl pours me another glass of Shiraz and then wanders to the bar to order a brandy.

If I had made my outburst in an American tavern, I might have been assaulted. But here, well, I am only guilty of bad manners. Pierre Daninos writes about English reticence, opining that "men who are ceaselessly battered by the wind and rain and shrouded in a permanent fog end up themselves turning into raincoats which shed criticism as easily as an oilskin sheds water." Nothing ruffles these people. But I broke a sacred code and intruded upon the privacy of bystanders. Had I been a cross-dresser in pink pantaloons, stockings, and gaudy makeup who kept to myself, no one would have minded. But I crossed a line. And judging by their disdainful expressions, I have been scorned and upbraided.

Mabel is waiting for us at our B&B, still apprehensive about the possibility of the police calling. Of greater concern to me is that there is no heat in our room. Somewhere I have read that the English hate heat but love a bright fire. In our room I observe that the solitary pillow on my bed is rather flat. So I go back downstairs to speak to Mabel.

"Uh, Mabel, do you think that I could have one or two large, poofy pillows? I suffer from acid reflux and need big high ones."

Her eyes grow steely. "Poofy, you say?"

"Well, yes, you know, very soft and large, please."

"And I suppose you'd like them well rounded, too, would ye, love" — a mischievous twinkle in her eyes. "Well, then, love, I will see what I can do."

Mabel bustles into the nether region of the dark, chilly hallway and emerges with two large, rose-tinted pillows, which she hands to me.

"Thanks so much." I dare not push my luck and ask for the heat to be turned on.

When I enter the room upstairs, Karl is in his narrow bed already, staring at the ceiling. He is unusually quiet.

"Sweet dreams, Karl. I am sure knackered."

But Karl tosses and turns most of the night, thinking about poor Tiffany.

2

HORSESHOES, WOOD PIGEONS, *and* PARIS

Peace is the walk.

Happiness is the walk.

Walk for yourself

And you walk for everyone.

— THICH NHAT HANH —
The Long Road Turns to Joy

I AWAKE WITH A START. Outside my open window the distinctive *Ooo-oo* urgings of the wood pigeon tell me it is indeed an English spring morning. It's mating time.

Other grunting sounds intrude. What kind of bird is that? Then I realize that it is only Karl in the adjoining room doing his morning push-ups — all fifty of them.

"The wood pigeon call reminds me of our grouse in Canada," muses Karl at the breakfast table. "I sure would like to try some pigeon pie."

"That may be wishful thinking. Though I grant you, these wood pigeons we see flying out of the hedgerows are plump enough for eating, a far cry from domestic pigeons. My grandfather used to keep pigeons on his farm in the Fraser Valley; he let me feed them nuts and crumbs."

Mabel sets down a cafetière — "French press" to North Americans — and invites me to have another cuppa. Five years ago one would have been served instant coffee at a B&B, but the English are now into better brewing.

"And what shall I be telling the police if they enquire about ye?" Mabel asks.

"Don't worry, Mabel, we will call them, and in any case, they know we're walking the Macmillan Way."

After one more cup of java, we heft packs. Mine is a little lighter, I confess to Karl, as I have just thrown away my extra pair of Nikes and a bottle of Pepto-Bismol.

"You should have kept the Pepto," says Karl, "given your sensitive stomach."

He is referring to the fact that I can't handle more than half a bottle of wine with the evening meal without waking with a splitting headache, whereas he can down a pre-dinner pint of Guinness, a double Scotch, and half a bottle of Shiraz with the meal, then finish off with a double shot of brandy — and yet wake up humming the "Colonel Bogey March," raring to go.

"My stomach's not sensitive — yours is just cast iron, Karl."

A lone magpie stalks about on the lawn as we leave — surely the ugliest, most ungainly of British birds. My wood pigeon is still calling his mate. But it is the distinctive song of the thrush that bids us adieu down Mabel's path to the road. From here we decide to briefly explore the town and ogle the impressive Georgian-style buildings, including the Stamford Union Workhouse, built in 1836.

During the Victorian era, numerous workhouses were established for the poor, perhaps out of guilt over the presence of poor people in a country grown rich from industrialization and trade. The British have long had a schizoid streak when it comes to the poor. The same Victorian society that condoned children performing dangerous jobs of toil and drudgery — such as chimney sweeping and coal mining — was determined to bring relief to the poor, homeless, and sick. London alone saw schools, birth houses for indigent women, residences for the elderly and infirm, Coram's Foundling Hospital, the Lock Hospital for venereal disease, the Bethlehem lunatic asylum — known as "Bedlam" — and even a School for the Indigent Blind, all founded by private charities. As the historian Ben Wilson observes, "Few other peoples lavished so much money on charity as the British."

Stamford is the first of five market towns we will pass through en route to Chesil Beach — the others being Stow-on-the-Wold, Cirencester, Tetbury, and Sherborne — and the only one that was administered as part of the Danelaw. In 1066, when the Normans arrived, only 10 percent of the population resided in towns. Yet market towns were key to the survival of the surrounding villages and farms. By royal decree, markets and trading could occur only in these designated centres.

The weekly market provided an opportunity for women and children to sell their cottage wares to supplement the family income. The Victorian writer William Howitt wrote, "There are few things which give such a feeling of the prosperity of the country, as seeing the country people pour into a large town on market-day," boys and girls with "baskets of tame rabbits, and bunches of cowslips, primroses, and all kinds of flowers, and country productions imaginable." The pubs did a roaring business on market day, and Howitt further observed that farmers left the market for home "three times as fast as they came in, for they are primed with good dinners, and strong beer."

The railway was late in arriving at Stamford, but this proved a blessing because the town was left unblemished by the sooty Victorian railway centres and Corn Exchange buildings one sees around the country — huge, ugly buildings that have more in common with Soviet than traditional English architecture. Here, ancient timber-framed structures interweave with Georgian delights. There are myriad twisting alleyways and open squares, lending much of the town a medieval flavour. Stamford was proclaimed the first Conservation Town in England, in 1967.

Stamford wool was famous for its quality throughout the kingdom, and the town was also renowned for centuries as the producer of most of England's glazed pottery. Today chain stores are interspersed with a host of independent shops with tasteful exterior decor. There may be much chintz and bling, but the presentation is low-key. Even the McDonald's has a lovely Georgian façade.

Just south of Stamford we cross a meadow and walk smack into a historical legend. A plaque identifies this spot as where the Celtic queen Boadicea pursued the remnants of the Roman Ninth Legion as they fled across the River Welland in AD 61. Boadicea was the wife of Prasutagus, king of the Iceni tribe of Britons, who ruled over present-day East Anglia. The Iceni had submitted to Roman rule in AD 43 and had become a vassal state. But when Prasutagus died in 61, Roman legionnaires seized Boadicea and gave her a public beating, likely using the flagrum, a short whip that was exceedingly painful. Soldiers then raped her two daughters. The Iceni were insulted, and they revolted, led by Boadicea as their new queen.

Boadicea was amazingly successful as a warrior queen. First she led the Iceni and a second tribe, the Trinovantes, into a siege that totally destroyed Roman Colchester (Camulodunum). The Roman general Suetonius heard of this and rushed to London (Londinium) to defend it, but then decided he had insufficient troops and evacuated the city on the Thames, leaving it to be burned by Boadicea, who led some 100,000 soldiers. For almost two years Boadicea pillaged Roman settlements. She was eventually defeated in the Battle of Watling Street, after which she either committed suicide or died of illness. The spirit of the Celts was epitomized by this brave woman, who is quoted as declaring, "It is not as a woman descended from noble ancestry, but as one of the people that I am avenging lost freedom, my scourged body, the outraged chastity of my daughters . . . But heaven is on the side of a righteous vengeance . . . If you weigh well the strength of the armies, and the causes of the war, you will see that in this battle you must conquer or die. This is a woman's resolve; as for men, they may live and be slaves."

So great was Boadicea's fame that nineteen centuries later Queen Victoria willingly portrayed herself as the Celtic queen's successor. Prince Albert commissioned a giant bronze statue of Boadicea and her daughters standing in her war chariot; completed in 1905, it stands next to Westminster Bridge. The fury and wrath of the warrior queen is captured by the warlike chariot, which points toward the Houses of Parliament as if to warn the governing powers of a woman's wrath. (Margaret Thatcher was said to be fond of the sculpture.) The inscription reads:

Regions Caesar never knew
Thy posterity shall sway.

On this balmy Sunday morning, Boadicea and her Roman foes seem far away. Field after field of delightful meadows full of buttercups are bordered by the gently winding stream. For the first time on Macmillan we encounter numerous walkers on our path, elderly and young couples alike rambling along, many of them with picnic baskets, strollers, and romping dogs. Laughing children run in the meadow, rainbow kites trailing in the breeze. It is all very festive.

We are greeted by a chorus of twittering skylarks as we locate and follow upward a hedged pathway toward Easton on the Hill. Karl plunges ahead like a beagle on the scent. I stop for a moment to watch a pair of larks as they climb skyward. The air is so fresh I can taste it. And somewhere beyond the briar hedge the scent of new-mown hay wafts pungent to my nostrils.

One's humour ebbs and flows on a long-distance walk. Robert Louis Stevenson writes of this in his essay "Walking

Tours": "In the course of a day's walk, you see, there is much variance in the mood. From the exhilaration of the start, to the happy phlegm of the arrival, the change is certainly great. As the day goes on, the traveller moves from the one extreme towards the other."

The Buddhist monk Thich Nhat Hanh stresses that walking is essential therapy for all human beings. In *The Long Road Turns to Joy* he exhorts, "If you see something along the way that you want to touch with your mindfulness — the blue sky, the hills, a tree, or a bird — just stop, but while you do, continue breathing mindfully. If you don't breathe consciously, sooner or later your thinking will settle back in, and the bird or the tree will disappear. Always stay with your breathing." My mother always told me to take deep measured breaths throughout the day. She herself suffered from weak lungs. I must remember to follow this advice — a Buddhist monk and my own mother can't both be wrong.

Yellow celandines, wild violets, and cow parsley line the verges where the hedgerows dissipate. Farther on, rose hips appear in the hedge. On a hawthorn branch I notice the mangled corpse of a sparrow, its ravaged body dangling. Karl opines that it may be the work of a shrike, a predatory bird that likes to impale its victims on a thorn and store up a larder. It has earned the reputation as the "butcher bird."

Skylarks continue to sing above us over the open fields. The male ascends to a great height before diving in free fall toward the female, putting on an aerial acrobatics show to impress his intended. The skylark population in Britain has plummeted by about half since 1980, largely as a result of changing farming methods that have seen reduced crops of barley and wheat, which provide the stubble needed by larks for foraging. A second factor is the spraying of herbicides and insecticides that destroy both insects and weed-producing seeds upon which larks depend.

The lark is important in English literature and history. William Wordsworth honours the bird in his poem "To a Skylark." Ralph Vaughan Williams also gave tribute in his famous musical piece *The Lark Ascending*. From the aerial show above, I can now better appreciate how Vaughan Williams received his inspiration. The skylark is the quintessential English harbinger of spring, and Vaughan Williams captures its grand aerial antics perfectly in his composition. An anonymous elderly Englishman posted this comment online after hearing a recent performance by the London Philharmonic Orchestra: "Always takes me back to my childhood — lying on my back in wonderment, on a grassy hillside on a hot summer's day, watching and listening to a skylark circling higher and higher, singing louder and louder . . . that marvellous music from the heavens on a background of blue sky. A long time ago, with the occasional Lancaster Bomber passing high overhead."

We are walking ancient paths, byways, and lanes exactly one hundred years after the first appearance of motor cars on English roads, in 1904. In *Cider with Rosie*, Laurie Lee notes that he and his family were born into a silent world, with long and dusty distances between villages and "white narrow roads rutted by hooves and cart wheels, innocent of oil or petrol." Then that world was shattered. Field horses screamed as noisy brass-lamped cars crawled down the lanes and coughed their way up the hillsides. The very warp and woof of society was irrevocably altered. No one could be truly isolated any longer.

Villages we encounter typically boast a Norman church on a hill, a pub that sells local ales and beer, a picturesque brook, a cricket or soccer pitch, perhaps a vicarage or rectory, a village shop with a post office, many cute cottages, and, just outside the village, an old stone or brick mansion, refurbished and owned by a stockbroker or lawyer, with an Audi and a Land Rover in the driveway.

Most villagers today fall into three categories: farmers who have retained a chunk of land adjoining the village sufficient to sustain an income; retired folk; and wealthy urbanites who are part-time only, arriving from London and environs on weekends. Although there is no longer the sense of community that existed prior to the Enclosure movement, there is at least a quiet understanding among these three groups to try to preserve the best of the English countryside.

The village represents the first organized communal event in human history. It was the catalyst for civilization, and ancient villagers would look askance today at the limited role the village plays within the national matrix. Yet that role is still important. Even in the cities, people revert to "neighbourhoods" that mimic the village and give each district a distinct flavour — one need look no further than London and such colourful neighbourhoods as Chelsea, Soho, Greenwich, Hampstead, Covent Garden, Bloomsbury, and Southwark. Prince Charles's experiment to create the ideal English village at Poundbury in Dorset is not as utopian as it may sound. Planners in both North America and Europe are trying to design communities that are self-contained, are less dependent upon the automobile, and use local building materials and traditional designs.

The term *global village* was coined by Marshall McLuhan, who anticipated the growth of technology that would connect the world but recognized the village as the most basic form of community; for it is within a community that one is judged by one's fellows. The popular American singer Katy Perry proclaims, "I am every woman. It takes a village to make me who I am."

DIARY: *Over a stile in a hedge full of honeysuckle, avoiding mudholes in field, then across a tarmac drive to enter Easton on the Hill. The village sits high above the Welland Valley, with a variety of tawny-hued stone houses.*

The National Trust administers a priest's house here that dates to the fifteenth century. The building is a combination of church and residence. The church itself is spacious. A display of the local Collyweston slate and its history is found inside, so there is an educational purpose as well as a religious one. Like most English churches we will encounter along Macmillan, this one is a hybrid of Norman and Gothic. England's parish churches have six styles of architecture: Anglo-Saxon, Norman (sometimes called "Romanesque"), Transitional, Early English Gothic, Decorated Gothic, and Perpendicular Gothic. The last three styles are collectively called "Gothic."

Everyone recognizes the ubiquitous square Norman tower, but usually there are elements of other styles as well. Round arches hint at Anglo-Saxon or Norman construction, whereas the "pointy arch" is Gothic. Some churches have a chapel, others just an additional altar, while the more impressive ones boast a spire. Interestingly, the north face of the church was regarded in medieval times as the "devil's side." No reputable person was ever buried to the building's north.

Every parish church is unique in its interior design. Some possess carved pews, intricate floor tiles, choir stalls, wall paintings, stained glass, monuments, lecterns, and fonts. Quite often an effigy of a knight or other major figure prominent in the early history of the parish is found inside. The font is typically the oldest part. Some churches we visit have misericords, carved brackets beneath the hinged choir seats upon which it was acceptable to lean during a "standing" part of the church service.

The Church of England is officially recognized as the state church. The "C of E" maintains 45 percent of England's Grade I listed buildings — chiefly churches and cathedrals, which total some 16,000 structures. Although church attendance has waned, the church buildings are used for a potpourri of community, cultural, and interfaith purposes. A survey in 2003 revealed that 86 percent of the country's population had visited a church building or place of worship during the previous twelve months. So whether it's a concert, a lecture on African pythons, or finding some quiet time, these wonderful historic buildings are still much used and obviously cherished. Churches that have been completely abandoned are cared for by the Redundant Churches Fund.

The *Guide* advises that we are now overlapping with the Jurassic Way, an 88-mile footpath that runs from Stamford to Banbury. The Way commemorates the rock formations that run in a southwest–northeast direction from the English Channel in Dorset to the Humber in Yorkshire. The limestone belt actually began for us at Kates Bridge. The closer to the heart of the Cotswolds we travel, the more the quality of the stone improves, until it attains the rich golden hue so characteristic of storybook villages like Bourton-on-the-Water and Lower Slaughter.

During the Jurassic period of geological time, the portion of central England we are walking was covered with a shallow, warm sea. This followed a lengthy era when Britain was a sandy desert much like Arizona or Mongolia today. In a cataclysm of events, this desert was transformed from a dry wasteland to a watery environment teeming with life.

Ammonites, brachiopods, plesiosaurs, ichthyosaurs, oysters, birds, and other species that crawled out of the ocean all died in vast numbers over the millennia, and left their bones behind. These became embedded in soft clays and limestones, some of which became fossils.

This Jurassic rock strata was discovered and named by William Smith, a countryman who spent his life exploring subterranean England. Smith produced the first geological map of the country in 1815. That map was a harbinger of the change that was to come to the accepted order of things. It was clear from the rock strata that the Earth was more than a few thousand years old. Charles Darwin published his theories on evolution later in the century. The literal Biblical view of creation was no longer credible.

We cross the lovely Collyweston Bridge over the River Welland to enter the county of Rutland. Rutland is the smallest county in England, though from 1974 to 1997 it was part of Leicestershire. When Parliament merged Rutland into Leicestershire in 1974 following a committee's review, Rutlanders conducted a Gandhi-like protest of civil disobedience, continuing to make out their property tax cheques to "Rutland County." The government ultimately bowed to this smouldering rebellion and restored Rutland to full county status in 1997.

Rutland has the highest average family birth rate of any English county: 2.81 children, compared with only 1.67 in Tyne and Wear. It also has a fine reputation for physical fitness. I don't know if this makes a case or not for the more physically fit being more sexually active. Rutland has also been placed at the top of the heap by statisticians as being the most contented county in England. So: happiness, fertility, and fitness — Rutland comes out on top. It is noteworthy that the county is composed of only two major towns, many small villages, and numerous farms. So: minimal pollution and a healthy rural lifestyle. Could Rutland be the model for the healthiest form of community in the twenty-first century?

Our route takes us through several wet barley fields and then over a footbridge to cross the River Chater. We are entering the village of Ketton. Cement works here employ some 220 people and supply the United Kingdom with one-tenth of its Portland cement. The local limestone quarries also produce Ketton stone, which was used to build several Cambridge colleges. We see giant dump trucks and excavators working quarries in the distance, like big Dinky toys.

We are now just a short distance from Fotheringhay, where Mary, Queen of Scots, was imprisoned and tried before being beheaded on February 8, 1587. The famous Talbot Hotel in nearby Oundle has a macabre link with Fotheringhay Castle, as the main staircase of the hotel is the very one Mary descended at the castle on the way to her death; her ghost is still seen retracing those final steps. (The staircase was installed in the Talbot when it was rebuilt in 1626, at the time of the castle's demolition.) Mary's executioner lodged in this inn the night before he performed his grisly duty.

The wind picks up as we march along, and great sweeping views across Rutland Water open up through the trees. Waves are being churned into whitecaps, the sky changing from an oyster-shell hue to angry, inky blotches of nimbus rolling in from the North Sea.

"Dirty weather coming, John," says Karl. "We better hoof it to our lodgings."

The Rutland Water reservoir is a vast nature reserve that is the breeding site for numerous species. It is also a fisherman's mecca. The surrounding landscape is one of gentle, undulating wolds and alternating flat, grassy fields. Once heavily populated, the hundreds of lost and deserted villages in the vicinity attest to the ravages of the Black Death in the fourteenth century.

Rutland Water was a low-lying region of marsh and lake prior to 1976, when it was flooded and transformed into a reservoir 4.19 square miles in area, making it England's second-largest lake after Windermere, in the Lake District. Some twenty thousand wild birds reside here year-round, and countless others stop over while on migration. The prized bird to spot is the osprey, which was introduced in 1996; breeding couples now return annually to raise their young. This magnificent bird boasts a five-foot wingspan at maturity.

Wetlands to the west of Rutland Water are now a nature reserve which is home to the Anglian Water Birdwatching Centre. The British Birdwatching Fair is held here annually, the largest of its kind in Europe. I am told that two of the highlights of the recent summer exhibition were the killer cat and stuffed canary carpet displays (not at all politically correct). The fair is the birdwatchers' equivalent to the Glastonbury music festival.

Heavy gusts of wind and rain are now upon us. Karl disappears from sight ahead of me and I don't catch up to him for a good half hour, when I find him standing motionless at the outskirts of our destination village in front of an official-looking sign which reads: "Whitwell — twinned with Paris."

Our B&B host is Julie, a bubbly, athletic woman in her forties who keeps a trim cottage with her husband and two collies. My first question to her pertains to the opening hours of the Noel Arms village pub. My second question relates to the funny sign.

"Is this some joke, or is it a different Paris?"

It transpires that Julie is uniquely qualified to answer both questions, because she and her husband at one time managed the Noel Arms. She gives me a newspaper — the *Daily Mail* from August 18, 1992 — that exploded the Whitwell story onto the national stage.

"Some cars skidded into the hedge," we read, "but mostly they pulled back slowly, and had their pictures taken at the sign. You see these places everywhere, and often nobody's heard of the city's twin before. All it ever means is that officials get a trip once in a while to drink wine for several days and visit the local sewage farm."

The Whitwell village elders, led by Sam Healey, proprietor of the Noel Arms, voted to twin Whitwell with Paris. They then erected the signage, and patiently waited for the mayor of Paris, Monsieur Jacques Chirac, to visit, as is the custom with the twinning of cities. Finally, the Whitwell elders received a reply from Chirac's office advising they had never heard of Whitwell. The letter was a little on the frosty side; in fact, the villagers found the tone a tad offensive. (After all, noted Healey, even though it boasts but nineteen houses, Whitwell is clearly the place to be.) So the village elders wrote back and advised M. Chirac that if they did not hear back from his office by a fixed date, they would assume that M. Chirac had agreed to the twinning. That date passed without response, and so the official twinning ceremonies were scheduled in the village.

The day of the ceremony was so replete with liquid refreshments that about all Healey could remember is that everyone ended up as "drunk as lords." He woke up in his coal shed the morning after. He did recall that they staged the first can-can dances ever seen in Whitwell. Healey wrote to M. Chirac and told him he'd missed a great party and the committee would deputize someone to officially open the new toilets at the

Noel Arms for him, since it appeared that M. Chirac would be unavoidably absent.

The news report concluded with Healey saying, "It isn't a bloody joke. It's serious. We put up the signs, one at each end, and Victoria Dickinson came and painted all these nice French flags on the wall. The road signs cost forty quid each, and we've had a lot of them pinched. We're thinking of making a sign saying 'Paris — twinned with Whitwell,' and sticking it up at Charles de Gaulle Airport. Why not?"

Even Rutland County Council got into the spirit of it all, by replacing the hokey wooden signs with formal, legal metal ones. Whitwell had arrived.

Julie verifies all this. She is also very kind and turns on the heat for us this evening.

Morning dawns with a bland tapioca sky that hints of a dry day on the path. We are soon wending our way along a cycle track through a copse skirting the lake.

DIARY: *Our entry into the trim town of Oakham coincides with the first rays of sun striking the buff-toned façade of the Brook Whipper-in Hotel in the market square, where I enjoy a fine panini tuna sandwich. The serving of tuna sandwiches for lunch on Saturdays is a tradition in many market towns. A barrel-chested green grocer at the market next door sonorously proclaims, "90p. for 3 cauliflower!" I love the picture-postcard octagonal Butter Cross with its pyramidal roof, beneath which lay stocks that were used to punish miscreants.*

Oakham historically wielded a degree of autonomy normally associated with a city-state. Its authority emanated from Oakham Castle, whose only surviving structure is the Great Hall, built in 1190. We leave our dirty walking boots at the door and tiptoe inside to explore.

The Great Hall is the earliest structure of its kind associated with an English castle to survive intact. Sunlight streams through the high window at one end, highlighting the rounded Doric arches that support the ornate ceiling, which consists of elaborate cross-sectioned beams strung out in the Elizabethan style.

But the real feature of the Great Hall is the 230 horseshoes clustered all over the walls. Most are plain, but a few are encrusted with jewels, and glitter subtly in the soft light. The explanation for this unusual display is a centuries-old tradition requiring any peer of the realm visiting Oakham to forfeit a horseshoe to the lord of the manor at the castle. Even Prince Charles recently had to hand over his horseshoe. The tradition is linked to one of the earliest owners, the Ferrers family.

We move on to inspect the famous Oakham School, founded in 1584 by Robert Johnson, an archdeacon who believed — unusually for his day — that every child should have an opportunity for education, and who set aside much of his church's income to establish a school plus two grammar facilities in Oakham and Uppingham. His injunction was clear: "The schoolmaster shall teach all those grammar scholars that are brought up in Oakham, freely without pay, if their parents be poor and not able to pay, and keep them constantly to school." He persuaded Elizabeth I to endow the school permanently by royal charter. The Oakham School became the first private secondary school in Britain to allow coeducational instruction for all grades. Then it strutted its stuff further in 1995 by becoming the first public (that is, private) school in Britain to go online. A chapel and a memorial library respectively honour the sixty-nine schoolboys killed in World War I and the eighty-two killed in World War II.

Like any ancient market town, Oakham has had its share of notables and eccentrics. One Jeffrey Hudson of Oakham was so small that he was once served up to Charles I in a fruit pie. While entertaining the king and queen for dinner, Hudson's master, Lord Buckingham, advised their majesties that he had a special surprise in store. Two servants carried a massive pie into the room, placed it on the table, and out popped Jeffrey Hudson clad in a full suit of armour. The queen was so delighted by this that she claimed Hudson for her own court, granting him the title of Queen's Dwarf. Royal courtiers referred to Hudson as Lord Minimus. When the queen was forced to flee to exile in France in 1643, Hudson accompanied her as a trusted aide. Later, he led a colourful life abroad that saw him twice captured by pirates and sold into slavery, only to escape back to England. At the time of his death at age sixty-three, Hudson measured three feet six inches in height.

The day is getting on as we finish our inspection of the town's artifacts, but Karl insists on checking up on the Oakham constabulary to ensure that they have picked up Tiffany's clothes from our green lane near Stamford. So we traipse all the way to the police station, only to find that at 5:15 PM the station is already closed and one must call a special number in case of emergency. Karl and I just stand there dumfounded.

"Bloody hell! Have you ever heard of a police station in a major town that simply closes at 5 PM, John? What — do they expect all crime to stop for the evening or something?"

"I don't know, Karl. Maybe they don't have enough business to keep the staff engaged, but my hunch is that they are bogged down with both crime and paperwork and don't want to be interrupted by some bloke coming in at night to report a stray dog and such."

In fact, the "Closed" sign epitomizes the English aversion to the masses having access to shopping, sustenance, or authority outside of severely prescribed hours.

After booking in at a local hotel, Karl and I sample the fare at its upscale restaurant. How about braised lamb shank with a minted pea purée? I was about to say there are no mushy peas offered anymore, but trust the English to sneak in their pea concoction under the guise of gourmet. I settle for grilled figs, pistachio nuts with local honey, and goat's cheese for starters, then move on to wood pigeon breast, foie gras, black pudding, and roasted potatoes, with New York cheesecake for dessert.

Karl fulfills his wish and enjoys wood pigeon as well. The bird has a taste similar to a Cornish game hen, and a texture like liver. Our server advises us that she enjoys roasted wood pigeon on toast. The ingredients, she says, are as follows: two oven-ready wood pigeons; robust herbs such as thyme, sage, and rosemary; four garlic cloves ("bashed not peeled"); olive oil; butter; two thick slices of sourdough bread; and 150 millilitres of red wine. Sounds like heaven on a stick.

Of the pigeon family, only wood pigeons can be legally killed for food. Recently a woman in a London park was arrested for feeding domestic pigeons with seeds, then grabbing them, wringing their necks, and stuffing their bodies into her voluminous handbag. One wonders if she bothers to pick up roadkill.

Don't laugh. Roadkill cuisine has become big in Britain. Waste not, want not. Fergus Drennan has hosted a BBC production, *The Roadkill Chef*, instructing viewers on the cooking of casseroles from squashed badgers, pheasant, and rabbits, among other animals. Another BBC broadcaster, Miranda Krestovnikoff, recently hosted a dinner party where guests were treated to the following dishes: fried rat served with garlic and soy sauce, the rat having been picked off the B3347 in Hampshire; fox sautéed in garlic, found dead on a road near Wimborne, Dorset; and badger *chasseur,* served with tomato sauce after being removed from the A354 near Salisbury. Roadkill is touted as being high in vitamins and proteins, with lean meat and little saturated fat, plus the wild dead are free of hormonal drugs and additives. But if you are the driver who runs down that luscious-looking badger, it is illegal for you to eat it. Any other motorist, however, is legally allowed to give it a go. Once dead, the only animals it is illegal to eat in Britain are humans and swans. Only the Queen can consume swan — it is an act of treason for anyone else to kill or eat the stately bird.

Relaxing over his plum brandy, Karl is the picture of contentment.

"Next thing, Karl, you'll be eating Welsh rabbit."

"I will have you know, John boy, that Welsh Rabbit is now known as 'rarebit,' and that it is neither Welsh nor rabbit. It is a concoction of melted cheese with butter, milk, and Worcestershire sauce spread over buttered toast."

"Ugh!" But the word is barely out of my mouth before I realize that the concoction just described by Karl is what was served to me by my grandmother when I was eight years old — and which I positively loved.

3

HARE PIES *and* BOTTLE KICKING

Ill fares the land, to hastening ills a prey,

Where wealth accumulates, and men decay:

Princes and lords may flourish, or may fade;

A breath can make them, as a breath had made;

But a bold peasantry, their country's pride,

When once destroyed, can never be supplied.

— OLIVER GOLDSMITH —
The Deserted Village

DIARY: *Oakham is a memorable, tidy little town where one could comfortably settle as a safe harbour. Rutland in fact could have served as inspiration for Tolkien's Shire in* The Lord of the Rings. *The county resembles a Wild Wood in its insularity, seemingly detached from the broader world . . . Ascending a long hill on Oakham's fringe, we pass by a primary school and hear the laughing, frolicking sounds of children at play immediately below us — and yes, there is the ubiquitous soccer ball being kicked about with wild abandon. Oh, to be young again!*

From here, our route traverses large swathes of croplands and copses, with small stone villages scattered hither and thither. We will soon leave Rutland, slice through a corner of Leicestershire, and then explore the lonely undulating grasslands of Northamptonshire before reaching the fringe of the Cotswolds.

Karl and I remark upon the constant intersection of other footpaths joining ours, some with clearly marked names, others anonymous. It is like veins of a body radiating in every direction. Many of these veins have existed from neolithic times. Rome added the arteries to the veins when it built the long, straight connecting roads, such as the Fosse Way. Writing in the early 1950s, Geoffrey Grigson opines: "Roads, lanes, paths. We use them without reflecting how they are some of man's oldest inscriptions upon the landscape, how they are evidence of the wedding between men and their environment."

We cross a stone bridge over the River Gwash. On the outskirts of the tiny village of Brooke lies the twelfth-century parish church of St. Peters, set at an odd angle in a field. The massive oak door creaks; a pigeon flaps in the belfry. Inside is a slanted limestone floor worn smooth by the tread of centuries; rare old box pews denote a well-preserved ancient house of prayer. Outside, we wander the graveyard. Many of the lichen-covered tombs are now bereft of lettering. It's a lonely spot. A Victorian lamp hangs on a crooked post, resembling a gibbet and serving no apparent purpose.

The utter silence is interrupted by the rumble of a rusty brown pickup down the churchyard track. A young, powerfully built man gets out and greets us. He is the groundskeeper — and is straight out of *Lady Chatterley's Lover*. His biceps bulge like sinuous tree roots. He carries a .22 rifle which I assume is for shooting rabbits, for I notice three of his victims lying in the truck bed next to a gas-powered lawnmower. Even his wary aloofness reminds me of the gardener in D.H. Lawrence's novel.

"You must be finding a lot of rabbits around here," I remark.

He says nothing and fiddles with his tailgate, obviously impatient for us to leave the grounds. Karl mentions that we are walking the Macmillan Way for three hundred miles.

"Thee's walkin' all the way to Dorset and the sea, then?"

"Aye," Karl says with a smile.

"Can't say's I've travelled much about, but once took the train down to London, I did."

"Have you lived in the area for long?" I ask.

"'Tis right. Been huntin' and tendin' gardens, field work, whatever a man can find."

We bid him adieu and leave him to his work.

Walking through Brooke, it is so quiet we whisper, afraid

to wake up canines or humans, though it is already mid-morning. The appearance of such villages has not changed significantly since the medieval age.

As for the copses, hedges, and flora of the countryside, that is another story. Woodlands have been decimated over the centuries, and the surviving copses are a mere fraction of the size they were in 1850. Hedges too were ruthlessly destroyed after World War II.

The primary hedge ingredient is hawthorn. This genus is shrouded in mystical folklore. The English used to call it the "bread and cheese" because young leaves were placed in sandwiches, much like lettuce today. The hawthorn relies on pollination by dung flies and midges, attracted to the scent and to the brown and purple anthers. Evidently, to a carrion fly these colours resemble decaying flesh. The blackthorn bush is related but is not indigenous to England. A Eurasian shrub with white flowers, its small, bluish-black, plum-like fruits are harvested chiefly for flavouring alcoholic beverages such as sloe gin.

All in all, if you ignore the horrible slashes of the motorways and "A" roads desecrating the country, both Wordsworth and Constable would be able today to gaze across the rolling countryside and receive inspiration. And much barley is still grown, because since Anglo-Saxon times the populace have consumed beer in copious quantities. Nearby Northampton alone boasted 160 inns and alehouses in the eighteenth century — about one for every thirty inhabitants.

In every village, from medieval times, there were three types of occupational rights: the right of every person to roam the lanes, the footpaths, and the church grounds; communal rights, such as the village green, the common oven, the wells and town pump, the stocks, and the open fields; and strictly private rights — the manor house of the lord and the cottages and crofts of the peasantry. The struggle to keep the paths and tracks open to the public has not always been an easy one. The Enclosure movements of the eighteenth century at first severely disrupted the footpaths. There ensued many stormy battles with big landowners. Legislation was passed in 1815 which allowed any two justices of the peace the power to close a footpath that they believed was no longer "necessary." In a Hansard record of 1831, it was recorded that this power had been regularly abused by the practice of one magistrate commonly saying to another, "Come and dine with me; I shall expect you an hour earlier as I want to stop up a footpath."

Jane Austen recognized the propensity of greedy landowners to close public paths, and referred in her novel *Emma* to conscientious nobles doing the right thing by not prejudicing access to the common folk. Sir Arthur Conan Doyle wrote of the hypocrisy of landowners — what we might call the NIMBY ("not in my backyard") syndrome today — in the speech of Mr. Frankland of Lafter Hall in *The Hound of the Baskervilles:* "It is a great day for me, sir . . . I have established a right of way through the centre of old Middleton's park, slap across it, sir, within a hundred yards of his own front door. What do you think of that? We'll teach those magnates that they cannot ride roughshod over the rights of the commoners, confound them! And I've closed the wood where the Fernworthy folk use to picnic. These infernal people seem to think that there are no rights of property."

There are still problems with farmers ploughing over their fields and failing to demarcate the walking path — which by law they are supposed to do. We are experiencing this problem in some of the rapeseed fields in particular. Thanks to the

Ramblers, this issue has been kept in the spotlight. Not that landowners like Madonna and others won't keep trying to fend off walkers. But most owners accept public footpaths running through their estates as an embedded country tradition and an integral part of rural life.

Villagers are confronted today by many newcomers who dream of quiet but sanitized country living. These newcomers complain about everything from the smell of manure to cattle-truck dust to cocks crowing — even the loudness of church bells. One wealthy car dealer, Frank Sytner, recently retired with his wife to the nearby village of Ridlington in search of the quiet life. But the couple did not care for the sheep, the smells, or the mud associated with a farming community. Mr. Sytner sued a neighbouring farmer for inadvertently spilling some mud on a lane leading to Sytner's prize horses. Mrs. Sytner also complained in court of the annoying sound of cows in the field. When the judge pointed out that perhaps the cow ruckus was normal for the countryside, she responded: "Yes, it's unfortunate, isn't it." The judge threw out the case.

Ian Johnson of the National Farmers Union opines that tolerance between the wave of newcomers to the countryside and the existing hierarchy of farmers and squires is badly needed. Although many townies adapt well, others, like the Sytners, move to the country, asserts Johnson, "but they don't want to be near the nasty niffs and noises . . . They don't want any movement in the country. They want to ossify it, crystallize it, or preserve it in aspic. They want their picture postcard there for immortality." So put on those designer wellies and get muck on them!

What Canadians would call Red Toryism is described by author Raymond Williams, in his *The Country and the City:*

"In Britain, identifiably, there is a persistent rural-intellectual radicalism: genuinely and actively hostile to industrialization and capitalism; opposed to commercialism and the exploitation of environment; attached to country ways and country feelings, the literature and the lore." Prince Charles epitomizes this mould.

The squires and the radicals with Tory tastes are now at one with socialists who wish to preserve the countryside. Perhaps this unusual political alliance began in the nineteenth century, when the austere Duke of Wellington joined with the poet William Wordsworth in denouncing the carnage wrought by the ubiquitous railway lines upon England's "green and pleasant land." Wordsworth abhorred the intrusion of the smoky, dirty trains into the countryside and declaimed in a sonnet, "Is there no nook of English ground secure / From rash assault?" The Red Tories and socialists, alas, part company on issues like fox hunting.

A mile beyond Brooke we say hello to an elderly, spry lady sitting on her porch who invites us into her garden for a cup of tea. She says that she walks in North Wales and fights to prevent any new roads or despoliation of her hillside there, where she keeps a caravan for part-time rental plus personal use. Her name is Nora.

We sit and chat about the countryside and village life. Nora's cottage is surrounded by wildflowers, and above our tea table stands a charming Elizabethan-style chocolate and white dovecote with a pigeon perched on a ledge, alert for some tea crumbs.

Nora is a keen observer of village trends: "It's funny how the new people coming into a village to live want to retain village traditions but always want to improve things. Like here, they want a community centre, as if that will keep young people in the village and in line. The young people will still get in their cars and drive to Stamford for partying."

"That's the way with young people all over the world, Nora," Karl says with a smile. "Young folk love their cars. Thanks for the tea; and maybe we'll see you one day at your caravan in Wales."

Refreshed by Nora's tea and talk, we continue down a green lane lined by a hedgerow blanketed with white mayflowers on one side and open farm tracts on the other. My olfactory senses are pervaded by the pungent, distinctive odour of steaming, newly ploughed fields mingled with hedge blossoms, radiant in the sunshine, that takes me back to weekend jaunts to my grandparents' farm in British Columbia's Fraser Valley. Heaven for a ten-year-old city boy was sitting under the horse chestnut tree with Grandfather as he smoked his pipe of Borkum Riff while I sipped Grandma's iced raspberry-vinegar cordial. Surely there is a thread of kinship here among rural areas the world over: that definable odour of spring — perhaps one of the few occasions when Man's agricultural activity blends harmoniously with the richness of Nature's bounty of bursting blooms and the nascent stirring of the land.

The scene before us characterizes much of the landscape each morning: a stile or gate, misty fields of green alternating with cadmium yellow swathes of rape unfolding into the distance. Other than the wood pigeon's occasional *Ooo-oo*, there is utter, ineffable silence. But the rapeseed plants are sopping, and the path which runs diagonally through the centre of the field is often hidden by the five-foot-high stalks that we shove aside with our sticks.

Rapeseed has become a dominant field crop in England. In Canada, it is known as "canola." The plant name derives from the Latin name for turnip, *rapa*. It is a variety of the

Brassica family and the third-largest source of vegetable oil in the world. It was first grown in England in the fourteenth century; in the nineteenth century it became a lubricant for steam engines, and today is grown for vegetable oil, animal feed, and biodiesel. The rapid expansion of rapeseed fields in England is attributable to the European Union's appetite for ever-increasing supplies of biodiesel for both heating systems and motor vehicle engines.

Finches flutter about as we pass through Prior's Coppice Nature Reserve, and then it's onto a bridleway recently churned up by horses. Restored medieval fish ponds flank both sides of the track before we cross the River Chater. Fish ponds formed an important source of the diet of ancient and medieval people in England.

The Way now winds along and over the Eye Brook before ascending a steep hill into Belton-in-Rutland. Cool rain and a slippery track combine to make this a gruelling grind.

We secure lodgings at a stone cottage B&B in Belton. The landlady is pleasant but brusque. I dare not ask her for the heat to be turned on early, despite our damp, bedraggled state. I would like some heat before bed; the last uphill climb exhausted me. A sign in my ensuite warns: "Guests may not wash clothes in the basin." To hell with that! The only way we can keep clean is to wash our socks and underwear each night.

We have decided to take a cab to Uppingham, as the Crown Inn there has been recommended to us by the landlady. Before we set out for dinner, Karl insists that the cab driver be directed to the green lane where we found Tiffany's clothing, just to make sure that the Oakham police have picked up the garments.

"Since we can't seem to rouse anyone at the Oakham police station, John, we have to be satisfied they are doing their job. I have to know."

"We could just call them in the morning. It must be a good thirty miles back to Tiffany's lane."

"No, John, I have to know tonight that they have done their job and picked up the clothing."

"Okay, Karl. We will go back there."

And indeed we do. The cab arrives at our B&B around six o'clock. The cabbie is swarthy and sixtyish, sports a captain's beard, and wears a Greek fisherman's cap. He resembles Captain Smith of the *Titanic*. I show him the location of the Tiffany site, marked with an X in my *Guide*, and off we go. He does not seem to find our request at all unusual, and keeps up a steady stream of conversation about his relatives in Canada, who work in the Alberta oil and gas fields.

We pull up to a spot in the road where it curves. Tiffany's lane is marked with a bridleway sign attached to which is the familiar Macmillan sticker. Karl and I both get out and trundle up the dark, mucky track, casting furtive glances around us. The cabbie has positioned his vehicle with headlights shining up the lane to give us more light, but it's a surreal, chilling scene right out of Stephen King's *The Dark Half*. This portion of our otherwise delightful walk has taken on a sinister aspect. About two hundred yards in, we search on the right side below the hedgerow and then reconnoitre for another hundred yards or so.

"Karl, the clothes are gone. The police definitely picked them up."

He just grunts and says he wants to search farther toward the road, but eventually agrees that the clothes are gone. By this time, the rain is pelting down. I can see the cab driver's dim visage behind the wheel as his windshield wipers kick in.

"Okay, John, I'm satisfied. Now I could use a good stiff Scotch."

The Crown Inn has great food and two known ghosts. The pub crowd is orderly. It is *de rigueur* in England for the barmaid to display generous décolletage, and we are satisfied that the Crown has passed muster in this regard. The buxom blonde swinging the Guinness is cheerful and friendly. She also smiles at me without any subtle mockery of my foreign accent when I order Karl's double Scotch and my half pint of lager. Wherever one travels, the first thing the natives do is analyze your accent. The flip side of this is that to a villager, we are all foreigners unless we live within a radius of five miles. In these small rural backwaters, a Yorkshireman is a source of wonder, even gossip. But a North American is simply beyond comprehension and can be safely ignored.

We both order the beef Wellington, which is delicious — essentially a filet steak lathered with pâté and duxelles, wrapped in a puff pastry and baked. I have mine with a touch of curry. The dish is named after the Duke of Wellington, perhaps because he was known to love a mix of beef, truffles, mushrooms, pâté in pastry, and Madeira wine. Others suggest that it was just a patriotic chef who wanted to assimilate the French recipe for *filet de bœuf en croûte* during the Napoleonic Wars. Regardless, I could eat this every night, washed down with a spicy Shiraz.

Next morning there is a promise of sun. A winding path leads us out of Belton. There must be horses about, as there is a pervasive odour of horse manure when we emerge from a copse into open fields. In the tiny village of Allexton, the Norman church has been abandoned and is now under the care of the Churches Conservation Trust. The churchyard is overgrown; thistles, brambles, and St. John's wort compete with ivy growing right up the oolite stone walls. Inside, the church is bleak and stark. Little light penetrates, and the black-and-russet tiled mosaic floor is cracked and stained.

Outside, Karl and I poke about a bit in the graveyard. Despite the playful swoop of swallows, there is a problem here. By the vestry door at the north end of the church, the overgrown weeds reach up and partly cover the grand tomb of Thomas Hotchkin, who died in 1774, having, it is stated, "been most miserably cut and mangled, of a fistula." Hotchkin gained his wealth from his West Indies sugar plantations and slave trading. A rotten smell of decay, redolent of dead rat or mouse, emanates from near his tomb, upon which rests a large urn. Perhaps fitting for a slaver's tomb, I muse. The panelled vestry door glows magically like the Black Gate of Mordor, evilly beckoning us, and there are dark red blotches resembling blood near the old brass door handle. Above us a crow starts cawing and does not cease. I shiver and signal to Karl that it's time to leave. He doesn't argue. This is one morbid place.

We footslog through field after field. The landscape is now rolling, and I can see ten miles toward the Northamptonshire skyline. Karl curses the many rabbit holes, as well as the farmers who do not leave the required swathe in their fields for the prescribed path.

"The law evidently says that we can be fined for trespass if we leave the trail, but the bloody farmer can't be bothered to show where it is," he says. "So I say to hell with it. Just make for the far stile by whatever route is fastest."

It is indeed a conundrum, and there are so few walkers on this section of the Way that one can see the farmer lapsing into the habit of ignoring the path with his crop planting. However, we also note the same large boot marks we saw yesterday on the path, and my bet is that the chap who leaves them knows where he is going and we should follow his marks if in doubt.

Both my feet hurt from blisters. The last rabbit hole I stepped into gobbled up my left foot, which is now a tad sprained. The other foot stepped in a wet cow pie while trying to avoid a badger sett, and the boot is bespattered with dung.

Two jackrabbits are so absorbed with boxing one another that they ignore us as we approach to within a few feet — such is the male ego, I suppose, even in the rabbit world. These are, in fact, hares competing to impress the females during mating season. As a former bantamweight pugilist, Karl is highly amused by their boxing antics.

"They show good form standing like that, cautiously circling one another on their hind legs. They even feint and pivot."

"One of them kicks his legs out as well — like Mike Tyson on steroids." I wonder whether the females are hiding in the tall grass watching the show.

DIARY: *Down into the village of Hallaton, passing a large duck pond and a conical market cross resembling a nuclear rocket silo. Found the Fox Inn, where we enjoyed a pint of local brew and learned all about the famous bottle-kicking and hare-pie-scrambling contests. The village is also famous for the Hallaton Treasure, a hoard of some 5,000 Roman silver and gold coins and jewellery. The odd part is that the coins were in the possession of the local Celtic tribe, the Corieltauvi, well before Caesar's conquest, and one Roman coin was dated to 211 BC, making it the oldest Roman coin ever found in Britain. The site was also a Druidic shrine.*

Hallaton's quirky tradition involving ale and hares dates back to 1698. The event also involves a second village, named Medbourne. Folk music, a church service, fierce wrestling, and

59

liquid refreshments combine to stir up the locals in a blend of pride, passion, violence, and virility.

For almost two hundred years until 1962, the Hallaton rector was required to host the event, because a parcel of land was gifted to the rectory in 1770 on the express condition that the rector provide two hare pies, a quantity of ale, and two dozen penny loaves, to be scrambled for on Easter Monday each year after he had preached his divine service. The land, called Hare Crop Leys, was donated by two ladies who wished to give thanks to God for delivering them from goring by a bull by intervening at the last moment in the form of a hare — the hare having diverted the bull's attention, allowing the women to escape the field in which they were walking on a footpath.

The event consists of two segments. First, a parade leaves the Fox Inn, led by a warrener carrying a staff topped with a hare. (It used to be a real dead hare but is now a carved replica.) He is accompanied by assistants who lug baskets of bread and hare pie and three bottles of ale. The bottles are actually kegs, each weighing five kilograms. Upon arrival at the church, the pie is blessed by the vicar then tossed to the assembled crowd in bits and pieces. How much ends up actually eaten and how much is left on the ground for the dogs is an open question.

The second stage of the event is the macho phase of bottle kicking. The parade proceeds to Hare Pie Bank. Bottle kicking is a rough-and-tumble game. The normally friendly relations between the two villages turns to dark hostility in Hallaton Brook, where it can get downright vicious, and also on the hilltops, where the participants engage in a fierce, rowdy battle to wrestle and wrench the casks of ale back to their own village. It's down and dirty in rugby-like scrums, with no referee. Torn fingernails, sprains, bruises, and cracked ribs are common. Once one bottle is won by a side, it is hustled up to the top of the hill and a second, lighter bottle is then fought for — and a third bottle in the event of a tie. After the winning village is declared, everyone rushes back to the Fox Inn for liquid refreshments.

The tradition has been so fiercely defended that when one rector threatened to cease provision of the ale and pies, he was threatened by the villagers: "No ale and pie — no rector." The rector hastily relented. Villagers know their rights. It appears that they always did.

The village of Peatling Magna, near Hallaton, supported Simon de Montfort against King Henry III in 1265, in Montfort's revolt to enforce Magna Carta and protect barons and their villeins from arbitrary exercise of royal authority. When the king's men entered Peatling Magna after defeating Montfort at the Battle of Evesham, they were given a cool reception — as they were in fact at Hallaton. The villagers told the armed men to leave, on the basis that they were not representative of the *communitas regni,* or community of the realm, which the villagers believed entitled everyone to basic rights. The villagers sued the king's representative, Peter de Nevill, and were actually given a hearing in the royal court. Although they lost the lawsuit and had to pay a fine, they took a stand to assert the protection of the following pledges of Magna Carta:

No free man shall be seized or imprisoned, or stripped of his rights
or possessions, or outlawed or exiled, or deprived of his standing
in any other way; nor will we proceed with force against him, or send
others to do so, except by the lawful judgment of his equals, or by
the law of the land.

To no one will we sell, to no one deny or delay right or justice.

Until recently, most historians have assumed medieval villagers to be coarse, ignorant, and utterly servile. Well, they may have been illiterate, perhaps coarse, but evidently not so servile. The distinguished English historian Michael Wood, in his work *In Search of England*, argues that historians have seriously underestimated the lust for freedom possessed by common people in the Middle Ages.

Further, the derogatory terms *serf* and *villein* (the origin of *villain*) are much misrepresented in history class. Serfs and villeins thought the term "free man" in Magna Carta applied to them and not just to some tiny group of lords and knights. As Frances and Joseph Gies write in their *Life in a Medieval Village*, the "unfreedom of the villein or serf was never a generalized condition, like slavery, but always consisted of specific disabilities . . . The villein remained 'a free man in relation to all men other than his lord.'" The authors conclude that "a rich villein was a bigger man in the village than a poor free man." The prototype of the stalwart peasant, loyal and pious but stubborn, is perhaps best presented in the medieval poem *Piers Plowman*. The peasant was also independent in thought, as recognized by Oliver Goldsmith when he wrote the line "A bold peasantry, their country's pride."

In medieval times, England's villages lay at the heart of the open field system, where common fields were available for grazing animals and growing corn and wheat. All of this disappeared for villagers, beginning in the late sixteenth century and culminating in the Enclosure statutes of the early nineteenth century. Freedom of tenure was a concept that villagers had practised from Anglo-Saxon times, even if they did not technically own any of the common land on which their animals grazed or their crops were planted. Yes, they had to do work for the local lord's demesne, but they got to work their own "furlong" as well — and eventually, instead of having to work the lord's land, they paid him a form of tribute each year for the right to work land that over time might become their own, either by leasehold or by fee simple.

Enclosure rendered the poor destitute and retarded the evolution of the peasants' landholding rights. When the Industrial Revolution arrived, it was the poorest peasants who first drifted to cities like Manchester and Birmingham to seek subsistence wages. A similar movement is occurring in the countryside of China today with the drive to industrialization in cities like Chongqing.

Hallaton slumbers in peaceful splendour on this late May morning. On the outskirts of town, however, we spy a sobering reminder of the brutish bottle-kicking festival. A plaque on a stone pillar reads:

In memory of Anthony James Hough,
24 July 1971– 09 April 2002.

"Karl, I read in the pamphlet that an Anthony Hough died of a suspected heart attack in the heat of a scrimmage at the 2002 bottle-kicking contest."

"Poor bugger."

We are escorted by thrushes, crows, and rooks flirting and scolding and soaring overhead. The path plunges through a gap in a disused railway embankment, where we cross an old Roman road to proceed across a minute stone span over the River Welland. We have now left Leicestershire and entered Northamptonshire. The sky remains veiled yet bright, like some coquettish bride. The day's experiences create a rush in my blood. I yearn to pound the trail ahead and drink in the ecstasy of the English spring.

Throughout Northamptonshire there is a paucity of farm animals. Large, sweeping fields of varied crops predominate. A few tracts are overrun with crimson clover and common vetch, plus purple and rose lupines here and there in clumps, vying with the ubiquitous thistles. We are pleasantly surprised today to encounter many butterflies and moths, one of which is the Jersey tiger moth, as beautiful as any butterfly, with vivid orange markings. A day-flying species, it is highly resistant to chemicals.

There is a familiar leitmotif to this landscape. Everything is topsy-turvy. Roads and lanes twist and curve, elongate and contract. Hedgerows hide their own secrets as well as blocking the view. Grassy uplands, growing crops, and fallow fields twist and contour in the most idiosyncratic, capricious, and erratic manner possible. The only ordered logicality to the landscape is found in the Fens. Elsewhere, a village one mile from one's home can be literally lost in some coomb that few people ever visit — or leave, for that matter. Many rural inhabitants, like Lady Chatterley's gardener at Brooke, seldom venture beyond a limited periphery — reluctant like Ratty to ever leave the Wild Wood.

It was and is all about the shire. The shire or county is equivalent to a North American county in only rough terms, because whereas across the pond the county is merely an administrative territory, in England the shire was paramount, often coming before country. As Kipling wrote of his fellow countrymen, "One spot shall prove beloved over all." Most of the shire boundaries were settled before the end of the reign of Edward the Elder, King Alfred's son, who ruled from 899 to 924. And so the identification of the English with the shire as a distinct home territory has endured for over a thousand years.

The Normans, after 1066, adopted the Anglo-Saxon administrative units but changed the name from "shire" to "county." The chief officer was the sheriff — hence the evil Sheriff of Nottingham from Robin Hood's era — who reported directly to the Crown. The sheriff was not replaced in his duties until 1888, when county councils were established. The loyalty expressed by the English to their home turf has spilled over from village and countryside to the urban cores. A man plays football for Birmingham and England, not England and Birmingham. And of course, within one's shire, loyalty is first and foremost to one's village or town.

In a succession of high, muddy fields near Braybrooke, the sticky wet rape plants obscure the footpath. I holler at Karl to stick to the proper route, but I really just want him to slow down. In any case, he pays no attention.

I finally rationalize — it may be trespass, but it's the farmer's own fault, so I follow Karl's easier route around the field. I remember A.E. Housman's lines:

Laws for themselves and not for me,
And if my ways are not as theirs
Let them mind their own affairs.

Fortunately, we hear no shotgun warnings in these Northamptonshire fields. In fact we often walk all day and barely see a soul. Even the normally ubiquitous crows and rooks shun our company. Mind you, I do receive a scare: upon topping a rise in a high field I find myself staring at a grim-faced soldier near the path, clad in scarlet uniform, bearskin hat, and wellies, brandishing a real musket, fresh off the battlefield of Waterloo! I approach him cautiously, and it is only when ten feet away that I am certain that this apparition is a scarecrow — one very sophisticated scarecrow. I don't know if the rooks and crows are impressed, but the dude certainly had me fooled.

DIARY: *Saw a sign for cyclists on a post: "Over Kelmarsh betwixt woods and spinneys." How quaint.*

The *Guide* cautions: "Watch for holes in the path — badgers abound here!" Too late for Karl, as ahead of me I see him suddenly lurch and fall to his knees. But he picks himself up, cursing, and dusts himself off.

"Are you all right?"

"Damn rabbits! Twisted my ankle a little — nothing much."

"The *Guide* warns that these are badger setts."

Karl grimaces. I hear another muffled curse, and then off he goes, stamping his walking stick furiously, his pace unslackened.

Brampton Ash village is full of hundreds of colourful hens running free range on a covered run. Karl spots a milk delivery van in the lane and hails the driver, and before I know it he is quaffing back fresh milk from an old-fashioned glass milk bottle. I follow suit. Milk never tasted so good. We return the bottles empty to the van before climbing a long, steep hill out of the village.

We are halfway up the winding hill when I hear a clattering racket. Around the bend bearing down on us is a pony trap being driven by a slender, rosy-cheeked woman, her long raven hair flying in the wind, with an elderly, hollow-cheeked man resembling Frankenstein's monster standing on a platform behind her. Karl and I dive into a ragged hawthorn hedge to save ourselves. I wave as they go thundering by, but they seem oblivious to our presence.

"That girl could be the free-spirited Bathsheba right out of *Far from the Madding Crowd*."

"It's certainly strange, John, that neither of them even gave us a glance. If we hadn't rolled smartly into the hedge, I swear they would have run us down without a thought."

We soon turn right at a group of unusual red-brick barns called the Red Hovel. On the far side of the busy A6 we hit a spinney (a small area of scrubby bush) and navigate a flimsy plank bridge over the River Jordan. At Braybrooke we find the earthwork mounds of Braybrooke Castle, which was once a fortified manor house owned by the Latimer family. An interesting stone monument here commemorates the turn of the millennium by giving the history of the village in a nutshell — an outdoor sculpture with carved representations for each topic and event. The story is presented as follows with my gloss:

Chetelbert the Dane, first recorded resident; *13th century church; The river Jordan,* named by the Baptists, with a chapel built in 1788; *The bridge,* originally a pack bridge; *The knight,* Thomas Latymer; *A Lollard* taking copies of the translated Bible to Thomas Wycliffe at Lutterworth; *The Lollard Bible* translated into Middle English from the Latin by Czech scribes living in the castle — a heretical occupation, which could get you hanged, drawn and quartered or burnt at the stake; *The castle in flames,* possibly an accident with gun powder; In the castle gateway are a set of wickets to represent the local cricket club; *A carp,* farmed in the castle fishponds as food for local inhabitants; *A roll of fabric* representing the weavers of the village who made cloth for the soldiers fighting the Napoleonic Wars; *Ammonite,* representing the Jurassic Way; *Plate* made by the village potter from local clay; *The sun and flying swan* represent the two pubs of the village; *In the present day* the fields are used for rearing beef and lamb on the rich grassland surrounding the village; *Morris Dancer's bell* representing Braybrooke Morris Dancers.

What a wonderful way to summarize a village's history. Additional images interspersed on the face of the column depict animals of the countryside: badger, fox, hare, even a fairy.

Usually I try to line up our bed and breakfasts three or four nights in advance, but sometimes we get stuck, and this is where the *Macmillan Accommodation Guide* is of great help. Just past Braybrooke we can walk northwest on an authorized diversion to Market Harborough, where I have booked a B&B. We will then rejoin the main Way in the morning near Great Oxendon.

Karl is apprehensive.

"Are you sure this is legitimate? I said I would walk the entire Macmillan Way, and I damn well mean to."

"Karl, even the *Guide* provides this as an alternative — it's a spur route; and we will end up walking several miles farther anyway."

He grunts acceptance, and we trudge toward the market town that used to be part of William the Conqueror's Rockingham Forest, which stretched from Market Harborough all the way to Stamford. In forty-five minutes we see the steeple of St. Dionysius Church looming ahead, and on our approach discover next to it a beautiful half-timbered building called the Old Grammar School, dating from 1614. Here there is a covered market area; the upper end of High Street is a wide boulevard of unspoiled Georgian-style buildings. It is late afternoon and there are many people on the street. I notice a couple of rough, burly, tattooed men pushing baby prams with their partners.

Our B&B is a few blocks west of the town centre, and we find it just as a downpour strikes. The frumpy landlady greets us as if she is surprised to see us, but welcomes us in. I immediately plan my attack on her precious central heating system.

After a pleasant cup of Tetley tea with biscuits, we are all sorted out, ready to head downtown to dinner. On High Street there is every kind of shop: Oxfam, a Waterstone's bookstore, a Lloyd's Bank in Venetian Gothic motif, pharmacies, a bike repair shop, and a café called Zizzi's where people are enjoying beer and mochas outdoors even in the drizzle. Numerous white-haired couples are lounging on benches clustered around the Old Grammar School. West meets East down a side street, where stands the quintessentially English Swallow Cottage — climbing roses and all — offering "Traditional Cantonese Foods and Hot Food Take Away." (The English love chicken chop suey served with chips.)

We decide to try out the Red Cow Hotel. Its façade is a gaudy mélange of orange bricks and cream-coloured stone. The pork pie is overcooked, and we are distracted by the loud blare of the telly broadcasting a soccer match. But it is a fun place, with darts being played and crowded tables occupied by loquacious diners. Many locals are here for dinner: families; a young buck wearing a tartan sitting on a barstool; a fiftyish, red-faced, short, stocky man with a peroxide blonde looking older than her aspirations; and a Prince Charles look-alike with a doughty, horsey brunette fawning over and pecking him. Much Guinness and lager are flowing freely. Does this scene represent the safety valve for an otherwise docile race?

"Karl, this brochure states that the town was known far and wide for its corset factory, which, commencing in 1876, supplied most of Britain's ladies with their corsets and stays for a good century. In later years they exclusively produced the 'liberty bodice' as a modern alternative to the corset. The factory shut down in the late seventies."

"You don't say? Did the factory close down because of outsourcing to China, or do the ladies just not wear corsets anymore?"

"I believe the latter. In any case, the factory building still dominates the centre of town but now houses a library, museum, and government offices. It should be just down the street from here."

"Trust the government to take over the expensive real estate. It's nice to have a library and all, but those bureaucrats at city hall aren't producing GDP like the corset-factory workers did."

"Are you going to finish off with your brandy tonight?"

"Hell, yes. I wonder if there's a pay phone that works so I can call home."

Karl is uncle to Steve Yzerman, at the time of our walk one of the leading stars in the National Hockey League. Steve's Detroit team is usually in contention for the Stanley Cup. The oldest, most coveted sports trophy in the world is a gift of Lord Stanley of Preston, Canada's governor general in the late years of the nineteenth century. His Lordship became so keen about ice hockey that he decided to financially support fledgling hockey clubs. Lord Stanley purchased with his own funds a decorative punch bowl made in Sheffield, England, which Cup, he proclaimed, should be presented each year to the top hockey club in Canada. The first Stanley Cup was presented to the Montreal HC in 1893, and Karl's nephew has already won it three times with Detroit. Since the British papers don't cover ice hockey and this is playoff time, Karl is always phoning home to obtain both hockey and family updates.

"There's a pay phone by the bar, Karl."

"Do you think we should call the Oakham police again about Tiffany?" Karl asks. "I read in one of the London papers this morning that there's been reports of taxi-cab rapes of young women in London and outlying counties."

"Look, Karl, these things take time and all we did was find some evidence. Tell you what — when we get home, I'll follow up with the Oakham police and email them an enquiry as to their progress with the investigation."

Karl grunts, unhappy with my response.

"Tell you what, you go make that phone call home and I'll fetch you your brandy, as there's a lineup at the bar."

Karl makes his call and returns pensive.

"Everything all right at home?"

"Just fine on the home front, but Detroit is not doing so well in the playoffs."

Karl downs his plum brandy quickly. "I'm ready to turn in, John."

We stumble out of the Red Cow. On High Street, I now recognize from my brochure the stately brick edifice of the former Symington Corset Factory, its charming façade adorned with a fine copper steeple and Palladian windows. The products of this factory represented the mainstay, so to speak, of a British woman's appearance for over a century. The Urban Dictionary defines corset thus:

Undergarment worn throughout ages, to redefine the shape of a woman's body (mostly into an hourglass); usually by cinching the waist, and pushing up the breasts. Originally lined with whale bone for support, and laced up at the back . . . Current-day it is no longer JUST worn as an undergarment, but is commonly worn as part of an outfit usually during the nocturnal hours. Favored garment by the goth or gothic genre.

We encounter two lady goths dressed as Brides of Dracula along High Street, but I am certain they are not wearing corsets.

4

PRINCESS DIANA *and* ELDERBERRY WINE

You're traveling through another dimension not only of sight and sound, but of mind; a journey into a wondrous land whose boundaries are that of imagination. That's the signpost up ahead — your next stop, the Twilight Zone.

— ROD SERLING —
The Twilight Zone

I WAKE UP TO the peal of church bells ringing "God Save the Queen." But it's not Sunday. It is June 2, the anniversary of Elizabeth II's coronation, and it also happens to be my birthday. (I share that honour with both Thomas Hardy and the Marquis de Sade. But I digress.)

We rise early and leave Market Harborough via Little Bowden on the Brampton Valley Way. Numerous allotment strips are being worked along here as vegetable gardens, something that has become very popular in England, a throwback to the old Commons principle that preceded Enclosure. Townspeople cheerfully dig in their plots and weed their zucchinis, potatoes, and corn. Lime and chestnut trees demarcate a finely clipped cricket green as we make our way south and leave the village proper.

Through a fine mist I discern the high brick buildings comprising Her Majesty's Prison Gartree, a maximum security facility that holds more lifers than any other prison in Europe. Some four hundred of its inmates are aged over fifty. Various activities are designed to provide some meaning to the prisoners' lives, including an active prison garden program. There is even some limited interaction between the inmates and the allotment holders we have just passed.

Near Great Oxendon we rejoin Macmillan Way. We climb over a stile, follow a muddy path through scrub woodland, and then descend to a broad flat valley, part of a fourteen-mile linear park that once formed the route of the railway between

Market Harborough and Northampton. Almost immediately looms the gaping black maw of the Great Oxendon Tunnel, the first of two quarter-mile tunnels designed by George Stephenson and opened as a railway route in 1859. Karl marches ahead like some commando. It is pitch black, and I have to touch a side wall and grope my way along to the distant point of light where Karl's figure is faintly visible. "Blimey, it's dark!" I mutter out loud. I feel like a sewer rat. I can't see a foot in front of me. I keep stepping into puddles. On top of everything else, my feet hurt like hell from blisters. Yet Karl just whistles blithely onward, his dark figure silhouetted against the oblong panel of light in the distance, Tilley hat jauntily tilted, the very picture of verve and élan. He is utterly oblivious to the plight of his younger mate.

When I emerge from the first tunnel, he has already disappeared into the distance. Some three miles later, I enter the second tunnel, which is equally dark and puddled and as unnerving as the first. When I reach the rusty grillwork at the far end, I am splattered with mud and in ill humour but thankful to be out of the darkness. Then the path plunges sharply downward and I experience a vertiginous moment, like Alice must have felt falling down the rabbit hole. At bottom is an eight-foot brick wall on the right and a hedge on the left; tall black trees stand in the field ahead, enveloped in thick mist, poised and intimidating like so many Ents. Can the Dark Riders be far behind? I almost expect to hear horns in the distance and see Rohan riding forth out of the gloom to save me.

It takes another half hour to finally catch up to Karl.

"You might have slowed down for me, Karl. I could have slipped and broken an ankle in one of those dark tunnels."

"Really?"

"You remind me of Alec Guinness in *Bridge over the River Kwai*. This isn't supposed to be a forced march!"

"You realize, John, that there's a Canadian connection to the 'Colonel Bogey March'?"

"How's that?"

"Well, certain Canadian regiments adopted the tune over the years as their march past, and there was a diplomatic brouhaha in 1980 when the Japanese prime minister visited Canada and a military band played 'Colonel Bogey' for the occasion. Apparently, the Japanese felt that with the famous movie and all, the Canadians were sending a pointed message about the inhumane treatment that Allied prisoners of war experienced from the Japanese during the War."

"How politically incorrect on Canada's part."

"Quite."

"Anyway, could you please slow down!"

Karl just looks at me and smiles. The moment passes.

One mile to the west of us sits Kelmarsh Hall, a stately eighteenth-century mansion in the Palladian style. Nancy Lancaster, niece of Nancy Astor, designed the interior. Her decorating firm, Colefax & Fowler, is credited with popularizing the modern English country house look, colloquially called "shabby chic" — an eclectic blend of period and contemporary furnishings. Kelmarsh Hall has gained prominence recently as the site of English Heritage's annual Festival of History, where some two thousand performers dressed in period costume re-enact jousting, fencing, archery, and other period activities. It is now billed as the largest heritage event of its kind in Europe.

We cross over the Kelmarsh Cycle Path, betwixt fields and spinneys. We see no walkers, but a group of male cyclists fly by, clad in colourful spandex.

This region has seen a marked ebb and flow of population. Bronze Age dwellings have been unearthed here; then there is a long gap until the Saxon era. The land was largely cleared by the Middle Ages, but the Black Death decimated the population. Disease and the Enclosure movement combined to allow estates such as Althorp to become gargantuan. This in turn led to corporate-scale sheep farming.

Agriculture experienced a revolution in the eighteenth century with the application of scientific techniques to animal breeding. Robert Bakewell, a Leicestershire landowner, referred to his sheep as "machines for turning grass into mutton." One benefit of Enclosure was that animals could be managed better within fenced fields than on open, common ground. Improved animal breeds appeared, such as Hereford cattle and Southdown sheep, and inventions such as the seed drill (in 1701) also contributed to greater efficiency.

A mile past Maidwell we pass beneath an ornate gateway on a firm, wide track. Here sits the famous eighteenth-century Cottesbrooke Hall; we stop to peer at it down a tree-lined avenue. This impressive building is linked by tradition to Jane Austen's *Mansfield Park*. The red-brick pile standing in magnificent repose is thought to be the estate highlighted in the novel. Austen likely never visited the hall, but did write to her sister and a friend for detailed descriptions of this area. More tangible Jane Austen associations lie ahead of us on Macmillan Way.

The world abruptly closes in when our narrow path drops downhill into an overgrown wood. Stinging nettles clog portions of the trail. Just when I think we are lost, we exit the copse into the village of Creaton, which boasts a population of 488. Creaton holds close associations with George Washington, the first American president. The president's great-great-grandmother, Amphyllis Twigden, was born and grew up here. Amphyllis married Rev. Lawrence Washington, whose son John emigrated to America and became the great-grandfather of George. The foundations of her cottage are still visible in the centre of the village across Grooms Lane.

The path is again hard to follow after we exit Creaton. The *Guide* tells us to "continue up hill, through large gap in fragmentary hedge-line coming in from left." Fragmentary, all right — non-existent! Then we are urged to climb over a stile "by a water trough," but I can find no such trough, and to further complicate matters, there is a new gate on the wrong side of the field and no stile leading to the meadow beyond. By this time Karl has disappeared over the horizon, completely off path.

I trend left, following a faint track that leads into the Holdenby Woodlands. Then I find a meandering trail through the woods that winds in a promising direction. I also stumble upon a grove of wild garlic stalks, which I begin to munch. A furtive pheasant cock crosses my path. Bluebells glisten; thrushes twitter. Could Bilbo's Shire be more enchanting? Does it really matter if I am lost for a while? I am more worried about Karl, who might turn back and begin searching for me. But for now, this is pure euphoria, and for a few irresponsible moments I am at one with Alice when she asks the Cheshire Cat,

"Would you tell me, please, which way I ought to go from here?"

"That depends a good deal on where you want to get to,"
said the Cat.

"I don't much care where —" said Alice.

"Then it doesn't matter which way you go," said the Cat.

Alas, my compass now tells me that the path is veering away from Holdenby village, where I should be. So after ten minutes I find a deer track that heads in the right direction, then peters out. I trip and fall on some barbed wire from an old fence, fight my way through brambles and nettles, and finally emerge a good twenty minutes later, scratched and bruised, on a paved lane with wide grass verges. A little farther on I find Karl — sitting on a bench near the entrance to Holdenby House estate, drinking a can of Guinness and grinning like a sly fox.

"What took you, John boy?"

"A minor diversion. And you're looking rather chuffed with yourself. How long have you been here?"

"Oh, a little while — enough time to sniff out the village and grab a beer. No pub, though. What's with the scratches on your arms?"

"It's nothing, Karl."

"Why are you leaning over my bench?"

"I am noting down interesting inscriptions on benches I have seen en route — this one celebrates a local resident who liked to walk."

Some of the inscriptions I have seen are rather funny: "Mistaken Accidental"; "Little black poodle waiting for the Star"; "Born in a puddle"; "She used to sit here sometimes"; "Jacket potatoes shared here"; "My first love." I got a chuckle out of a plaque near Market Harborough which read "She sat too long."

Holdenby House is a country mansion with a falconry centre. But it is closed to the public today. I wanted to visit this estate where Charles I was held for four months just before his execution. The Scots had brought Charles here in 1647 and handed him over to Cromwell's Roundheads. With its 123 windows and 14 towering chimneys, the pile was called the finest home in England in 1583, when Christopher Hatton, chancellor to Elizabeth I, built it. He refused to move in until the queen visited. Hatton had made his fortune by helping to finance the piratical ventures of Sir Francis Drake. In gratitude, Drake changed the name of his ship to *Golden Hinde* to commemorate the gold deer emblazoned on the Hatton coat of arms.

Alas, Hatton went bankrupt and died in 1591. The British Crown then purchased the home for the monarch's personal use. The estate was used as the set for a BBC production of Charles Dickens's *Great Expectations,* for which the director piled eighty tons of mud and ivy by the long driveway to make the place resemble the dilapidated home of Miss Haversham.

I stand at the gates and count the chimneys atop the massive pile. From here, walkers must navigate along a tiny road with the stone wall of Althorp Park to the left. Althorp is an immense estate of 14,000 acres, with oak woods, a little lake called the Round Oval, and the imposing mansion of Earl Spencer, brother of Lady Diana. The late princess is allegedly buried on an island in the Round Oval. The oldest tree on the estate is the Crimea Oak, seventy-two feet high and planted by Sir John Spencer in 1589 as his contribution to grow more oak trees for the Admiralty to replace ships sunk during the Spanish Armada crisis. The current earl planted an avenue of thirty-six oak trees in 1999 as a memorial to Lady Diana. Each tree represents one year of her life.

We enter the minute village of Great Brington. Here we are immediately swept up in swirling debate at the post office shop, where the strong rumour floats that Diana is in fact buried in the church at Great Brington next to her father. This could not be revealed, the story goes, lest the church be constantly jammed with tourists. So an urn allegedly containing her ashes is displayed on the island in Althorp Park. The park is open to visitors only in the summer months. One can walk down to the folly shrine to Diana, place flowers in her memory, and gaze across the water to the island.

Some nineteen generations of the Spencer family are buried at the church, and the theory is that Diana was secretly cremated and her ashes interred in the family chapel. Locals note that a strip of wet concrete suddenly appeared in the chapel at the time of Diana's purported interment at Althorp Park.

The postmistress tells us that we are the first Macmillan walkers she has seen who are walking the entire route. She says that it's now officially okay to pronounce the name of the estate as Althorp, because in 1998 Earl Spencer changed the pronunciation from AWL-trupp to AWL-thorp, though locals wouldn't have expected North Americans to get the correct English accent right. We buy a couple of postcards and leave the villagers to continue their playful badinage.

The church is absolutely fascinating. The first thing one notices is the series of Spencer tombs in the north chapel, great monuments enclosed by spiked iron railings, including the tomb of Diana's father. There is no doubt as to what family rules this neck of the woods. But there is a second matter of interest, particularly for American visitors: a gravestone marking the burial of Lawrence Washington, the great-great-grandfather of George Washington, who died in 1616. This comes after just having passed through Creaton, where Amphyllis, Lawrence's wife, lived. We view the Washington coat of arms on the slab, with its alternating rows of stars and stripes — George Washington later chose this motif for the American flag. So in this tiny rural village are direct links to both Diana, Princess of Wales, and George Washington, the father of the United States of America. And people complain that history is dull?

"So what do you think, John?" Karl asks as we leave the church. "Is she buried there or not?"

"Well, I personally think that, being English, the family did the sensible thing and ordered up two urns — one for the island on the estate and the other for the church. I did that with my own mother's ashes recently, as she wanted half of her remains buried in New Brunswick with her ancestors and the other half buried in the Fraser Valley so my dad and the immediate family could visit her."

We leave it at that.

DIARY: *Dinner at the Saracen's Head pub in Little Brington. About 7:30, couples begin arriving for dinner — women dressed nattily for dinner and drinks, the men in cotton shirts and tweed jackets. Inside is a full-size red telephone booth that is advertised by the owner as actually working! Karl takes advantage of this.*

The dining room has great ambience. Shelves of books line the stone walls. A black dog named Henry rolls over in front of the bar and begs for ice cubes. A suave English yuppie in his forties, dressed in jeans and tweed jacket, sits down carrying a bottle of Bordeaux, his female friend at the table obviously not his wife. She is neatly attired in brown leather skirt and beige blouse, smoking fags.

Our meal consists of Long Buckby rump steak, game garnered from the nearby village of Flore, and veggies from the pub's own orchard and kitchen garden. I ask the server about "bubble and squeak," as I have seen it on the menu at various pubs. I am informed that in the eighteenth century it consisted of fried meat and cabbage, but in this century it's a mash of fried potatoes combined with other veggies left over from the Sunday roast.

"It sounds execrable," I say. The server laughs and says that she often buys it at the Tesco supermarket in a packaged, microwaveable format.

The pub performs an extremely important role in rural English social life. Labourers, businessmen, professionals, and homemakers all drop in to their local watering hole in the evening to have a pint, talk about the latest soccer scores or politics, or simply to gossip. I once found myself in avid conversation at a bar with a couple, and it transpired that the bloke was a barrister and his wife a High Court judge. No matter. The pub levels social distinctions. Richard Jefferies called the alehouse the labourer's "stock exchange, his reading-room, his club, and his assembly rooms."

The local pub has also from time to time acted as the rallying centre for political agitation and a haven for smugglers and fencers of stolen goods. In the 1830s, when rural violence erupted over the displacement of jobs by new machines, public houses were at the very centre of agitation as, it was often said, "nurseries of naughtiness."

What can compete with the joy, colour, and ambience of the English pub? The sheer outlandishness of the names numbs the mind. How about this little sampling: The Gallows Inn, The Dapple Cow, The Merry Mouth, The Hatchet Inn, The Maid's Head, Barge Aground, Cat and Bagpipes, The Tippling Philosopher, Trouble House Inn, The Indian Queen, The Trip to Jerusalem, The Book in Hand, The Mortal Man, The Saracen's Head, The Quiet Woman, The Jolly Taxpayer, The Man in the Moon, The Foaming Jug. Pubs change their name from time to time; in Great Brington, following the death of Princess Diana, the Fox & Hounds quickly became the Althorp Coaching Inn.

Until 1550, British taverns and inns were unlicensed. Anyone could open a public house, though if it became disorderly, the local JPs could close it down or debar the proprietor from selling ale or spirits. The beginning of a licensing system carried a fixed code of conduct. In the sixteenth century, a tavern keeper was forbidden to shelter travellers, while an innkeeper was forbidden to allow people to "tipple" in his house — tippling could occur only in the alehouse. Even today an innkeeper is required by law to get up and supply a traveller with food and/or shelter at three in the morning, whereas a tavern keeper has no such obligations. A "free house" may sell all brands of beer and is not tied to one supplier.

OUR QUIETUDE on the trail this morning is shattered by the pop-pop-pop of guns blasting below us in the Nene Valley. The noise is from a rifle range. A few moments later a much louder explosion breaches the calm of the hedgerows, and several wood pigeons crash out of the hawthorn in fright. We are puzzled; it sounds like artillery shelling. Upon emerging from a copse into orchard fields, it becomes apparent that the three explosions in close succession emanate from the nefarious "crow cannon," which I recognize from my twenty-eight years of living on a hobby farm in British Columbia.

Propane-fuelled bird cannons have stirred controversy in rural areas around the world, and in North America have led to petitions, civil suits, even bloodshed. They are the only reasonably effective way of keeping starlings, rooks, pigeons, and crows from devouring field crops. In Australia, residents had to petition the government to stop the cannon firing on Christmas Day. Man can send spaceships to the moon, but thus far the birds have outwitted us in harassing our crops — even falcons have been tried in Britain and North America, with varying degrees of success. Other methods, such as scarecrows and flashers, are ineffective. The only alternative remedy is netting, but this gets very expensive with large acreages and the nets must be replaced every five years or so. That said, the crow cannon only *reduces* crop destruction. Up to 30 percent of some crops are lost even with the cannons in action.

Though wood pigeons are vilified for devastating crops, rooks are more common, descending in vast flocks to eat cultivated cereal, fruit, and earthworms. This makes for much Sturm und Drang drama in English fields. The rook differs from the North American crow — it has a bluish-purple sheen, grey-white skin near the eyes, and shaggier feathers. Rooks are colonial birds that nest together in groups of up to thirty.

I asked a farmer at our B&B the previous evening about the rook problem. He replied that the rook, though much hated by farmers, is a more dignified bird than the crow — a carrion crow prefers the eyes of live lambs to earthworms and is the ultimate murderer. Rooks cluster together for the greater good, and the phrase "rook parliament" originates from the almost human manner in which an avian trial is held for a wayward or sick rook. Just before clawing the feathered victim to death, the entire rookery empties into the sky like in Hitchcock's *The Birds,* in a cacophony of cawing and furious beating of wings. Farmers also regard mass desertion of rookeries as a sure prelude to disaster — climatic or otherwise. That said, an annual cull of rooks with 12-bore shotguns and .22s barely makes a dent in the population.

The nursery-rhyme stanza "four and twenty blackbirds baked in a pie" actually refers to rook pie, which until the twentieth century was a staple dish of the poor. Dickens refers to it in *The Pickwick Papers.* The landlord of the Fox & Hounds in Acton Turville, Gloucestershire, hosts an annual rook pie night, complementing the rook flesh with sausage, brandy, sherry, and spices. The travel writer Paul Theroux enjoyed rook pie at the Crown Inn near our destination at Abbotsbury, Dorset; but recently the proprietors of that inn received several poison pen letters and threatening emails from birds' rights activists, which made them so distraught that they have ceased offering this traditional country delicacy to their guests.

The third noisy encounter of the morning unfolds as we leave a copse via a kissing gate and stand on an overpass staring down at the twelve or so lanes of the frenetic M1, the great motorway connecting London with the North, which resembles a speedway track. This stretch experiences a daily volume of 100,000 vehicles. I must be dazed from the bucolic world in which I have been cocooned, because I cannot relate to this motorway scene — it must be in some twilight zone — and I hustle in panic across the concrete span to reach a spinney on the far side, like some recluse hastening to his primeval cave or Ratty retreating to his riverbank.

The spinney holds an unexpected surprise. A tall, rather seedy-looking bloke stoops bathing in a brook, completely in the buff. His rusty red Cortina rests on a green lane nearby. Through the hatchback, I can see clothes and paraphernalia completely jamming the vehicle. The poor chap seems slightly bewildered, and makes no attempt to cover up his crown jewels as he pauses to talk with us.

"You blokes sound foreign."

"We're from North America, walking the Macmillan Way."

"Ah, and where would that be?"

"Er," I stammer, "it's a long-distance path."

His eyes dart from Karl to me and back; he seems a little wild, but not exactly dodgy.

"Blimey! Fancy that. Can't say as I like walking much. Not now, at any rate. The wife and I had a big row last night; she told me to sod off. So I packed up all my clothes and left. Don't know where I'll go."

We wish him well and leave him to his morning ablutions.

"The poor fool," Karl says after an interval. "Wonder where he'll bed down tonight."

"Likely right where we left him — in his car on that green lane."

The lonely village of Flore is approached through a field of barley along a red-soiled path. We stop for a moment to view the Adams Cottage, a thatch-roofed building reputed to be the home of the ancestors of John Adams, second American president. Then we cross a bridge over the River Nene and skirt the town of Weedon by walking along the Grand Union Canal.

Radar was first demonstrated and proven effective near Weedon in 1935. A memorial plaque south of the village commemorates the trial runs of a Handley Page Heyford biplane piloted by Robert Blake on February 26 of that year, whereby the repeated passage of his plane disrupted the electromagnetic energy field transmitted from a nearby radio mast such that the position of his aircraft could now be tracked. When one considers how close Britain came to succumbing to the Luftwaffe in the Battle of Britain in 1940, it can be argued that radar may have made the crucial difference between victory and defeat.

Just outside Farthingstone, we arrive at a rolling expanse called Glebe Farm, our B&B. A hot soak in the big clawfoot tub eases the blisters somewhat. After ablutions, Karl and I go for a stroll on the grounds and meet up with Colin from Derbyshire, a young man in his twenties, who is camping out in his tent here for the night. He jumps up to greet us. I notice his freshly washed socks hanging out to dry. We had met this tall, lanky walker briefly on the trail in the late afternoon. His long legs take enormous strides, and he is planning on completing Macmillan at the rate of twenty-four miles a day — about twice our pace. He should arrive at Abbotsbury and the sea after only twelve days' journeying! It turns out that the distinct boot marks Karl and I have been following belong to Colin.

Colin is well equipped to cook his own food, but we persuade him to join us for dinner at the local pub. The proprietor of Glebe Farm kindly offers to drive the three of us to the village, so we all pile into his Land Rover. We don't mind the friendly collie that accompanies us, nor the dog hairs.

Over hearty plates of lamb stew, we learn that Colin lives with his mother and works in the computer maintenance field. He loves walking and has conquered many of the high reaches of Derbyshire, the Lake District, and Wales. He is also curious about hiking the mountains in Canada, where he would like to explore the wilderness. The dinner is memorable. We enjoy the amiable companionship of Colin, and also discover English country wines. We consume first a bottle of elderberry wine and then a bottle of elderflower wine, both made from the elderberry bush.

Karl makes raspberry wine himself, and when he asks the publican how the elder wine is made, the fellow points to a rather grizzled old man at the next table. "Ask Harold, he's the local connoisseur for the country wines."

Harold promptly joins us, samples some of our elderberry, and pronounces it as "not bad, mate, though it could have stood a bit longer, but not bad. We here call it the Englishman's grape; it's been used in wine for hundreds of years. My missus also makes elderberry pie, jam, tarts, and jelly. Some country folk still call elder the Judas tree."

"What about North American elderberry? We have lots of it in our West Coast forests."

Harold scratches his thin beard. "Don't rightly know about that, mate; but I would think any variety should make for good wine. Try making the elderflower as well. My missus swears by it. Some farmers still carry an elder branch around when the flies are bad in the barnyard."

Colin adds, "Me mum makes elderflower cordial in summer — she calls it 'elderflower champagne.' She makes it bubbly, all effervescent like. Better than the store stuff."

Next morning, our friendly Glebe Farm landlady serves us a wonderful breakfast, full English without the grease, and lovely hot rolls. Even Karl succumbs.

Conscious that Colin hit the trail before eight o'clock, we reluctantly leave Glebe Farm, only to stop abruptly in our tracks a few hundred yards along. A weird radio beacon has popped into view — a flat, glistening steel apparatus that looks extraterrestrial. We decide to investigate and find a tarmac path leading to a chain-link fence guarding an ugly little white building supporting a gargantuan mushroom cap above hundreds of metal rods extending in every direction — and no one around for miles. Have the Martians landed? Perhaps it's an MI5 listening post?

We soon reach Canons Ashby, named after the Black Canons, Augustinian monks who built a priory here in the twelfth century. The priory became a popular stopover for pilgrims and students from Oxford University. It was closed in 1536 with the Dissolution, and the remaining Black Canons were evacuated. A John Dryden, ancestor of John Dryden the poet, later inherited the priory and built the present manor house, now managed by the National Trust. Dryden the poet often visited his uncle here and enjoyed the unspoiled view of formal gardens and extensive woodlands.

"I don't know much about John Dryden, Karl, other than what I learned in high school — he was a poet and a satirist. But I do remember one line of his that I rather cherish."

"And what line is that, John?"

"'Beware the fury of a patient man.'"

"Are you making a dig at my impatience again?"

"No, but if the shoe fits, you know?"

"Ha! Life's too short to dawdle."

We wanted to visit Canons Ashby House, but it is closed. However, the Trust kindly allows walkers to pass through the grounds without charge. A famous statue of a shepherd boy playing a flute stands on the front lawn.

While lingering in the sunshine here, we cannot help but observe several National Trust workers on the grounds trying to fire up a weed-killing machine that belches a lot of smoke but kills no weeds. Seven workers move along at a snail's pace with this monstrous devil, but the weeds are still very much present after they pass. If all seven workers used a simple handheld weed-eater — even an old-fashioned scythe — they could have finished the job in under an hour.

That said, the National Trust has become the driving engine for preservation of hundreds of heritage buildings and sizable tracts of nature reserves. Incorporated in 1895, the Trust's purpose is "the preservation for the benefit of the Nation of lands and tenements (including buildings) of beauty or historic interest, and, as regards lands, for the preservation of their natural aspect, features and animal and plant life. Also the preservation of furniture, pictures and chattels of any description having national and historic or artistic interest."

It boasts the largest membership of any charity in the country, with 3 million paid subscribers and 40,000 unpaid volunteers. The Trust owns more than 600,000 acres of countryside, 600 miles of coastline, and over 250 heritage buildings, and 13 million people visit its properties each year.

The writer A.A. Gill decries the Trust as a backward-looking keeper of the nostalgia industry, but it is hard to be critical of the one agency in the world that works indefatigably to not only preserve historic structures but keep the countryside green and frozen to development. It may be that the Puck of the garden has replaced the Green Man guarding the ancient forests, but one can only work with repairing, redressing, and preserving what we have left to us. Bemoaning the sins of one's ancestors is surely a nihilistic exercise. The Trust is the envy of like organizations in countries such as Canada, where it is difficult to find patronage beyond meagre government resources to conserve heritage sites.

Our route out of Canons Ashby takes us down a steep hill on a minor road that leads to the valley below, where we cross over a stile, then a narrow plank over a stream, known as a "sleeper bridge," to enter the derelict village of Moreton Pinkney. This place has seen better days, though there is a pretentious manor house with a Victorian tower and a couple of pubs: The Crown and England's Rose, renamed from Red Lion in honour of Princess Diana.

A footbridge leads over a gentle stream to follow a hedge-lined track. A sign at a farm gate warns: "Danger — Guard dogs loose." A little later on, another sign: "Trespassers may be seriously injured." We stop to consider.

"Somebody's trying to tell us something, Karl. Maybe walkers have strayed too often off the path here."

Karl just gives me that half-smile of his, takes a swig from his Thermos — he won't admit it, but I know there's ale in there — and sallies forth, oblivious to the fierce barking that erupts from kennels halfway across the next field.

The path continues relentlessly downward to become a wickedly wet bridleway. At the bottom is one vast series of mudholes. From this fetid primeval ooze it is a long, long climb up a slippery scarp to the pleasant village of Eydon. It seems that every cottager is in her front yard this Saturday, edging herbaceous borders, killing weeds, and generally cleaning up. We pass a village green where the medieval stocks are still intact. I cast them a nervous glance, for I am dirty, grungy, and dishevelled enough to be ensconced there as some tramp despoiling the spiffy village vista.

We quench our thirst on an outdoor picnic table at the Royal Oak. A farmer on a tractor wielding a huge, yawning bucket motors down the street and loads up people's excess sod. A bloke at the next table tells me that the village elders appoint a specific day in spring to spruce up the place, and that most cottagers join in. Some poor lad we watch is being excoriated for spraying rat poison all over his mother's flower garden.

John Grindlay runs the Eydon Kettle Company from his home here. His STORM kettle is portable and allows one to boil water anywhere, being an improvement on a design that originated in Ireland. If we were English and absolutely had to have a cuppa every hour along the trail, this would be a necessity for the backpack. I point this out to Karl, who is singularly unimpressed.

"To hell with tea — where's our next real drink?"

"Coming right up, at the Griffin in Chipping Warden." With that, he quaffs the last dregs of his Guinness and hoists his pack.

At the other side of the village, we begin our descent into the valley of the infant River Cherwell. "Infant," says the *Guide* — I'll say! When we cross over a footbridge, this majestically named stream is no more than a ditch clogged with willows, alder bushes, and bulrushes. This is the first stream on our journey that flows southward, emptying into the Thames at Oxford.

I remark to Karl on a large herd of cows in the field we are approaching.

"Stop calling steers 'cows' — steers are castrated male bulls," he says. "Cows are female."

"Then what are bullocks?"

"Bullocks are the same as steers."

"What about castrated females, then — are they heifers?"

"Dammit, no! They don't generally castrate the females — a heifer is just a young female that hasn't yet given birth."

And with that, Karl clumps down his walking stick and marches ahead.

"Oh, bollocks!" I shout after him. "Why don't we just call them all 'bovines,' then?"

Just before ascending a bridleway up a hill, I catch up with Karl. He is standing poised with his walking stick, pointing to a field below, from which a ghetto blaster is blaring the original Don McLean version of "American Pie." Dozens of gaily painted caravans and lorries occupy a vast meadow. Gypsies, or "tinkers," as they are sometimes known, were historically associated with green lanes, because the tracks were wide enough to accommodate their trademark horse and cart. Nowadays they use lorries or cars to haul their caravans (trailers in Britain are called "caravans"), and the green lanes are too muddied up by horses anyway.

"What do you think, Karl? There must be fifty caravans down there."

Little waifs, dogs, and horses gambol about, while gaudily clad women with long black hair, glittering hoop earrings, and ankle-length cotton dresses mill around what looks like a communal cooking fire. An aroma redolent of borscht, sausages, chips, and horse manure wafts our way.

Karl smiles. "Live and let live, John. They don't seem to be harming anyone; and I like the self-sufficiency I see down there. I wouldn't mind tasting some of that borscht, either."

"That doesn't sound like you — where's your Dutch orderliness and cleanliness?"

Karl laughs and shrugs. "I guess I admire their resourcefulness."

Atop the hill, sheep roam everywhere. Although sheep are usually seen as cowardly creatures, a mother with young lambs will run fearlessly toward you if you come too close, to divert you from her babies. And why do they shit every time you approach them? Are they all incontinent?

Clearly visible on the hillside just beyond us is a golden track that resembles the yellow brick road in *The Wizard of Oz*, and for a moment I turn euphoric. Then we descend into a miasma that alters the spirit.

Just a half mile or so short of Chipping Warden, we encounter a bevy of tumbledown farm cottages. Then we cross a brook and enter a wide track through a spinney, where we navigate through several mouldering, derelict concrete air-raid shelters, huddled together and forgotten. It's dark, dingy, and clammy in this scrub spinney, and we cannot exit the place fast enough. It gives me the creeps. And there is much evidence of mice and rats about. The shelters exist because of the nearby airfield, one of the most important in RAF Bomber Command during World War II.

We bear left from the evil spinney and enter Chipping Warden, where we stop to refresh ourselves at the Griffin Inn. Wide greens fronting ochre-hued thatched cottages give the place real character. The word *Chipping* is often found in village names in England, as it is the Old English word for "market."

The big-cheese landowner in Chipping Warden during the eighteenth century was the Duke of Beaufort. The chap had serious marital problems. A bill was moved in the House of Lords in 1744 to dissolve his marriage with Frances Scudamore. Witnesses from Chipping Warden included a farmer who testified "That in the beginning of June, 1741, he observed a Man afterwards found to be Lord Talbot meet the Duchess as she was walking alone in the Fields near that Place; and thereupon mentioned adulterous Familiarities which passed between them." The House Journal carefully omits details as to the "Familiarities," but records that witnesses testified "as to the sending for a Midwife to the Duchess; her being delivered of a Daughter." So it was not just the common folk who used the footpaths for their dalliances.

It was an altogether humiliating exercise for both husband and wife. The common people began twittering about fornication in the fields. When hubby sued for divorce, Frances countersued, alleging the duke was impotent — and he then had to go through the execrable ordeal in March 1743 of demonstrating before court-appointed examiners that he was physically capable of having an erection.

The origin of the term "lover's lane" lies with the green lanes and footpaths where lovers met for over a thousand years throughout Britain. In E.M. Forster's novel *A Room with a View*, Lucy and Cecil pause "where a footpath diverged from the highroad." The path was a more intimate alternative to a public walk along the road. Lucy chooses the propriety of the highroad because she is not yet ready for courtship intimacies and the pleasures of the path. Paths, in fact, were graded in terms of how well used they were in order to estimate the chances of an unwanted encounter while engaging in a moment of intimacy. Tennyson's poem "Marriage Morning" attests to the differentiation:

Woods, where we hid from the wet,
Stiles where we stayed to be kind.

We are having a squishy time trudging through fields of muddy sod mixed with sheep feces. Dirty weather adds to the ordeal. Raindrops the size of mothballs pelt down. After two hours of drenching, bone-chilling rain, we reach our B&B, a large stone farmhouse set back from the lane beside a clump of elm trees. I am now officially a water rat. A rosy-cheeked, middle-aged landlady greets us with a smile. She is all business and ushers us in to the parlour for the customary tea and biscuits. I am still shivering and have a premonition of a cold, miserable night. So I pose the taboo question:

"Do you suppose that we could have some heat in our rooms so as to dry out? I'd like to hang my wet clothes on the radiator."

Shocked silence. "We generally don't turn the heat on between the May bank-holiday weekend and September," she replies with chilly hauteur.

Oh-oh! Cross-cultural angst. Is it perversity, tradition, or mere frugality that promotes this English mindset? I wonder.

"Uh, well, we are very wet, you see."

"There is a big tub in your room, so you can take a nice hot bath. As for your clothes, they should dry out by morning. Tell you what, if they are not progressing well by the time

you two are back from the pub, I can pop them in the dryer."
Her bright eyes flash with what she considers an eminently
sensible solution to the problem.

Karl shrugs and says he is going to his room to have a hot
soak. But my mettle is up.

"Look," I say, "perhaps we are just wimpy North Americans,
but if I don't get warm soon I am liable to get pneumonia.
We've been walking in a chilling downpour for a couple of
hours. Let me pay you ten pounds extra for putting the heat
on tonight."

"What?" The woman's cheeks become even redder and
puffier. "Why, that's just not done, you know, this time of
year!"

But I can see she is thinking, and probably needs the
money. Now, perhaps, we will discover if the national mania
over heat is based upon frugality or just custom. Her wheels
are definitely turning.

"All right now," she says, after a long pause. "I will turn
on the main thermostat to heat your rooms for precisely two
hours — take the chill off, perhaps — and that will cost you
five pounds extra. Heat is very expensive in Britain, and the
thermostat controls the whole house, so it does seem like a
waste when one can always put on a jumper."

And that definitely spells the end of discussion.

5

ROLLRIGHT STONES, WITCHES, and BANBURY BUNS

Ride a cock-horse to Banbury Cross,

To see a fine lady upon a white horse;

Rings on her fingers and bells on her toes,

And she shall have music wherever she goes.

— MEDIEVAL BANBURY NURSERY RHYME —

THE ELDERBERRY WINE so fortifies me that I hardly notice the frigid bedroom and sleep like a baby. Next morning we decline breakfast and opt for an early start. Our path intersects the delightful Oxford Canal. A gaudily painted canal boat bedecked with potted plants is just passing through a complex-looking lock. Karl laughingly points with his walking stick toward a couple of Holstein cows leaning over the steep bank, their big brown oval eyes fixated in curious wonder upon this strange craft passing below them. Thank you, my bovine ladies — you're looking beautiful this morning.

The canal was completed in 1786 and linked the coal fields of Coventry to the Thames at Oxford. Today one can walk for miles along its 78-mile towpath. Like so many of the byways and green roads of England, canals have become pleasure corridors when once they were chiefly used for freight. The last time that animal power was used to haul a flatboat down the Canal was in 1959, when the *Friendship* was drawn by a mule. The Oxford is one of the favourites in a national canal system that draws tourists from all over the world to sample the slow pace of travel through England's countryside. Its special delight is that, unlike most inland waterways, it meanders and twists in wacky loops amid myriad hills, allowing boaters to enjoy unique, bucolic landscape perspectives. One might even glimpse fairies in those hollow hills.

Farnborough lies at the very fringe of the Cotswolds. The village sits on the south scarp of the Burton Dassett Hills. It is unworldly in its charm, highlighted by the savoury butterscotch stone walls of the church. The spire is Victorian but the remainder of the structure is medieval. At the entrance to the churchyard is a lychgate — typically a covered, little structure, and in this case slate-roofed. Inside are cherry-red pews that gleam in polished splendour.

Farnborough Hall is another of those mega-piles built by the rich in the eighteenth century. Alas, it is closed. We decide to compensate by taking refreshment at the Inn at Farnborough, a sixteenth-century pub, where we sample some genuine Warwickshire hooch known as "hooky." The menu claims, "The Inn also serves 'proper coffee' by trained baristas." I didn't see a barista anywhere, but Samuel Pepys would have felt at home here knowing he could enjoy strong coffee. Of course, Pepys would have had to first sort out which Farnborough was on offer. (There are five towns of the same name in England.)

A couple of hours later we stand gaping like scared skydivers on a viaduct over the M40 motorway, the vast freeway connecting London to Birmingham, and I experience another vertiginous moment. Vehicles rush feverishly below us, spewing their carbon imprint over the countryside. The noise is deafening. The moment passes: a long field with a red rock path, a stile, an apple orchard, and presto! We arrive abruptly in the ancient village of Warmington, a million miles in time and space from the M40.

Nick and Helen are waiting for us at their B&B, which adjoins a pond that is home to three white ducks who wander tamely about the green all day. Helen settles us in and kindly offers to wash and dry our clothes. Nick is an accountant who works from home via the computer, travelling to London by train twice a week to meet with clients. They are quintessentially polite, helpful, and low-key.

We walk to a pub recommended by Nick only to find that although drinks are served, the kitchen is taking two weeks off. (This drives North Americans up the wall — how do you build and maintain a business if you are so erratic in service?) I ask the barkeeper to recommend another pub, and he says to go to Horley, but when we arrive there we are told they don't serve food either; so we catch a cab to Wroxton, where we actually find victuals.

The White Horse Inn is warm and sumptuous. Golden lamps glow in every window. Karl and I both tuck into a scrumptious fisherman's pie. Instead of wine, I wash my fare down with two iced Smirnoffs, while Karl orders a couple of double Scotches. Then I finish the other half of Karl's pie, not because he didn't like it, but because he has a tiny stomach and is what one would call a "grazer." His grazing habits do not extend to alcoholic beverages.

It's time to hit the sack. I order a cab back to our B&B.

"My feet feel like they've been ravaged from a forced march."

"How do you think all those Roman soldiers felt, marching forty or fifty miles a day with packs heavier than yours?"

"How is it that you have no blister problems?"

"Because I am a tough old logger from the woods — my calluses have built up over decades."

"A tough old logger with brass balls is more like it! I think I will dump some more clothes and get some blister treatment tomorrow in Banbury."

"You'd do better to dump some of those useless books."

"Never."

We have decided to stay in Warmington for two nights so I can treat my feet and Karl can take a day to drive up to Yorkshire in a rental car. Karl has a family tradition of burying capsules with notes and coins all over England for his children to find. He began this tradition long before the advent of geocaching, a GPS-based system for hiding treasure in containers that hit the scene in North America in 2000. One of his daughters reciprocates and buries a capsule or two for Karl to find using a treasure map she gives him. The current one is for a certain Yorkshire abbey, where the capsule is buried near a bench beneath a large oak tree a specified distance from the abbey entrance.

BANBURY HAS BEEN AN important market town for over 1,500 years. It lies at the junction of two ancient roads — the Salt Way and Banbury Lane — and once had the largest cattle market in Europe. Nearby Cherwell Valley produced the famous Banbury cheese.

An impressive market cross, a church that resembles a cathedral, and a strange monument of a young woman astride a horse combine to impress the visitor. The market cross itself is a replica, as a Puritan MP removed the original in the sixteenth century. The Puritans, like Henry VIII before them, destroyed so much of England's architecture. It took the prudish yet pragmatic Victorians to replace the market cross, in commemoration of the marriage of Victoria to Prince Albert.

The Banbury Cross nursery rhyme has survived. William Gladstone sang the popular rhyme to his children every day as they took "rides on his foot, slung over his knee," and in the 2011 film *Anonymous,* Queen Elizabeth I is heard singing the final lines while dancing in her bedchamber. Speculation still rages as to whether the statue of the "fine lady" on the horse celebrates Elizabeth I or Lady Godiva. My money is on Godiva.

At Boots pharmacy, I find a blister prevention spray that will give me a new layer of water-resistant skin each morning.

Contrast this with the nineteenth-century folk remedy prescribed by Francis Galton in *The Art of Travel:* "Blisters? Simply make a lather of soap suds inside your socks and break a raw egg into each boot to soften the leather." Yuck!

During the last week we have encountered many humble chapels and meeting houses that denote the historical presence of Methodists, Baptists, and Quakers — people who were regarded by Anglicans as only slightly more palatable than Roman Catholics. The Quakers were imprisoned at Banbury in the seventeenth century for attending services at their meeting houses. John and Charles Wesley frequently roamed this part of the countryside, preaching at first in open fields. For them, their fellow Anglicans had become too detached from scripture and had morphed into the "frozen chosen."

Banbury was a hotbed of religious dissension during the seventeenth and eighteenth centuries. It wasn't until 1689, with the Act of Toleration, that Nonconformists were exempted from attending Anglican church services. Jonathan Swift wrote in 1710 that the residents of Banbury showed "continuous zeal." In 1790, rather than pay additional taxes to repair the unsafe foundations of the town church, the citizens opted to blow their church up with gunpowder.

Banbury still holds a traditional "mop fair" each autumn — a form of labour exchange that dates to the fourteenth century. After the Black Death wiped out entire villages, labour shortages emerged and landowners searched desperately for workers. In market towns throughout England, people would congregate on the appointed day in the town square to bargain with prospective employers. Food, refreshment, and entertainment soon turned these hiring meets into vibrant fairs. An individual would signify his or her employment preference by displaying some emblem — a shepherd held a crook or tuft of wool; cattle workers held clumps of straw; a field labourer held a shovel; while dairymaids carried pails, and housemaids held mops or brooms. If a bargain was struck, the employer had to seal it by handing over a few shillings to his new employee.

Intense partying occurs on the first weekend in July with the Banbury Hobby Horse Festival. Since 2000, Morris dancers have adapted their traditional costume ritual to the peculiar traditions associated with the lady on the white horse. Many costumed animals appear on the streets during this raucous weekend — Eustasia the unicorn, Vibria the dragon, and other such creatures. There is a colourful parade, street vending, raucous music — and on the bandstand appears a fiery preacher who vehemently denounces the gaudy, pagan festival, claiming that people are "following those jingling bells to hell!" He is in deadly earnest. One year even the preacher smiled when one of the Four Horses of the Apocalypse handed him a note proclaiming "The end of the world is neigh!" The contrary preacher has himself become an important actor in this riotous event.

The moral degeneracy of Banbury was bemoaned for centuries. In 1628, when a huge fire destroyed much of the town, the presiding vicar, William Whately, gave a two-hour sermon on the depravity that had merited God's "severe judgment."

Banbury's character has amused the English in other ways. A proverb from 1662 takes note of the culinary passion of residents for baking their renowned cakes and buns: "Banbury zeal, cheese, and cakes." A Banbury Tinker in English folklore is someone who tries to mend things but only makes them worse.

The Elizabethan-styled Reindeer Inn is one of the chief architectural wonders of the town. I stop here for a pint of lager and admire the antique charm, especially the great Globe Room, with its awesome panelling and decorated doorways. After being suitably fortified, I feel compelled to go down the street to sample the famous Banbury cake, a spiced, currant-filled pastry similar to an Eccles cake. Formerly made exclusively in Banbury, these cakes have been baked since 1586, and were once shipped around the world.

Now, I am expecting something mouth-wateringly sensuous. I know, silly mistake. The English do not like excess — in their food or much else. So when I bite into the pastry, it is a tad disappointing. And a little dry. Bill Bryson writes of English taste, "They are the only people in the world who think of jam and currants as thrilling constituents of a pudding or cake." And James Joyce has his hero in *Ulysses* feed the gulls with the Banbury treat: "He halted again and bought from the old applewoman two Banbury cakes for a penny and broke the brittle paste and threw its fragments down into the Liffey. See that? The gulls swooped silently, two, then all from their heights, pouncing on prey."

Of course, one can always order a spotted dick. This popular dessert includes dried fruit — again, currants or raisins — but at least it is usually served with custard to make it palatable. Hospital bureaucrats at Gloucestershire NHS Trust renamed the dish "spotted Richard" in 2001, concerned that people would confuse it with male genitalia. After a wave of protest over such prudishness, the Trust restored the true name in 2002, so "spotted dick" it remains.

Then there is the famous cream tea, served with a scone, jam, and "clotted cream" — a culinary mystery. Why the English are so stingy with the fat content in most dessert items and yet encourage clogging of arteries with clotted cream is beyond my comprehension. The cream would be classed as pure butter in North America, as it has a typical fat content of 64 percent. Lathering such richness on a dry biscuit mixed with gooey jam is not my idea of gastronomic decadence. Yet the monks of Tavistock Abbey in Devon were making clotted cream in the fourteenth century, so it has a lengthy tradition.

Odd culinary tastes still prevail. Take Marmite, a black, gooey spread favoured by schoolchildren much like peanut butter is in North America. It is utterly revolting. One food reviewer calls *A Clockwork Orange* a Marmite film. In a typically self-effacing English way, even the Marmite website has termed it "noxious gunk," and the manufacturer provides a forum for people to rant about how much they hate it.

That said, one of the greatest myths — horrid English cooking — is no longer tenable. Between the time I first began to visit England in the 1980s and today, there has been a sea change in restaurant and pub food, so that some of the best gourmet dinners I have ingested have been at remote country pubs. Continental cuisine has raised expectations and become dominant, though it's still possible to be served mushy peas and soggy carrots. The advent of the gastropub in the late nineties sealed the deal. Pub grub was no longer sufficient.

The first reputed gastropub was The Eagle in Clerkenwell, London, which opened in 1991, and the concept took off from there. At first, steak and ale pie, shepherd's pie, lasagne, bangers and mash, and Sunday roasts were served. Then the better establishments expanded to gourmet delights like baked Dijon salmon, chicken tikka masala, filet mignon with balsamic glaze, Cornish game hens with garlic and rosemary, and a favourite treat — beef Wellington. Tikka masala has now overtaken good old fish and chips as the national dish of England.

KARL RETURNS in late evening from Yorkshire, having successfully recovered his daughter's time capsule from the abbey grounds, though not without incident. Evidently, he attracted much attention when he tunnelled like a mole into sacred ground in front of perplexed tourists. He had just retrieved the buried capsule when an abbey official, puzzled by a stir in the courtyard, came onto the grounds to investigate. By this time, Karl was carefully replacing the grass turf, both capsule and spoon tucked nicely away in his pocket.

"So what did the official say to you?"

"He just stood over me as I finished replacing the turf, his eyebrows arched, looking very worried."

"So what did you do?"

"I stood up, cleared my throat, and told him that the Yorkshire soil was of great interest to me as a Canadian agronomist with special interest in forestry."

"But you're no agronomist."

"I know, but it turns out that his uncle emigrated to Canada years ago and went into forestry in Ontario, so that shifted the conversation to a topic I know everything about — trees."

I shake my head. "Karl, how is it that you can shift so quickly from stubborn Dutch stoicism to whimsical Irish blarney?"

Next morning after breakfast I apply the blister spray to the feet and voila! It does indeed feel like I am wearing new skin. We take our leave of Helen and Nick and are quacked at by the ducks patrolling the green by the pond.

The walk out of Warmington toward Edgehill is quite an ascent. A lone beech tree is our marker as we make a turn, poised above a high escarpment. There are stunning views over the Avon Valley. My blisters are less painful.

Unfortunately, Colin the über-walker's footprints are no longer visible, as rains have washed them away. We soon face the weather again: sheets of rain lash us in windy gusts as we traverse steep rolling fields where myriad sheep tracks sometimes take us off trail.

We emerge from a copse to arrive in the centre of the ancient village of Ratley, startling an elderly man walking his collie. He looks us up and down as if we were a pair of mesolithic vagabonds.

The rain abates and the day is turning warm. We look forward to refreshment at the famous Castle Inn in Edgehill. But first we descend into dense woods for two miles, and then plunge farther down long, steep wooden steps known as Jacob's Ladder. A hike of a good half hour back uphill takes us to Edgehill village. The Castle Inn is mercifully open. I admire the imposing golden oak door, above which hangs a crimson sign dating the inn to 1747.

"As the good duke said, John, never miss an opportunity to take a pint and a piss."

Karl happens to be a great fan of the Duke of Wellington.

"Now Karl, that's not quite how the quote goes — the duke said nothing about a pint."

"You can trust the Iron Duke, John, to know the order of things." With that I can't argue.

The local squire built the inn as a castellated octagonal folly in 1749 to commemorate the Battle of Edgehill. The walls of the bar area are decorated with weapons, including pistols and swords. Tradition has it that Cromwell planned the battle sitting in the back of the Reindeer Inn in Banbury. Visitors staying in the turret of the Castle Inn still report being awakened by the sounds of fighting below, reports given credence by being recorded at the Public Record Office over the years.

The English take their ghosts seriously. They are even assigned file numbers.

We each take a Guinness outside to the terrace garden, where we kick back and bask in the pale sun. Below us lie the terraced slopes of the battlefield where a thousand men died in 1642. Edgehill was the first major battle of the Civil War. The two sides, a total of 28,000 troops, were quite evenly matched. Both sides claimed victory, but historians agree it was a draw. The battle set the tone of indecisive combat over the next four years, until Cromwell eventually prevailed.

The fields now are peaceful, aglow in the mellow afternoon light. In the distance, soft, rounded hills mark the Vale of the Red Horse. The cacophony of clashing swords, screaming horses, and bloodcurdling cries is hard to imagine in this bucolic setting.

Alas, we must heft packs. The path dips down steeply behind Castle Inn, then descends into deep beech woods until joining a muddy track merging from the north. The track is called King John's Lane, because the famously despotic monarch spent many of his days hunting in this region.

"You know, Karl, King John was an evil bastard who greedily tried to seize the throne while his heroic brother Richard the Lionhearted was off fighting the Crusades. After Richard died, the barons rebelled against King John, and he was forced to sign the Magna Carta in 1215. The charter was never intended to protect the common man, yet it ultimately became embedded in the justice system and conflated with ancient Saxon concepts of fair play."

"You're the lawyer," says Karl, "but I don't see a whole lot of rights percolating down these days to the common man or woman. Try and fight city hall. Nor did the Magna Carta address the plight of the workers displaced by the Industrial

Revolution, or, for that matter, the condition of agricultural workers like those Poles up near Boston scrimping a living from picking lettuce in the Fenlands."

"No argument there, Karl."

I once visited Runnymede, where King John signed the Magna Carta, with my wife and eldest son. The chief memorial is on a high hill across from the River Thames. The barons and knights had gathered on a meadow to meet King John to demand their rights. As I sat there and contemplated the scene, I saw the gaily painted banners of the barons with their tents and courtiers and pages. The lonely king's pennant was set apart, while the placid river wound its meandering course in the background. My son, meanwhile, scrambled about on the slope above us and I became rather emotional, realizing that much of the freedom he will enjoy will have emanated from what occurred at this spot so many centuries ago. As I pondered this, plane after plane taking off from Heathrow flew low overhead, one every sixty seconds — a different age, to be sure, but Man still faces the same basic struggles of existence: political equality, economic justice, and a fair balance between citizen and state. Ironically, but for King John the ogre, the evolution of British and all human freedom may have taken a much longer path toward fruition. For many, of course, the path is still untrodden.

FROM SUNRISING HILL there is a panoramic view westward over Warwickshire, where bright yellow, beige, and green fields alternate like a quilt tapestry beneath the Malvern Hills. This is Shakespeare country. Stratford-upon-Avon shines resplendent beside the silvery Avon, a storied stream that winds through meadows before merging with the Severn at Tewksbury. For the first time, we are confronted with evidence of substantial horse ranching and equestrian activities — cinder tracks, horse-jump runs, and well-fenced paddocks.

We push on. Two little boys are so completely absorbed dangling fishing poles over a brook that they do not notice our approach across the narrow footbridge. As we cross, the breeze sends a shower of white hawthorn blossoms in a cascading spiral upon us.

The scene beyond the brook is right out of Constable's painting *The Cornfield:* Ahead of us is a flock of sheep being herded by an English collie along the path. A tall elm tree stands as sentinel. The eye is entranced by the seemingly endless slanting fields beyond and a sky pulsating with fast-moving, creamy pillows skirling eastward. Darker clouds loom ominously on the western horizon. The only part of the scene denoting the twenty-first century is a farmer in tweeds and wellies standing beside his Land Rover, watching his dog and sheep while speaking on his mobile.

Of the English painters, John Constable was the master of skies. No part of England is far from the sea, and the sky is ever changing as layer upon layer of clouds pile in from the Atlantic, the Irish Sea, and the North Sea. Even when the sky is blue it seems pale. Sarah Lyall believes that the climate influences the English to be less "perky" than Americans — "The moodiness makes for lovely landscape painting, but the sun's failure to rise all the way in the sky brings on a natural melancholy." There is some truth to this. However, I would say that the climate tends to produce a mellowness, as opposed to melancholy.

We trudge on toward Epwell on a squishy lane full of mud-holes and horse turds.

"Why do you suppose that farmer back there was all dressed up in tweed?" mutters Karl. "Surely, that's impractical.

Do they just see themselves as gentlemen farmers here who don't want to get all mucked up?"

"It's a tradition, Karl, I suppose. Particularly in wealthy horsey communities like the Cotswolds. And it's not wholly impractical, since tweed is made to be durable and reasonably rainproof."

"Perhaps — but a farmer should dress like a farmer, not like Sherlock Holmes."

Tweed, in fact, is making a comeback in Britain. The fabric originated in Scotland and quickly became popular with the upper and middle classes, who wore tweed Norfolk jackets and plus-fours for cycling, hunting, golfing, and motoring. Mr. Toad was even styled by Kenneth Grahame in a Harris tweed suit. After 1918, the fabric declined in popularity until it was revived by the academic set. During the seventies and eighties there was another brief revival, this time in the form of loud and herringbone tweeds. Now tweed is popular among the smart horsey set and academics as well as with hipsters, vintage tweeds being especially in vogue. Harris tweed is still made on the Outer Hebrides and is the only fabric in the world protected by an act of parliament.

I reflect that thus far on the walk we have been haunted by the ghosts of every past era — "haunted" both literally and figuratively. Oscar Wilde once wrote, "He to whom the present is the only thing that is present, knows nothing of the age in which he lives. To realise the nineteenth century, one must realise every century that has preceded it, and that has contributed to its making."

One cannot walk a mile in this country without history intruding to startle or absorb the senses. Along our path, every vestige of the past presents itself — sometimes vividly, as with a monument such as Edgehill and the carnage of the

English Civil War; sometimes more subtly, as with a simple sign proclaiming "King John's Lane." Every key moment in English history seems to pop up en route — and every age in that history: neolithic barrows; Celtic place names; Queen Boadicea's meadow; Roman roads and ruined villas; medieval castle ruins; Anglo-Saxon burial sites; Viking villages; centuries-old churches, still standing; Elizabethan architecture; Victorian piles and monuments; twentieth-century war bunkers and airfields — all taking their turn in the never-ending saga of history.

Our route now follows a green lane that forms the boundary between Oxfordshire and Warwickshire. This track is part of a trading road dating to neolithic times. It bears the insipid name of Ditchedge Lane. Superb views unfold on both sides of the ridge we climb, particularly to the west toward the Cotswold hills, where the folly known as Broadway Tower crowds the skyline. It stands near Broadway, the centre of Cotswolds chic, haute couture, and fine antiques. It is to Broadway that wealthy North American antique hunters flock, some shipping entire container loads of high-priced brass, raiment, and centuries-old oak across the pond.

GUIDE: *At bottom of long field, follow path along small sunken section of track and through gate onto minor road. Bear left and over bridge beside attractive ford.*

We stand on an ancient packhorse bridge over Traitor's Ford on the River Stour, where Parliamentary sympathizers were executed during the Civil War. Some believe that its original name was "Traders Ford," since a cattle market was once held here. The spot was used for a scene in *Three Men and a Little Lady*, a 1990 Hollywood comedy featuring Tom Selleck.

Karl and I clamber off the bridge, doff our packs and boots, and wade into the water to cool off. Just as we do so, I am accosted by a couple of big dogs, one of which resembles a cross between a German shepherd and an Irish wolfhound. At first I think they are just playing, but when the bigger cur chomps at my leg, it is time to do battle. I slosh to shore, grab both walking sticks, and thrash and yell at the canines, only routing them after the blackthorn stick does its work on the wolfhound's rear quarters. Then I look around anxiously to ensure I am not going to be arrested by some animal rights activists. The dogs romp away into a nearby barley field.

Karl has remained oblivious to my aquatic battle, as he is performing washing ablutions midstream below the bridge, quite enjoying the experience. He finally looks up at me, a bar of soap in his hand, and smiles. "Cleanliness is next to godliness, my mother always told me."

Just beyond Traitor's Ford we meet a man with a spaniel who says he is walking his dog this weekend to "get away from the kids." He lovingly coddles and coos his springer and proudly tells us that the inn he is booked to stay at this evening welcomes dogs within. I wonder how much coddling and cooing he gives to his children or, for that matter, his wife.

The British government recently issued an alarming bulletin to the public over the nation's children — increasing numbers of whom are evidently growing up aimless or dysfunctional. Some relate this trend to the traditional distance that English parents place between themselves and their children. The Victorian notion that "children should be seen and not heard" still holds traction in large swathes of English society.

Sadly, even *The Wind in the Willows* was written by a father who found it so awkward to communicate with his son that he sent him off to boarding schools and refused to visit him. Grahame wrote his classic book in part as a substitute for being a parent, according to literary experts, including the BBC's John O'Farrell. Grahame wrote dozens of letters to his son, Alastair, detailing the adventures of Toad, but ignored Alastair's pleas to come and visit him. Fifteen surviving letters confirm that Grahame used Toad to deflect Alastair's pleas, which at age seven sound heart-rending: "You must come down for the weekend and pick a nice beef bone with me," wrote Alastair in 1907. Grahame later used his "Toad" letters as the basis for *The Wind in the Willows*.

Incredibly lonely and miserable, Alastair Grahame committed suicide at age nineteen by strolling down to the Thames near Oxford — home of Ratty, Toad, and Mole — where he lay down on a railway track and was decapitated by a train. How ironic that a novel borne out of a father's inability to handle a relationship with a son should have provided such incredible enjoyment and solace to millions of children around the world for over a hundred years — and brought Theodore Roosevelt to tears.

We beat uphill from Roman Row to the edge of Whichford Wood, where the last of the withering but still beautiful bluebells form an azure carpet in the open spaces of the forest, intermingled with white stitchwort and a few late-blooming wood anemones. The scene is one of natural harmony, with ferns, flowers, and leaves making a natural florist's bouquet.

Emily Brontë immortalized England's favourite flower in her poem "The Bluebell":

The Bluebell is the sweetest flower
That waves in summer air:
Its blossoms have the mightiest power
To soothe my spirit's care.

Our path is taking us through farmyards that reveal varying animal husbandry methods, including a few mucky eyesore operations. The typical farm buildings are a mixture of brick, stone, and wood. In this northern fringe of the Cotswolds, tidiness is not the priority, partly because these are working farms, not the playgrounds for the wealthy equestrian set we will encounter farther south.

Last night, after returning to our farmhouse B&B after dinner, we heard a great commotion in the barnyard. The farmer told us over tea in the kitchen that the noise was from the pigs. The taciturn chap tapped his pipe and casually advised us that pigs occasionally indulge in cannibalism and bite each other's tails off. He says it's not uncommon for him to find two or three pigs in the morning running about with blood all over them, and he has seen a mature pig take three good chomps to bite off the tail of a baby pig — apparently out of boredom. Mind you, he's proud of his pigs, which are Gloucester Old Spots, a large, black-and-white breed that has been prized for its exceptional quality meat for over three hundred years: prime pork.

"Do any other animals bite each other's tails off?" I ask.

"Not usually."

"That's ironic," I ponder, "because geneticists tell us that of all living creatures, humans most resemble the pig."

The farmer smiles. "Old Churchill had it right when he said he was fond of pigs. 'Dogs look up to us; cats look down on us; but pigs treat us as equals,' the grand old man said."

For the rural English, the family pig was akin to the family cow in North America. After Enclosure, villagers no longer had any grazing space. Keeping a cow required negotiation with some big landowner, but a pig could forage about the lanes by itself and find enough scraps to keep alive. The family fed its pig on food waste such as peelings, and watched it fatten. Once a year they slaughtered their animal, providing ham, sausages, bacon, and lard for many months. Writer Flora Thompson was typical of Victorian children, going to bed crying after the pig was killed, scalded, and butchered, since it had served as a family pet for the months preceding its demise. William Cobbett wrote in *Cottage Economy* that "a couple of flitches of bacon are worth fifty thousand Methodist sermons and religious tracts."

Another source of food for poor village families was the autumn harvest gleanings from the crop fields. Country custom allowed women and children from the village to enter the fields to collect the grain that harvesters had missed. Such gleanings provided wheat for flour and barley to feed the cottage pig. The gleaning tradition helped reduce the cruel impact of Enclosure and could make the difference between starvation and subsistence to a poor village family.

The gleaning tradition is still followed in parts of rural Canada. I have a dear friend who drives a field truck alongside a harvester machine every September in New Brunswick's St. John River Valley to bring in the potato crop. After the fields are worked, he takes his pickup full of burlap sacks and gleans the potatoes that the harvester has missed, filling the sacks and then delivering them around local villages to elderly folk, struggling single parents, and the food banks.

The village of Long Compton sits astride the busy A3400 road to Oxford — and totally ignores it. The golden Cotswold-stone cottages bask in late-afternoon sun, and villagers walk about with their dogs and wheelbarrows. At Wyatts Farm Shop we enjoy homemade ice cream that is sheer decadence.

We check into our working farm B&B, which the landlady, Eileen, operates with a quiet efficiency. Her aged husband,

Robert, runs the farm. It would be easy to write Robert off as some eighty-year-old down-at-heel codger in the early stages of dementia, but he seems more like a spry, amiable eccentric enjoying every moment of life. He thumps about his farmyard, his trusty thirteen-year-old border collie at his side, inspecting the poultry, the pigs, and his barns. He also smells of wine.

"When the old gal here gives out," he says, patting the collie's stomach, "I'll likely go with her. I want us buried together. Now, Eileen here — that's my wife — she wants to be buried more proper in the churchyard, but I've told her that my dog goes with me, and if they won't take my dog in the old churchyard, well then, they won't get me. Reverend Sassers in the village says I should reconsider, as there's only a few spots where dogs can be buried, and it's not right I be separated from Eileen, like — but to me it's a matter of principle."

When not tending to his farm animals, Robert can be found in his greenhouse. He shows us his winemaking operation. There are innumerable gallon glasses with bubbles of CO_2 going "pop-pop-pop" at ten-second intervals. Robert sits with his collie, a broad smile on his wrinkled face. He explains that he has batches of blackcurrant and elderberry wine on the go, and that he makes precisely five gallons per season.

We order dinner at the Grey Fox. Our palates are well prepared for a repast of the highly recommended breast of duck, washed down nicely with elderflower wine. Upon returning to the farmhouse, we stop in again on Robert in his greenhouse close by. We find him peacefully smoking a briar pipe as he sits mesmerized by the "pop-pop-pop." It appears that he hasn't moved an inch since we left him for dinner.

"Save a glass for us for next year," smiles Karl.

"My dear fellow, it never lasts that long. I always run short by January."

"Then why not make more than five gallons?"

"Say, now there's a good idea!" he laughs.

By this time, Eileen is standing in her apron in the farmhouse doorway, arms crossed, shaking her head and smiling.

I decide to change the conversation. "Robert, I understand your farm here goes back to Anglo-Saxon times. Have you ever found any old artifacts on the place?"

He pauses, watching the bottles. "Oh, now, I suppose a few coins over the years — from the plough, you know. The rocks, of course, keep pushing up, and new stuff comes to the surface."

The collie stirs and looks up at us as if to signal that our audience with his master is over. So we hobble over to the cottage, where Eileen offers us some cheese and apple slices before retiring.

It has been an enervating day. We have walked some long miles and are now finally into the magnificent Cotswolds, a magical honeycomb of hidden valleys, softly rounded hills, and quiet, refined villages.

Eileen has overheard our conversation with Robert about being buried with his dog, something she obviously has heard before, and seems fine about. "As long as it is what he wants," she says. "Bentley means a lot to him. At least it's better than becoming too attached to a fish."

"Fish?" I query.

"Yes, over in Blockley, just a couple of miles from here, lies Fish Cottage. Back in the nineteenth century, the owner of the house, William Keyte, trained a trout to rise to the surface of his pond like a dolphin whenever he approached. Keyte became very affectionate with this fish. When the fish died at age twenty in 1855, his son inscribed a memorial stone in memory of the 'Old Fish.' It can still be seen today: 'Under the soil the old fish to lie. Twenty years he lived, and then did die. He was so tame, you understand, He would come and eat out of our hand.'"

Perhaps, I reflect, the English anthropomorphize animals out of empathy for their plight. To humanize is not to demonize, according to David Hume, the eighteenth-century Scottish philosopher who had an enormous impact on the evolution of moral philosophy. As well as great classics like *The Wind in the Willows, Winnie the Pooh,* and *Watership Down,* there are the traditional folk tales of badgers' funerals, rooks' parliaments, magpies' weddings, and hedgehogs milking cows. Badgers, toads, voles, moles, bears, and rabbits all become vested with human characteristics and, hence, empathy.

Then there is the incredible influence of bird protection activists, who number in the millions. How do they feel about the serving of wood pigeons to delight our wretched human palates? Robins are protected by legislation, and it's a heinous offence to intentionally kill or injure any wild bird without special dispensation. The writer John Betjeman is said to have once asked, "Who runs the country? The Royal Society for the Protection of Birds. Their members are behind every hedge." And in this day's *Telegraph* I read of a ruckus in Thornbury, Gloucestershire, where three robins were "assassinated" by a squad of pest control officials at the Wyevale Garden Centre. The birds allegedly posed a public health risk by flying around the centre's cafeteria. The SWAT team action has been condemned by animal welfare charities and is now being investigated by government. Now we know who killed Cock Robin — it's a pest control company with the progressive name of Ecolab.

I fall asleep dreaming of witches' brew with Robert sitting in his shed smoking his briar pipe; I hear the pop-pop-pop of the CO_2 as Karl and I sit drinking elderberry wine.

NEXT MORNING, we encounter another mystery with links to witchcraft. Immediately after breakfast we hike up to the Rollright Stones, a circle of megaliths that stand high on a hill above the Macmillan Way. At the brow of the hill, we pass through a copse, on the other side of which stand these strange prehistoric monuments.

As with Stonehenge, tremendous effort went into hauling these boulders up here, and we really know nothing of their significance. The stones date from 3000 BC. The main group, known as the King's Men, is a circle of seventy-seven stones covered with mosses and lichens. A solitary stone stands across the lane, larger than the others. It resembles a seal balancing a ball on its nose. This upright, the King Stone, shows signs of vandalism, with many chip marks. During the Civil War, soldiers would break a piece off and put it in their pockets as a good-luck charm for pending battle. In the 1930s, the King Stone had to be fenced in to stop local troops from chipping it down to nothing.

The Rollrights have been a venue for witches to meet since at least Tudor times. This is considered hallowed ground by Wiccans, practitioners of modern-day witchcraft. The site is also supposed to enhance fertility. Young women were known to come here to touch the King Stone at night with their breasts. The archaeologist William Stukeley related in 1743 that young men and maidens gathered at the Rollrights on a specific day each year "to make merry with cakes and ale."

The presence of the stones has in legend been attributable to a local witch who cast a fatal spell upon a warrior leader and his retainers. The witch, Mother Shipton, taunted the would-be king by challenging him to approach the escarpment and look for Long Compton below. When he failed the test, the witch cackled:

"As Long Compton thou canst not see, King of England thou shalt not be! Rise up stick and stand still stone, for King of England thou shalt be none; thou and thy men hoar stones shall be. And I myself an elder tree!"

And with that, the king and all his men were turned to stone.

On our way down the hill we pass two black-cloaked, hooded figures whose faces are hidden. Karl nods a greeting, but they look away. A couple of Druids?

The main footpath now takes us past a quarry and through a gate over a cattle grid beside Grey Goose Farm. A short hop and we are sauntering up to the gates of Chastleton House, a Stuart mansion managed by the National Trust. The house was built in 1612 for a wealthy wool merchant. The Long Gallery is amazing, seventy-two feet long with a high, vaulted ceiling. On the grounds, we view an amazing array of box trees, carved as topiary into toys and chessmen clustered around a sundial.

The big attractions for me, however, are the two croquet fields laid out adjacent to the mansion, where a group of spirited fanatics are playing their guts out. Much of British sporting culture has of course permeated North America. Golf has been adopted by Americans even more fervently than by the British, yet the one golf course in the world still revered by all golfers is St. Andrews in Scotland, and in tennis, Wimbledon is still the über-event. Lawn bowling, which dates to the thirteenth century, is still immensely popular in England. The invention of the lawnmower, patented in 1830, led to a surge in popularity of many such sports, including lawn bowling, cricket, croquet, soccer, and lawn tennis. Prior to this invention, sheep were the chief means by which to create a smooth, level playing pitch.

Croquet has long been a pastime of English and North American families. The sport came to England from Ireland in 1852. It quickly became popular as a family and party activity because it could be played virtually anywhere on a well-clipped lawn, and the configuration might vary with the terrain. It was also the first outdoor sport that could be played by men and women as equals.

The rules of croquet were formalized right here at Chastleton House in 1866, by Walter Whitmore-Jones. They were then published in *The Field* magazine, as were the rules of lawn tennis, in 1877. The English are the most avid organizers of rules for games in the world, propelled by their manic anger against unfairness. Adam Smith coined the term "level playing field" in his (naïve) vision of capitalism, but it also defines the English sporting view of the world. The English have never reconciled their view of sports as a gentleman's game of amateurs with the cutthroat world of professional sport. The Academy Award–winning film *Chariots of Fire* exemplifies this angst.

6

HEART *of the* COTSWOLDS

Yes. I remember Adlestrop —
The name, because one afternoon
Of heat the express-train drew up there
Unwontedly. It was late June.

. . .

And for that minute a blackbird sang
Close by, and round him, mistier,
Farther and farther, all the birds
Of Oxfordshire and Gloucestershire.

— EDWARD THOMAS —
"Adlestrop"

A WARM DRIZZLE FALLS as we leave Chastleton via a picturesque meadow of buttercups, irises, and daisies. There is a distinct aroma of mint in the air. "June damp and warm does the farmer no harm" is an English folk saying, apropos this year.

I make for a stile to the left of two tall beech trees. The spire of the Stow-on-the-Wold church is discernible in the distance. My knees and ankles are aching and Karl's pace is not slacking. I reach a paved lane on the outskirts of Adlestrop. This is the village immortalized by the poet Edward Thomas, who was travelling through on the train in 1914.

The first thing I see upon entering the village is Karl standing beside a dross bus shelter sign, peering down at a plaque. On it are etched the famous lines of Thomas's cherished poem "Adlestrop." Thomas, who was killed in 1917 at Arras, remains a painful reminder that Britain lost the flower of a generation in the mass slaughter of World War I.

Thomas walked the footpaths with Robert Frost in Gloucestershire in 1913, inspiring Frost to write his famous poem, "The Road Not Taken": "Two roads diverged in a yellow wood, / And sorry I could not travel both . . ." When Frost sent Thomas the draft of this poem, Thomas felt compelled to immediately enlist in the army, as he viewed himself as having prevaricated between Frost's "two roads diverged" — in his mind, the rootedness of the comfy shire versus the road to battle for his country. Thomas has exercised a major influence upon how we view and write about the English countryside.

He once wrote, "Much has been written of travel, far less of the road."

During the dark days of 1943, Peter Scott, son of the famous Scott of Antarctica, spoke on the BBC: "For most of us, England means a picture of a certain kind of countryside, the English countryside. If you spend much time at sea, that particular combination of fields and hedges and woods that is so essentially England seems to have a new meaning." Even though most of the massive destruction wrought by the Luftwaffe in England was over cities, it was, says Scott, "that . . . countryside we were so determined to protect from the invader."[1]

By that time England had already become a largely urban society, but the idyll for most English people was still a cottage in the country. Songs sung by Vera Lynn to lift the spirits of the troops in World War II fantasized about the white cliffs of Dover and country lanes:

There'll always be an England
While there's a country lane,
Wherever there's a cottage small
Beside a field of grain.

It's almost as if the urban English always have the countryside at their back, beckoning. It is the refuge, the sacred shire, the Land of Lost Content. Linda Proud writes in *Consider England*, "The idea of a village, romantically dishevelled with tall nettles obscuring rusting tools, with ivy and vines invading walls,

---

1 During the Battle of Britain in 1940, young boys and men too old to enlist gathered on over ten thousand village greens nightly with shotguns and pikes, on guard all night against German invaders, ready to defend to the death their villages. They wore Local Defence Volunteer armbands.

with chickens, geese and ducks laying eggs under bushes, with a snuffling pig or two and some feral cats, is the form of a longing buried deep in the English soul. It means home and it means freedom."

William Blake's famous poem "And Did Those Feet in Ancient Time" betrays that same prejudice against urbanity:

And was Jerusalem builded here
Among these dark Satanic mills?

Blake contrasts the mills with England's "green and pleasant land." To this day, the poem that was transformed into a hymn, "Jerusalem," is the most popular song in the land, sung at funerals, weddings, clubs, sports events, and innumerable other functions. Nostalgia overwhelms this country — nostalgia not for power or for empire, but for the ancient green land. Hence the English aphorism "You are closer to God in a garden."

We find no rail station in Adlestrop, for it was demolished in 1966. The Cotswold Line tracks are still in use in nearby Evenlode Valley, but thousands of miles of rail trackage have been removed as part of an efficiency program that has severely reduced rail service. English country people have never forgiven the government for abandoning five thousand miles of track and closing more than two thousand railway stations following Dr. Beeching's efficiency report of 1965. His name is still vilified. The closing of these lines has left deep scars — long lines of weeds and grass, and stations left as boarded-up wrecks. But as in North America, it has provided a bonus to walkers, with the popular "rails to trails" trend. It is weird, though, stumbling upon abandoned brick and stone bridges mouldering in the woods, covered with ivy, moss, and brambles — and leading nowhere.

"What did Thomas mean by writing that the train 'drew up there unwontedly'?" Karl asks.

"I don't know. Nobody got on or off, but I suppose it could have expressed Thomas's mood, as if it was frivolous for the train to stop for no reason."

We potter over to the church, across from which is the gabled rectory, Adlestrop House, where Jane Austen stayed with her cousin, Rev. Thomas Leigh, on several occasions between 1794 and 1806. Another Austen relative owned the manor of Adlestrop Park. On these visits Jane attended this church, but she would not have seen the impressive clock hanging over the gateway, which was erected to celebrate Queen Victoria's Golden Jubilee, nor the prominent sign warning of a two-penny fine for "use of improper language in the belfry." Jane would have dusted her shoes off at the church entrance because the roads in the village were then unpaved and consisted of loose, chalky white limestone.

Jane Austen found her cousin's rectory a grand place, suitable for the high station that rectors such as Reverend Leigh still enjoyed in the late eighteenth century. The home boasted eight hearths, five maids, a butler, and two liveried manservants. From her room in the rectory, Jane looked out upon immaculately kept grounds, including a lovely walled garden. She was a great walker, and traversed paths now part of the Macmillan Way that led to nearby Chastleton House. She also enjoyed a private walk to a lake on the neighbouring Adlestrop Park estate. In her perambulations about the village, Jane would have noted labourers' cottages with thatched roofs, such as the still surviving Pear Tree Cottage, and the daily congregating of village women round the town pump to draw water and share the local gossip. Jane arrived for visits here from her home in Bath by coach and horses that delivered her directly to the door of the rectory along a road that is now a bridleway.

Mansfield Park has a scene depicting Adlestrop as a model country village. In rural estates such as Adlestrop House and the grandiose Adlestrop Park, Jane Austen, like George Eliot, found the ideal of country living and a moral society extant within a relatively self-sustaining community. Austen lived at a time when 80 percent of England's nine million people lived in villages or hamlets. The philosopher Roger Scruton opines that "the country house came to represent an ideal of English civilisation — one in which hierarchy was softened by neighbourliness, and wealth by mutual aid."

The walk from Adlestrop to Stow-on-the-Wold combines quiet country lanes with bridleways and pleasant footpaths. The day is sorting itself out and a certain luminescence is appearing in the western sky. We come across an elderly couple hunched over in a field of dandelions. The man's bearded face is weathered and tanned, as are his big, gnarled hands; his wife is portly and brimming with a robust red-cheeked vitality. I ask them what they are harvesting.

"Dandelions," grunts the man.

"Is that for dandelion wine?"

He stands up, scratches his thin beard, and then replies, "No, it's for the guinea pigs." Then he goes back to work, both he and his wife placing the dandelions in large buckets.

We decide to back off and move on. "Do you think he was pulling our leg?" laughs Karl.

"I honestly don't know, Karl. Maybe they do raise guinea pigs!"

The bluebells may be fading, but I am in love with them still, plucking a few and holding them up to the sunlight to admire their translucence, which reminds me of the agates and opals I collect from West Coast beaches and Fraser River sandbars. Interspersed with the bluebells are wild garlic plants, which I can't stop munching like a ravenous rabbit. Karl says I will make myself sick, and that my breath stinks.

The leaves of the garlic plants are spear-shaped and slender, and release a scent that seduces one to pluck and suck. This wild garlic is a species native to Britain and grows prolifically in ancient woodland. Garlic contains allicin, which is both antifungal and antibacterial. And of course chopped-up garlic adds real zest to salads and soup. After munching my fill I lope awkwardly along the winding path to try to catch up to Karl. I am wracked with momentary guilt, for I have trespassed off the path to enjoy the bounty of this private wood.

The owner has every right to complain about us walkers. Perhaps Madonna has a point in wanting to maintain her estate unsullied by muddy-booted ramblers. History records that even the most passionate democrats have ranted against public footpaths crossing their land. For instance, E.M. Forster, author of *A Passage to India,* purchased a little wood in Surrey, not far from London, but was tortured by the fact that it was "intersected, blast it, by a public footpath." This literary champion of the common man morphed into a strident property owner, on the prowl against anyone who plucked *his* blackberries, *his* bluebells, *his* hazelnuts. Forster derided the prevailing economic system that in his view caused him such conflict in his soul between empathy for the rights of the common man to access woodland and the desire of the owner to protect that land from public despoliation.

This introspection leads me to realize that the linear walk we have been taking, now well into our second week, is completely different from loop walks; it really is a journey in which one loses oneself to the landscape of history. We have passed through the Narnia wardrobe portal. The modern world is a thousand miles away. Thanks to Karl's problems with his mobile phone, we are deliciously cut off from the cares of daily life, emails left behind. Though I look forward to talking to my wife every week or so, I do not wish to hear about the mundane issues of family and household which she is facing. Selfish me.

The Cotswolds are classed as one of the world's areas of outstanding natural beauty. The name derives from the Saxon *cote,* a sheepfold, and *wold,* meaning a bare hill. The Cotswolds defines that range of hills in west central England some twenty-five miles across and ninety miles long, centred in Gloucestershire but including parts of Wiltshire, Somerset, Worcestershire, Warwickshire, and Oxfordshire. Sheep are the economic engine in the history of the Cotswolds. The splendid towns, fine churches, and magnificent honey-hued mansions were all paid for by wool profits from an era when England ruled the world of cloth manufacturing. In Westminster, the lord chancellor still sits on the Woolsack.

Huge flocks of sheep used to be driven from Wales, and it could take three hours or more for them to pass through towns like Stow and Banbury. By the fourteenth century, Europeans recognized the best wool as being English — and in England, the prime wool was Cotswold. After shearing, Cotswold wool was usually sent to ports like Southampton, from where it was shipped to the Continent. Local merchants grew wealthy and gave some of that wealth to the building of parish churches and other important buildings. A Cotswold epitaph for one such merchant reads:

I praise God and ever shall
It is the sheep hath paid for all.

After the demise of the woollen industry, this region of rolling and folding hills and coombs, of quiet villages and tiny lanes, quickly became a mecca for tourists and the retiring affluent. Horse riding, breeding, and racing are all the rage. The pubs overflow with well-dressed, tweedy locals and weekending Londoners.

The Cotswolds are home to a star-studded roster — Prince Charles, Prime Minister David Cameron, Arab sheikhs, industrial barons, and film stars such as Kate Winslet, Elizabeth Hurley, and Hugh Grant, to name but a few. Don't expect them to participate in ferret-racing, cheese-rolling, or nettle-eating contests. But by and large, they respect the long-time country residents and traditions. Of course, appearances in this country are invariably deceiving: the farmer's wife down the lane might well have a degree in nuclear physics; her unshaven, eccentric neighbour puttering about his greenhouse in mismatched tweeds and smoking the briar pipe — meet the former ambassador to Iran.

The acerbic A.A. Gill is scathing in his comments about Cotswolds residents, particularly the part-time urbanites. He notes in *The Angry Island* that the area has become a playground for the rich to indulge their fantasies; it's all about "paddocks and swimming pools and pheasant shoots." The price of a small cottage in a quiet village is well beyond the reach of most working people. Gill mocks the Cotswold elite who enjoy the latest in home innovations, such as breakfast bars, Japanese grills, rotisseries, and, above all, the Aga stove — the equivalent of a church altar in the new country home.

The gentle side of sheep farming hits me on our way up to Stow. We stop to talk to a farm lady who is walking the path carrying a plastic bottle of milk and scanning the field slopes above. She is searching for a little lamb that was evidently so tiny after birth that it needs bottle nourishment to help it through. She asks us if we have seen it. We have not, but shortly after this encounter, I surreptitiously watch Karl stop a distance ahead of me to disentangle a slightly injured large lamb from some brambles by a fence, and he is surprisingly gentle. I don't say anything to him, but I have seen!

Imagine quaint country lanes, robins chirping, blossoms overflowing in orchards, and you will see our world today on the Macmillan Way. Imagine Arcadia — all that's missing are the Hesperidean nymphs. We pass over the gurgling infant River Evenlode and enter Lower Oddington. It's time to rest a bit in the churchyard. My eye fixes upon an enormous effigy of an unknown woman with Brobdingnagian feet sticking out from under her dress. Jumbled tombs are spread higgledy-piggledy throughout the rear of the graveyard beneath ancient yew trees.

"Mile 142, Karl, and just entering the environs of Stow."

"You choose the pub, John boy. I am parched."

"I can see it in my mind's eye. Tally ho!"

The long climb from the northeast up the main Stow road takes us past a vast meadow used by the gypsies for their annual Stow Horse Fairs. On a telephone pole I read a High Court order banning wagons and lorries from this field. Immediately beyond is a sprinkling of antique shops, chic clothing outlets, and towering Cotswold-stone buildings housing retailers at street level with living quarters above. Near the top of the hill is a rabbit warren of narrow alleys, ancient inns, and the town square. Stow has a reputation for severe weather: "Stow-on-the-Wold, where the winds blow cold and the cooks can't roast their dinners."

Stow stands at the convergence of eight ancient roadways. Traders have passed through here for centuries with their wares: salt from Worcestershire, fish from the Severn estuary, iron and charcoal from the Forest of Dean. At Stow they exchanged goods and purchased food, shelter and stabling, pottery, saddles, and harnesses. But in later centuries the wool trade dominated all. At one of two annual fairs, vast flocks of sheep would be driven to the town's environs and then into the town square down narrow alleyways. Some twenty thousand sheep would be sold on a good day. Foreign goods were sold too, and monastic buyers came from six monasteries within thirty-five miles of the town. The spring fair was one of the largest in the country. When the wool market died, the traditional fair declined and the gypsy Horse Fair became the residual event. Today it remains one of the largest gatherings of its kind in England — popular with artists, photographers, and those appreciating traditions of a raunchy, folksy nature.

We have decided to stop an extra day here and are booked for two nights at the Old Stocks Hotel, named after the stocks that still rest on the green outside. These are about 150 years old, having replaced the originals that were used to bind minor miscreants and humiliate them in front of their tomato- and egg-throwing fellow townspeople. Today some shop owners would like to use the stocks once again to pelt the gypsies and chavs who occasionally frequent their town.

We are given a warm welcome by Jason and Helen Allen. At the bar one runs into patrons of all types: a ruddy-faced mason who specializes in laying Cotswold stone; an elderly couple up from Dorset for a weekend; Camera Club seniors from Oxford; even a Roy Orbison look-alike who dresses in black with long sideburns and horn-rimmed glasses. The music is a blend of sixties and seventies classic soft rock — the Beatles, Chad & Jeremy, Leonard Cohen, Orbison, with a bit of Frank Sinatra and Vera Lynn thrown in. Relaxed and mellow.

The Old Stocks dates to the sixteenth century and has the usual floorboard creaks here and there, but by and large it is all you would expect in a small hotel. It has also been discovered by American travel guru Rick Steves, so one must book well in advance. I ask Jason — a dapper, quick-witted man given to sarcasm with uppity guests — what's with all the orange traffic cones around town, and, for that matter, all over the roads of England? There are even a couple of orange cones in my field of vision from our bow-window table in the dining room, lying obtrusively next to the rustic old stocks. I go out to examine them and find they are only protecting grass. I ask Jason to remove them, for the cones are detracting from the ambience of the town square — not to mention the myriad tourists who want to be photographed sitting in the stocks.

Next morning I am sitting enjoying my poached eggs on toast and notice that the orange cones are now even more offensively placed: perched on the very top of the stocks! Jason has undoubtedly done this just to perturb me. So I decide that it is time for some colonial self-help action and trundle outside to determine how to remove the offensive objects. Jason must have seen me, as they subsequently disappeared altogether.

The streets are quiet at the moment, but I envision what it must have been like on that spring day in 1646, when the Royalist forces of Charles I, commanded by Sir Jacob Astley, were trapped in the square in front of me and slaughtered — thousands of horses and men fighting at close quarters, the heavy clashing of sword against sword, the neighing of the horses, mingled screams. Astley finally ordered 1,600 Royalist troops to put down their weapons, and Roundhead troops then marched them to the church, where they were held overnight. Popular tradition has it that the blood ran so thick that ducks floated in pools down Digbeth Street.

After breakfast Karl and I stroll over to the church. The north door is flanked by two enormous yew trees standing like sentries. This is the most enchanting church entrance I have ever seen. (Tolkien, it is said, was so transfixed by these gnarled, knobby ancient yews — a primordial vision of tangled roots, trailing moss, and earthy fecundity — that this doorway became his inspiration for the portal to Moria in *The Lord of the Rings*.) After a visit we duck into the coffeehouse next door for some mocha java. I reflect that the town centre looks much like it would have in the seventeenth century.

Next door to the Old Stocks is the Royalist Hotel, reputed to be the oldest inn in England, dating from the year 947. An ancient tunnel leads from the bar to the church across the square. In some guest rooms and to the left of the hotel's massive fireplace, "witch's marks" are clearly visible. These medieval symbols were intended to ward off spells cast by witches. The obsession with witches reached its climax during the Civil War, when one Matthew Hopkins claimed to be "Witch-Finder General," ferreting out witches across the country. He was aided by zealous Puritan ministers and oddball fanatics.

St. Edward's Hall in the town square must surely be the only town hall built solely from the proceeds of unclaimed deposits at a town bank. Mysterious Fleece Alley dates from sheep-fair days. Swank shops and tourist nooks are the rule — upscale coffeehouses, bookshops, a chemist, stores like Groovy2Shoes, Styles of Stow, Laurie Leigh Antiques, Cotswold Baguettes, and one selling wood-burning stoves — though one would have to own a dukedom to afford wood in this country. Stow is all about Burberry and leather. No Oxfam here, please.

Stow is perpetually full of tourists — chiefly Japanese, North Americans, and elderly Brits from miles around who come here to stroll the streets, enjoy a cream tea, examine fine linens, and explore the curios, brass, and oak buffets in the cozy antique shops. "Look, Martha, imagine having to use one of those enamel chamber pots!" Of course, the tweedy rich don't browse; they come to certain shops by special appointment, blowing ten or twenty thousand pounds in an afternoon on such collectibles as a cobalt Ming vase, a Queen Anne glass bookcase, or a nineteenth-century edition of Gibbon's *Decline and Fall of the Roman Empire*.

We are treated this weekend to much activity in the town square, including Morris dancing, which dates back to medieval times and is still very popular in this part of England. Ironically, this quintessentially English dance originated with the Moors in Spain, *Morris* being a derivative of *Moorish*. Six men dress in costumes of white shirt and trousers, each with a hat colourfully garnished with flowers and ribbon. They wear gaiters with bells and carry sticks and handkerchiefs which they toss about, all to the accompaniment of a fiddler. Morris dancing had died out in Victorian England, but in reaction to industrialization, the late 1880s saw a revival of many rural customs, including quilting, folk music, and, of course, walking the footpaths. Although Morris dancing is still largely a male endeavour, we see a group of mixed young men and women practising the art. All participants are enjoying themselves immensely, as are the photo-snapping tourists.

Of course, there is that little problem of customer relations here. Unlike North America, the customer is not God, and should form a queue and wait patiently in line if there is anyone else near the counter. At the chemist's to purchase some Pepto-Bismol pills (to replace my bottle so injudiciously discarded en route), I ask the young clerk how things are going. She replies, "Just now, things are fine. But all morning it was simply horrible! Customers just kept coming in!" (One is reminded of the long-running sitcom *Are You Being Served?*)

There is still difficulty with servicing large groups of people, such as at restaurants, hotels, and food stores. Paul Theroux notes in *The Kingdom by the Sea* that the English "were brilliant at running a corner shop, but were failures when they tried their hands at supermarkets . . . The English do small things well and big things badly."

The propensity of the English to close things up has even pervaded the churches. In London a notice was recently posted on a church door: "This is the Gate of Heaven. Enter ye all by this Door. This Door kept locked because of the draft. (Please use side door.)" The moral here: If the English can find an excuse to close it, they will. Whatever and whenever the English can squirrel away from the public, they will — their castles, their wares, their thermostats, themselves.

This is an oversimplification. Our Old Stocks is operated efficiently, and the Tesco supermarkets are big, bright, and generally well run. Though it was a tad perplexing to go shopping at the Stow Tesco at nine-thirty on a Sunday morning and be upbraided at the counter when I brought my apples and water bottles up:

"Sorry, sir, we are not yet open."

The polite, brown-eyed cashier with the smart frock glanced at me pleasantly but firmly.

"I don't understand," I stammered. "I am here. You are open."

"No, sir, on Sundays we don't open until ten. Customers are only allowed to browse until we open."

"You mean I have to wait another twenty minutes to ring these few items through?"

"I am afraid so, sir."

"Right. Thank you so much. I am very sorry."

So I cooled my heels in the wine section of the store, admiring all of the Australian brands of Shiraz that we never see in North America. What an odd little isle! Yet it once ruled half the world.

I reflect on the use of "sorry" in England. It is used as an important safety valve for people's emotions. It is a way to apologize without losing face, or a means of embarrassing the other person when they are clearly in the wrong — as if to say, "Is my eye bothering your elbow?" — or as a means of conveying a lack of understanding of the other person's position. The English are masters at defusing a tense situation by using this word to allow the other person to back down after you have been the first to apologize — without, of course, meaning it. Just when you think the English are the politest nation in the world — as they are — you realize that the constant use of such terms as "sorry," "thank you," and "please" is really a very clever means of defusing an embarrassing situation, limiting confrontation, or achieving one's own devious ends.

Stow is a pleasant place, but twice a year it is traumatized. Below the town in the large meadow Karl and I passed on entry, the gypsies gather twice a year for the Stow Horse Fair. The group is disparate, as it includes true Romany gypsies, travellers — as the Irish strain is known — plus camp followers. Some two thousand of them arrive in mid-May in their caravans and lorries, with hundreds of horses and ponies in tow. The mud is something awful. The May host is the largest, and last year I visited their encampment. One needed high boots to walk through the camp gumbo, alive with colourful wagons, wagging dogs wallowing in mire, and little boys in costume riding piebald ponies. Stallholders offer wares of silver, gold jewellery, utensils, exotic peasant costumes, horse equipment, CDs, and birds, plus traditional victuals like kebabs and frankfurters.

In late afternoon during fair week, hordes of young people roam the streets of Stow, and the County Council sends a hundred constables to patrol the streets, a few of whom actually stand inside the larger stores. Many shops close for the week. A pub was wrecked one night during a bar fracas. And each evening, dozens of gypsy girls prance and promenade up and down the streets wearing very little clothing — high boots, tank tops, and short cut-offs — on the prowl, and evidently not for just a one-night stand. It's a tradition for gypsies to broaden the bloodlines by seeking spouses for their young men and women outside the immediate community.

Locals allege that the owner of the horse meadow only offers it to the gypsies out of spite, because the County Council refuses to let him subdivide the acreage. Numerous injunctions have been obtained forbidding more than a handful of caravans to park in the field, but they are studiously ignored. That said, the right to a horse fair is ancient: royal charter gave it to Stow in 1476. For travellers, this is their equivalent to the Caribbean carnival — but many locals and policemen don't see it that way.

True gypsies belong to a wandering race that may be Indian in origin; their language, Romany, is a corrupted dialect of Hindi. Gypsies arrived in Britain in the late fifteenth century and have been part of the cultural mosaic ever since. They originally prospered in metalworking, and later branched out into basket and peg making, horse-dealing, flowers and herbs, and fortune-telling, and excelled as pipers and fiddlers. William Howitt, a nineteenth-century educator, wrote, "The picture of the rural life of England must be wholly defective which should omit those singular and most picturesque squatters on heaths and in lanes — the Gypsies; they make part and parcel of the landscape scenery." There are thought to be more than 300,000 Romany and travellers in Britain today, and both groups are officially recognized as distinct ethnic minorities under the Race Relations Act.

Staying an extra night in Stow allows for a salubrious diversion to the lost medieval village of Widford. The remnants of this deserted village lie on the beautiful River Windrush a few miles southeast of Stow, in a lovely rolling meadow surrounded by copses of beech and oak. All that remains of Widford now is a few houses and the thirteenth-century church of St. Oswald's, which stands stranded in a field with no access road. The village was ravaged by bouts of the Black Death in 1348 and 1360, and never recovered.

In June 1348, two ships docked at Melcombe in Dorset. On board one of them a sailor carried with him from Gascony the germs of bubonic plague. Soon people were dying swift deaths all along the southern coast, the lymph nodes painfully swollen in their necks, armpits, and groins. This "Black Death" spread inland like wildfire, carried by fleas that infested black rats. Poor sanitation facilities and wayward garbage disposal had contributed to a sharp rise in the black rat population in the fourteenth century, causing the disease to spread extremely rapidly. Young and old, rich and poor, none were spared. Millions died across Europe. In Britain, between one-third and one-half of the population was wiped out within twenty-five years.

The Welsh poet Jeuan Gethin wrote in 1349 of the plague's onset, "We see death coming into our midst like black smoke, a plague which cuts off the young, a rootless phantom which has no mercy or fair countenance."

Hundreds of villages disappeared overnight. Many others dissipated over just a few years. The survivors barely had the energy to carry the bodies in wheelbarrows to be buried in common pits. Virtually no one knew the cause of the abomination, but of course the Church preached that God was punishing the wicked for their sins. A popular nursery rhyme of the period ran:

Ring-a-ring o' roses,
A pocket full of posies,
A-tishoo! A-tishoo!
We all fall down.

We walk about the deserted field where a few hummocks protrude from an undulating sward of buttercups and wild poppies. Hawthorn, honeysuckle, and plum cherry bushes are abuzz with bees; larks caper and cavort overhead. Backdropping the scene is the church, a tiny Early English Gothic structure. There was a chapel here as early as 642, when monks carrying the body of St. Oswald stopped to rest on their way to Gloucester for the saint's interment.

As I stand poised to click a photo of this enchanting scene, two gentlemen dressed in Victorian-era formal black evening clothes carrying hickory walking sticks suddenly pop into my line of vision, swaggering down a path through the field. One of the gents is tall and built like a bull, the other slight and barely five feet tall. I turn to Karl.

"Where did they come from?"

"Don't know, John — they just appeared from nowhere."

The two apparitions recede in the distance and we step forward toward the church. Inside we are immediately struck by its simplicity: scratched, time-worn box pews, carved corbels, and a rustic tub font survive. Archaeologists have confirmed that the site was used by the Romans as a bath-house connected to a villa.

The church is only accessible by walking path, and the ghosts of a once-thriving village lie buried, unmarked, their dwellings now just mounds in a grassy field. I can't get the two mysteriously dressed figures out of my mind. They looked like they were strolling to a Victorian theatre performance. Were they real, phantom, or did they just step out of a time capsule? Even Stephen Hawking is now on record as admitting that time travel is theoretically possible.

Next morning, back at Old Stocks, Jason and Helen bid us adieu.

"Now don't be getting into any mischief, you two — and John, I hope you don't run into any more traffic cones!"

"We will be back, Jason. Just keep those wretched orange cones off of the old stocks; the tourists deserve better!"

He laughs heartily and stands waving with Helen until we are out of sight.

We cross the busy A429 and turn south into a labyrinth of quiet villages, attractive Cotswold lanes, and fields so well clipped that they appear coiffured. The honey and cream cottages add a luminescence to the landscape even on a drizzly spring day. At Hyde Mill, swans glide gracefully on the mill pond formed by the River Dikler. We stand for a moment on a footbridge watching them.

"Congrats, Karl, we are now precisely halfway along our journey — 145 miles done, another 145 to go. Plus another 60 miles off trail."

"Where's our next drink, John?"

"Is that all you ever think about?"

"No, and that's a foolish question — I think about sex and hockey too."

Lower Slaughter is one of the most photographed villages in England. The water mill with its high chimney stands on the banks of the River Eye, and it is our luck to have the sun break through and reflect in the water as a group of equestrian riders cool off their mounts in the stream. Although the mill is of red brick, most cottages here are Cotswold sandstone and boast attractive mullioned windows, some with projecting gables.

Karl remarks that the well-manicured lawns, clipped boxwood hedges, herbaceous borders, and freshly painted cottages represent the finest in village pride. But I am uneasy with such perfection: villagers must get up at the crack of dawn to pick up every twig, trim every branch, mow every offending blade of grass, touch up the paintwork on every cottage window — even the spiffy little footbridges that access their homes bear the marks of recent paint jobs. Moreover, the picturesque mill wheel has been tweaked to revolve soundlessly. In short, it's too much like a storybook movie set. The name "Slaughter," incidentally, does not denote violence, but rather is simply a mangling of the Old English word *slough*.

Folks here do not like change or competition. A recent press report states that the parish council is fiercely fighting a young lad who insists on selling ice cream from his tricycle, seven days a week for six months of the year. Council argues that such "trading times" are excessive, and the resulting increased footfall will prevent grass from growing — and children might climb onto their trikes holding their ice cream cones and fall into the adjoining brook! I am amused by this, because when I was ten years old, I was busted by Vancouver City Council's jackbooted bylaw officer for selling, door to door, raspberries that I had picked on my grandfather's farm. I had neglected to purchase a pedlar's licence for $75 — a prohibitive sum for a child. Where can I sign up to contribute to this tricycle kid's legal battle? Why can't councils go fight adults instead of picking on kids!

The Cotswold stone belt reaches its apogee of perfection in Gloucestershire. J.B. Priestley passed through the Slaughters in 1933 and commented, "Even when the sun is obscured and the light is cold, these walls are still faintly warm and luminous, as if they knew the trick of keeping the lost sunlight of centuries glimmering about them. This lovely trick is at the very heart of the Cotswold mystery."

Cotswold stone tends to be a mélange of cream, yellow, gold, ochre, and various shades of grey. The villages seem to just grow out of the ground, so blended are the hues of nature with man's buildings. This effect is enhanced by the deeply sunken lanes plus the weathering process. There are subtle changes in the tints of the façades due to the variations of stone from quarry to quarry. All seems in harmony. And in springtime, white may-blossoms, yellow celandines, and wild violets line the verges of village lanes and paths.

It is a supreme irony in this traditionally class-conscious society that it is the humbler cottages of this region that tourists rave about — cottages originally built for the carpenter, the shepherd, and the labourer. Such dwellings were made of lesser-quality stone that has weathered to produce a quainter, more aesthetically pleasing look than the great houses of the rich built of the finest, unblemished freestone blocks. The patchy nature of the modest cottage façade gives it a unique charm.

Simon Winchester, in his *The Map That Changed the World*, confesses to an emotional reaction to Cotswold villages: "A huddle of warm-looking Jurassic stone houses, clustered amicably in some river carved notch in the meadows, can be so lustrously perfect, so quintessentially English, that seeing it brings a catch to the throat."

Lower Slaughter leads us into the Windrush Valley. To my mind, there is no stream in England more beguiling than the little Windrush, which bubbles and babbles and sings its way through one enchanting village after another, intent on bringing joy wherever its winding course may lead, eventually emptying into the Thames.

Though our *Guide* authorizes a diversion to Bourton-on-the-Water, the best-known village along the Windrush, we decide instead to visit the Notgrove Long Barrow. It's a sweaty grind up a steep hill on a humid June day. Notgrove is surrounded by trees at the summit. Only the faint outline of the ancient barrow is visible; because the stones were deteriorating, Gloucestershire County Council decided to dump loads of soil over them. This was a major site for the ancients. There is a forecourt, five internal chambers along a central passage, and a double wall surrounding.

The hilltop is dotted with wildflowers. I note knapweed and harebells entangled in the long grass, but it is the colourful riot of yellow-wort that gives the scene watercolour beauty. I can see why neolithic Man would have chosen to hold celebrations and be buried here.

Archaeologists have found three hundred long barrows in Britain, and believe their construction was the last phase in a long sequence of ritual entombment of the dead that occurred between 4000 and 2400 BC. Within the barrow was often a room-sized mortuary chamber support with wooden posts. The dead were placed here, but often they had been interred elsewhere and were brought to the barrow later.

All notable barrows in Britain are steeped in local legends that usually involve mysterious lights and music being seen and heard at night by villagers — many of whom were no doubt staggering home from the pub at the time. But the notion of ghostly beings originates with Celtic tales of the Sidhe, who were said to live in the "hollow hills." On this June morning, there is a certain synergy, an enervating delight, being up here with the breeze touching the face, the yellow-worts spread in profusion, and magnificent views of the gentle hills in every direction. About us, the gnarled yet stately oaks stand guard over the mysterious tombs. The sun bursts through long cumulus masses swirling overhead like horses' manes.

We descend to the trail from our ethereal revelry and soon reach the village of Cold Aston. I am a little confused by the entry sign that reads "Aston Blank." When I peruse the *Guide*, sure enough, "Aston Blank" is an alternative name for the place! How can a minute village of a few souls be so confused about its name? Well, it transpires that the village was known as Cold Aston from the thirteenth century, then changed to Aston Blank in the sixteenth century; in 1972 residents finally voted to change it back to Cold Aston again.

"But none of that explains why the entry sign still reads Aston Blank," notes Karl, "given that the name was officially changed back to Cold Aston in 1972."

"They'll get around to it, Karl. Maybe they left the sign as a sop to placate those residents who voted for Aston Blank."

Karl and I rest on a bench under a towering sycamore tree and watch the world go by. The place may be tiny, yet everyone seems to be completely lost, rushing about like characters in *Alice in Wonderland*. We sit fascinated as at least three trucks stop at the pub within ten minutes, the driver in each case asking directions for some house in the village (there can't be more than twenty houses here). Then we spot an old codger dressed in faded tweed walking along with his bicycle, his groceries in a basket on the handlebars. He appears confused and keeps heading down wrong lanes, totally disoriented. We cannot help him, as we are but strangers here. Finally, a lady watching from her garden patiently directs him past us to an obscure lane to our right, calmly explaining that he will find his cottage and wife waiting for him at the end of that road. He laughs embarrassedly as he approaches us and points to the red telephone booth beside the pub.

"I would've phoned me wife to come and fetch me home, but I can't remember me telephone number!"

"That's all right," Karl says with a smile. "The phone is likely out of order anyway."

And so the poor codger straggles down the lane. I suppose we will all end up like him one day.

We could be miles from civilization here — yet the busy A40 is only two miles away. J.B. Priestley was astounded to discover on his Cotswold travels that although the area was not mountainous or wild, it felt incredibly remote. Turning off a main road, one is plunged into "one of these enchanted little valleys, these misty cups of verdure and grey walls, and you are gone and lost, somewhere at the end of space and dubiously situated even in time, with all four dimensions wrecked behind you."

Karl and I regain our bearings by stopping for some ale and a hearty ploughman's lunch at Cold Aston's Plough Inn, where the burly proprietor tells us that the premises are haunted by a ghost named Old Harry. When I ask him if it is common for so many motorists to become lost in the village, he says that he spends a good part of his day directing people to their various destinations, like some traffic cop.

"That must cut into your time somewhat," I suggest.

149

"It's quite all right, mate." He smiles. "They usually end up coming back here for a pint or two later on, so it's actually good for business. No one forgets the Plough."

7

ROMAN VILLAS, RACEHORSES, *and* CIRENCESTER

Seek me no more where men are thick,

But in green lanes where I can walk

A mile, and still no human folk

Tread on my shadow.

— W.H. DAVIES —
"Return to Nature"

THE RUTTED TRACKWAY cuts deeply into the Jurassic limestone. Tinkers, traders, and soldiers have followed this route for millennia. A few miles south of Cold Aston, the trail drops abruptly down a steeply wooded slope, and I slip and fall on my butt, slithering a few yards into a small ravine in the adjacent wood like a sack of spuds. My camera is caked in a detritus of mud, needles, and leaves. By the time I reach the surfaced track below, I am knackered and bruised. Karl is standing there with an amused expression. He points to a page in his *Guide* informing me that we have just emerged onto Bangup Lane, an ancient track connecting Cold Aston with Turkdean.

"And I must say, John boy, you do seem a trifle banged up."

He seems chuffed, while my pride is injured — he's the old guy, so why am I the one falling down ravines? I don't know if I can ever get all the mud off my camera, and I shudder to think that the primordial ooze may have penetrated its interior. Why did I not have the presence of mind to bundle it up in the camera bag?

We slog along for two miles, past Bangup Cottage and Bangup Barn, then it's up another sunken lane overhung with dripping, moss-laden maple trees, to emerge in the village of Turkdean. No, I am not making these names up! The origins of many of them are completely lost. For instance, absolutely no one in this region has a clue as to the origin of the name Bangup. So many others are fascinating: Traitor's

Ford, Corton Denham, Sutton Montis, Chipping Warden, Compton Valence, Farthingstone, Lower Slaughter, Obthorpe, Sandford Orcas, Prior's Coppice, Tongue End, Upper Oddington, Wyke Champflower, Duntisbourne Rouse, Canons Ashby, Castle Combe.[2]

We leave Bangup Lane beyond Turkdean. Near a rusty horse trough we tear downward on a track that is slippery and steep; horses have churned the earth into a mucky mire. The hamlet of Lower Dean lies at the bottom, though the only sign of habitation is Castle Barn Farm. The *Guide* suggests a short diversion to Northleach, prime Cotswold walking country, so we hoof it down the track to explore this cream-stoned former market town.

An unusual attraction in Northleach is the Old Prison, which is unique in several ways. Firstly, it has made the longest journey possible for a prison — from a place of confinement to an upscale bistro and coffee shop. Secondly, it was built as part of a prison reform program in Britain that was to emphasize more enlightened treatment of prisoners convicted of minor offences. Hence the name here: "House of Correction." Northleach was the brainchild of a reformer named Sir George Paul, who became high sheriff of Gloucestershire in 1780. He was horrified by prison conditions and much influenced by John Howard, who first brought to national attention the terrible conditions of Britain's jails. Henry Fielding dubbed the prisons of the day "prototypes of hell."

---

2 On the subject of odd place-names: One year I stayed at a delightful thatched-cottage B&B in the village of Knockdown, Wiltshire. At breakfast I gingerly broached the subject of village name origin with the proprietor — an intelligent, red-haired company executive. "You know," he replied, "I've lived here some twelve years now and really haven't given a thought as to why the village is known as Knockdown. Please pass the salt."

Northleach House of Correction opened in 1791 and included a warden's house, female cells, police station, courtroom, and exercise yard. Sir George paid meticulous attention to detail, even ensuring the water supply by having a stream channel routed through the prison yard. Pumps were installed; windows were built larger than ever before allowed; air circulation was improved; and proper beds of horsehair, hemp sheets, and a blanket were provided to each inmate. A separate cell block was installed for women prisoners. For its day, Northleach was an enlightened prison.

The liberal prison regime at Northleach regressed after Paul's death in 1820. In 1823 hard labour was introduced — initially via a hand-cranked corn mill, and then in 1827 by way of the tread-wheel. The wheel accommodated sixteen men at once, climbing eight-inch steps like hamsters on a treadmill. The inmates wore themselves out on this notorious device. The machine was a product of typical Victorian genius, as it combined the moral duty of society to punish an offender with the equally cherished virtues of hard work and production — as the spokes turned, the gears crushed grain. Most prisoners worked a gruelling eight-hour shift, a regimen that often led to injury, illness, or death.

"To think that an exercise treadmill is now used voluntarily by millions to keep fit," says Karl, "when the whole idea of the machine came from that horrid prison device."

"Are you saying, Karl, that the prisoners should have been grateful for being kept in shape?"

"Hell, no! I don't care for treadmills or jogging — only walking, with a nice pint or two along the way. Speaking of which?"

Back on the Way, Karl pushes on at his commando pace, while I dawdle with my camera. I even stop to chat with a handsome-looking lady with Italian features who resembles Meryl Streep in *The Bridges of Madison County*. I spy her in black riding boots feeding some horses in her stable and ask if she would mind my taking her picture. She smiles and poses, tossing back her red kerchief over her long brown hair.

We stand in the sunshine chatting about photography and walking. She remarks that it must be terribly exciting to just pick up and leave with one's rucksack and explore the villages and byways. She invites me into her cottage for a cup of tea. Her husband, she says, is down in Devon looking at "more horses." She rolls her eyes; they are beautiful flashing black eyes. I decline the tea invite, but thank her.

"Sometimes I really do wish I could just go off like you. We never holiday. I don't mind the work, you know, but it's always just the farm, farm, farm — and Jack won't even go on a weekender up to Scotland with me. Oh, he's a good man, very good, but the farm is his real mistress. It might have been different if we could have had children."

Her hands tremble. I reach out and touch them for a moment.

Karl has stopped to wait for me half a mile ahead at a curious spot known as the Hangman's Stone. The "Stone" is just a large slab leaning against a rock wall. Tradition has it that a thief with a stolen sheep in his arms accidentally hanged himself while climbing over a stile that once stood in this wall.

"What took you so long, John?"

"Just photographing the lush countryside, Karl. If you slowed down, you might enjoy more of the sights."

"Wooden head, wooden shoes, and wouldn't listen, my friend."

The path takes us steadily downward. I stop every few minutes to drink in the sweeping views of surrounding hills and the valley of the River Coln below us toward Chedworth. We enter the village of Yanworth and are immediately struck by the neat, green-painted farm buildings and immaculate Cotswold cottages boasting window boxes, hanging baskets, low trimmed hedges, and finely edged herbaceous borders.

"Now this is my kind of village," smiles Karl. "We could be in Holland. If only everyone maintained their gardens and homes this well! Neat as a pin."

"I don't know, Karl, it's a little too regimented for me. Like those prissy cottages in Lower Slaughter. I rather favour the tangled, wild English garden look, with ivy taking off everywhere, wisteria overhead, and climbing roses out of control. Throw in a battered old sundial, and you have paradise."

The vista from Yanworth looking south is now more defined, a landscape of patchwork fields, copses, a shimmering lake, and little streams meandering about. The path continues across a working farm and then on to Chedworth Villa, which many rate as the premier Roman villa site in Britain. The villa was discovered accidentally in 1864, when a gamekeeper found fragments of pottery in the riverbank. But the real credit for the find goes to a ferret. A farmer had placed his ferret at the entrance to a rabbit hole to root out the rabbits. Trouble is, this particular ferret became lost in the hole. In the course of digging Mr. Ferret out, his owner found to his surprise that the rabbits were enjoying the high life in a warren situated in a Roman bedroom floored with fancy tiles; further digging revealed a treasure trove of Roman artifacts. The ferret should have been pensioned off for life as a reward.

Chedworth boasts unique mosaics, two bathhouses, hypocausts, a water shrine, and a latrine. A child's coffin was found in 1935. The villa was fully operational between the second and fourth centuries. The Romans practised sophisticated heating techniques here, including two separate bathing suites, one for damp heat and one for dry heat. The mosaic-tiled floor in the dining room, for example, was floor-heated by means of hot air circulating in the flues. A natural spring provided the occupants with a clean, fresh source of water, and became the site of a shrine to the water nymphs. A fascinating place!

The villas were the forerunners of the landed manorial estates of the country gentry. Fortunately for the villa owners, the Anglo-Saxons who followed the Romans were primarily farmers and had a real interest in maintaining agricultural production. The evidence indicates that there was little of the wholesale destruction of the villa farming communities such as occurred later on the eastern coast of England with the incursions of the Vikings. The Anglo-Saxon settlers even adopted the concept of the *villein* as part of their agricultural hierarchy.

Interestingly, one of the owners of Chedworth Villa has been identified as a man called Censorinus, and there is an inscription on a silver spoon found on site that reads "May you be happy, O Censorinus." This sounds like a birthday present or housewarming gift. Censorinus would have enjoyed a diet high in protein: deer, wild boar, eggs, and fish. He also ate oysters, snails, whelks, and mussels, as thousands of shells have been unearthed at Chedworth, plus a device for opening oysters.

Half a mile of thick woods separates Chedworth village from the villa site. En route we note much interesting flora — coppiced hazel, dogwood, bryony, and bluebells. I also stumble on a gigantic snail, which I later learn is unique to this locale and is called *Helix pomatia,* or the Roman snail. It is likely a descendant of the snails known to have been specially cultivated by the Romans for the table.

We tumble out of the woods into Chedworth village, which sits isolated in a sylvan valley. The welcoming Seven Tuns Inn faces a spring that bubbles out of a wall across the lane, and we refill our water bottles there. But a lady passing by tells us that the water is unfit for human consumption, so we empty them on the ground.

A piece of Chedworth village now lies in the state of Michigan. In 1930, Henry Ford purchased Rose Cottage, a dwelling nestled at the lower end of the village. He then had it transported, stone by stone — just like London Bridge — to a waiting ship, which took the cottage fragments across the pond, where it was reassembled at Greenfield Village near Dearborn, Michigan, a heritage community designed by the Ford family to celebrate traditional village life in America. The cottage can still be found there, surrounded by a Victorian flower garden planted with begonias, delphiniums, peonies, and herbs. Ford paid $5,000 for it.

Aside from its famous villa, the Chedworth area is known for another reason. William Smith became the father of British geology by mapping the story of the rock strata beneath Britain, including the fossil record. An important contribution to his understanding of the fossil record was "Chedworth buns," round, shell-like objects typically measuring three and a half inches in diameter that have been ploughed up by farmers in fields between Stow and Chedworth for over ten centuries. The local populace dubbed them "fairy loaves," but Chedworth Buns are actually the fossilized shells of urchins that lived in a warm shallow sea that covered central England 165 million years ago, during the Jurassic period.

The entry to the estate village of Rendcomb is dominated by the Italianate Rendcomb Court, now used as a coed boarding school. We check into Landage House, a lovely country mansion with an enthralling view of a pond, fields, and herds of sheep grazing peacefully below. There is even an outdoor heated pool. I could have stayed here for a week, swimming, strolling, and reading.

Too early for the pub, I stop at the village shop and buy a bottle of elderflower cordial to drink. Being parched, I quaff it down quickly. Karl stops me in the street and grabs the bottle from my hand.

"Good God, man, that's concentrate — don't tell me you drank it all!"

"Yes, and it was wonderful."

"John, tonight you're really going to need your Pepto-Bismol. That concentrate should have been mixed with water to make a whole two litres' worth!"

He was too right; my stomach groaned all night. Somehow all that concentrate did not mix well with a bottle of peppery Shiraz consumed over dinner.

The *Guide* provides for an alternative route south of Rendcomb in order to visit the market town of Cirencester, a place steeped in Roman influences. We decide to put on some extra mileage by traipsing five miles to town and then five miles back to rejoin the main path. This will add an extra day to our overall journey.

For once Karl is keeping a moderate, even pace. I enjoy the twists and turns of the River Churn as we wend our way through lush interlocking meadows dotted with hyacinths and wild irises.

The hamlet of Perrott's Brook lies in the isolated River Churn Valley. It is on the medieval route known as the Welsh

Way, which from 1400 was the chief conduit for Welsh drovers to herd their sheep and cattle to market in London. Up to two thousand animals at a time were driven along the track. Wagons also transported cloth and cheese products through here to be loaded onto Thames barges at Lechlade.

The Bear Inn in Perrott's Brook was ideally situated for accommodating travellers along the Welsh Way, and became a favourite coaching stop. It finally closed its doors in 2002 but is now a B&B. In the eighteenth century, there was a second inn across the road "compleatly fitted up and accomodated for the Entertainment of Gentlemen and Travellers," with "a Dog-Kennel neatly compleated and a Pack of Hounds kept to pleasure any Gentlemen that like the Diversion of Hunting."

So check into the inn on your horse and next morning it's tally ho with a pack of restive, rented hounds anxious to chase down a fox. I wonder how much that would have cost? Would one place a deposit down for the pack of hounds, as if one were renting a car?

The landlord of the Bear Inn performed double duty as a wheelwright to repair coaches and wagons. Undertakers frequently stopped at the Bear overnight while transporting bodies for burial at nearby Bibury, because the inn's deep cellar is situated on a brook. The pallbearers could deposit their corpses for the night knowing that the constant cold temperature would keep them intact until morning. Travellers staying at the Bear B&B today can view the old cellar where all this went down. It's a chilling venue for a Murder Mystery Night.

A well-documented duel was fought on the grounds of the Bear Inn in the late seventeenth century. Sir John Guise of Rendcomb was playing cards with his friend Sir Robert Atkyns of Sapperton, when a ruckus broke out and Guise demanded an apology in front of the inn's diners. Sir Robert refused, so Guise told him to draw his sword, saying, "You shall die like a dog." The two trundled outside with their friends. In a matter of moments Sir Robert had run his sword through Guise. The rector of Bagendon, who was present, wrote, "The impetuous soldier spitted himself on the lawyer's blade, which came out his back, and he fell into a saw pit." Amazingly, Guise survived the wound.

We make tracks for Cirencester, the largest town in the Cotswolds. There are enough bypasses and circle roads around it to make the head spin; they are very unkind to walkers. The townsite was the major centre for the Dobunni, the Celtic tribe which once dominated present-day Gloucestershire, Wiltshire, Somerset, and Avon. Contrary to the stereotype of "wild Celts," the Dobunni engaged chiefly in farming and crafts, and were not particularly warlike. They quickly appraised the overwhelming Roman forces after AD 43 and made a pragmatic decision: to submit and become integrated into the Roman plan of governance. They became the first major Celtic group to do so.

The Romans in turn recognized the conciliatory gestures of the Dobunni. As the Dobunni were frequently attacked by other more warlike Celtic groups, they readily accepted an offer by the Romans to resettle for protection in the immediate area of the fort built by the latter at Corinium, some five miles to the south of their main camp. The Romans astutely renamed the post "Corinium Dobunnorum." This precursor of Cirencester was one of the most important centres in Roman Britain. After the Romans left Britain, the Dobunni were slowly swamped by Anglo-Saxon settlers, who had successfully subdued all of the Cotswolds by the late sixth century. Corinium Dobunnorum was renamed "Cerne Cester."

The Cirencester parish church positively glows with cathedral-like majesty, thanks to numerous medieval chapels. The Perpendicular Gothic tower is 162 feet high. In a recess at the end of an aisle sits a silver goblet, the Anne Boleyn Cup, so named because it was given by Anne Boleyn to her physician, Dr. Richard Masters, in gratitude for his treatment of her daughter, Elizabeth, the future Virgin Queen.

The façades in the town centre are a harlequin hodgepodge of pink, orange, and white hues of various period design, including some handsome Elizabethan styles reminiscent of Stratford-upon-Avon. The streets are wide, spacious, and tidy. Upscale shops overflow with inventory.

Our next stop is the Corinium Museum. Mosaic pavements depict a centaur and Roman gods in various poses. We also view an unusual portrayal of Genialis, a mounted Thracian trooper in the Roman legion, trampling down a long-haired Celt. His tombstone lies just behind the stone carving. This is one of only ten stone tombs in all of Britain confirmed to contain Roman soldiers. But the most fascinating artifact is a wall plaster displaying a word puzzle:

ROTAS

OPERA

TENET

AREPO

SATOR

The interpretation of this anagram is: "Arepo the sower guides the wheels at work." This lettering sequence resembles inscriptions found on walls at Pompeii, and is the oldest evidence that the ancients enjoyed the kind of word games that are still popular today.

We emerge into the sunlight, dazed by the sheer extent of the Roman artifacts. I am fagged and crave caffeine. Karl wanders off in search of a phone shop to see if he can activate his mobile. I find to my delight that Cirencester is littered with coffee shops — Costa, Starbucks, and a number of independents, plus tea shops that are hedging their bets by innovating espresso machines yet don't want to lose the geriatric tea-and-crumpets crowd. As in Samuel Pepys's time, coffeehouses are experiencing a resurgence in the United Kingdom.

I stop for a mocha at an independent shop. The husky male owner with a fierce red beard resembles a Viking warrior. He states that the UK is now in the forefront of high-quality bean imports plus quality grinding and blending, with special emphasis on ethical practices and fair trade coffee. The ethically "green" pinnacle is reached, he says, when the grower recycles the leaves and roots of the coffee plants as manure dressing for next year's crop. It seems that the days of ersatz coffee in England are over.

Historically, the English love affair with coffee both predates tea and was more torrid. This surely explains why the Victorians tried to suppress coffee — no doubt believing that java overstimulated the senses and detracted from the temperate, sober, controlled society they sought to build. (Hey, any society that found dining-room table legs sexually stimulating and advised homeowners to cover them up would find coffee to be a licentious beverage designed to corrupt the masses.) There was no such danger from tea.

The coffee craze in England began in 1651, when a vendor known as Jacob the Jew opened a coffeehouse at the Angel Inn in Oxford. Things really took off two years later in London when the Greek servant of a British merchant opened the first coffee shack against the stone wall of a churchyard in an alley off Cornhill. Within two years, Pasqua Rosée was selling six hundred dishes of coffee a day, much to the displeasure of local pub owners. This coffee was a wicked brew — "black as hell, strong as death, sweet as love," as the Turkish proverb goes. Yet a London newspaper opined in 1701 how the "bitter Mohammedan gruel" nonetheless kindled conversations, inspired debates, sparked ideas, and, as Rosée himself stated in his handbill *The Virtue of the Coffee Drink*, "made one fit for business." Some observers credit coffee with bringing Britons out of their "drunken stupor," leading to the expansion of the economy and empire. In the early eighteenth century, up to eight thousand coffeehouses flourished in London, plus thousands more in country towns. By contrast, Amsterdam boasted only thirty-two in 1700.

The fervent, wide-ranging discussions of politics, philosophy, and religion grew so bold that Charles II tried unsuccessfully to suppress coffeehouses. The *Women's Petition against Coffee* of 1674 claimed that men had become "effeminate, babbling French layabouts." A counter-petition titled *Men's Answer to the Women's Petition against Coffee* claimed that coffee made men more virile.

In any case, the conviviality with which men of all classes now mixed can be said to have played at least a minor part in the transition to democracy. For it is in the coffeehouses of London, Glasgow, and Edinburgh that men like Samuel Johnson, David Hume, and Isaac Newton met and discussed their theories, elbow to elbow with dockworkers, fishmongers, and tradesmen. John Dryden and Samuel Pepys favoured Will's Coffee House in Covent Garden, which became known as the London Centre of the Wits. A pamphlet of 1674 called *Rules of the Coffee-House* proclaimed: "Pre-eminence of place none here should mind, but take the next fit seat he can find."

This ensured that men of all classes would rub shoulders in a relaxed setting. Lloyd's of London and the Stock Exchange were founded as a result of meetings of London businessmen at Lloyd's Coffee House (run by Edward Lloyd) in 1694 and at Jonathan's Coffee House (founded by Jonathan Miles) in Change Alley in 1762, respectively.

Tea first arrived in England from China in 1660, and was introduced in the coffeehouses. But tea, unlike coffee, was no social equalizer. On the Continent it was drunk by the fashionable rich. It gradually took hold in the sceptred isle, however, and by 1770 veritable "tea fleets" of ships were importing the brew. As the price of tea went down and people learned how easy it was to make their favourite blend at home, an entire tea culture developed, as did the baking of teacakes, crumpets, and biscuits.

Pubs deftly made inroads by merging with coffeehouses, and over time the ale prevailed over the java. By the Victorian era, middle-class wives had reined their men in from the coffeehouses to the pleasantness of tea in the garden at home, subject to the odd evening decamp to the local pub. Meanwhile, upper-class men formed private clubs and retreated to their privileged precincts to discuss the political issues of the day. Once again the masses were kept in their place and elitism prevailed.

Tea calms and refreshes. Coffee stimulates spirited discourse. Without tea, the Brits would not have muddled through the last world war. Without coffee, the RAF pilots would not have won the Battle of Britain. Without beer, all would have collapsed. But with the recent revival of coffeehouses, one can only hope that Britons will look up from their mobiles and laptops and rouse themselves from their navel-gazing stupor long enough to talk to their neighbours in the friendly kind of banter and badinage that characterized society in the seventeenth and eighteenth centuries. Brits consume an average of 4.2 pounds of tea each every year, but espresso sales now exceed tea sales in cash value. Wake up and smell the coffee.

It is hard to avoid the antiquarian shops in Cirencester. On a whim I purchase a late-fourth-century Roman silver ring and place it on my little finger, willing myself to imagine some Roman soldier wearing it into battle against marauding Saxons.

Karl just laughs. "What's your wife going to say — you always said you hated wearing jewellery, and I've never even seen you wear a wedding ring. Yet you don't mind wearing some anonymous dead Roman's battered band."

"That's not entirely true. I used to wear a wedding ring, but lost it ploughing my back field one day."

"So instead of replacing your wedding band, you're going to prance about with this bit of bling?"

"I'm hoping to feel the vibes of the past, Karl. Anyway, maybe I won't wear it every day. Did you get your mobile to work yet?"

"The damn thing can't be made to work over here. They say I'll have to buy a new mobile. They can't find a chip to work with my North American phone."

Our last stop in Cirencester is the Querns, a huge, bowl-like field that contains the remains of the Roman amphitheatre. Some eight thousand spectators could be accommodated here, watching the deadly clashes of Roman gladiators 1,800 years ago. In the medieval period the amphitheatre was used for only slightly less barbarous entertainment: bull-baiting. A bull was chained to a stake by the neck and then hunting dogs — usually bulldogs — were set loose upon the poor animal.

Dogs that were killed and maimed were replaced until the bull was killed or they ran out of dogs. Bull-baiting was a variation of the ancient practice of bear-baiting; both practices were banned by Parliament in 1835.

As we walk the amphitheatre, Karl can't resist doing his own baiting, asking, "Well, is your precious ring giving you some vibes as to what really went on in this arena during those Roman times?"

"I'm working on it."

At that moment we pass a buxom, middle-aged woman clutching a Starbucks cup and wearing a pink sweatshirt that is inscribed: "My body is not a temple — it's an amusement park." Karl winces.

Cirencester Park forms part of the enormous Bathurst Estate, including Pinbury Park. This ancient seat of the earls of Bathurst consists of 3,000 acres surrounding a mansion. An additional 12,000 acres accommodate equestrian activity. We walk down the Broad Ride, admiring the pristine setting. This was one of the earliest landscape parks in England, built by the first earl of Bathurst, who was assisted in its development by his close friend Alexander Pope. The famous poet and satirist was also a brilliant landscape designer, and helped Bathurst in building and placing classical Greek structures. Pope used his days spent at Cirencester Park to develop his perspective on nature and consider the sociopolitical importance of the landscape garden, which he wrote about in the 1730s.

Pope describes in a 1718 letter how content he was working at Cirencester Park: "I am with Lord Bathurst, at my bower; in whose groves we yesterday had a dry walk of three hours. It is the place of all others that I fancy." Bathurst and Pope would go hunting in the afternoon, and in the evening, draw up plans for the estate, including ingenious schemes "to open avenues, cut glades, plant firs, contrive water-works." In a letter from 1722, Pope said that he looked upon himself "as the magician appropriated to the place."

Ralph Vaughan Williams was born in Down Ampney, a few miles east of Cirencester, and Cirencester folk naturally claim him as one of their own. He is revered as perhaps the greatest composer England has ever produced. Vaughan Williams achieved a synthesis of lyrical, pastoral, and liturgical traditions with formal composition. One outstanding example of this is his famous *Fantasia on a Theme by Thomas Tallis;* another is his 1928 version of "Greensleeves" (the original of which many scholars believe was composed by Henry VIII for Anne Boleyn). *The Lark Ascending* captures the dynamism and acrobatic power of the skylark, which I have recently witnessed in the fields south of Stamford.

It has been a long, tiring day. Karl and I plod back to the town centre to dine and then crash. Before retiring for the night, I take my Roman ring off and put it in my jeans pocket. After walking around the Querns — imagining first the gladiators fighting to the death and then the blood-soaked bull-baiting — I somehow find the ring unsettling.

Next morning, the day dawns cool and misty for our hike back to Rendcomb to reunite with the main Macmillan Way. From the trail junction we meander southward to reach Duntisbourne Rouse. I am continually bewildered by the sheer number of paths that intersect our own. One can go anywhere on foot and be rewarded. In *The English Landscape*, Bill Bryson has commented that England boasts greater diversity and interest squeezed into a small area than anywhere else in the world. "Within a limited radius one encounters some remarkable diversion . . . And, this being England, more often than not it will have an engaging air of eccentricity about it."

Bryson speculates that someone has owned and used every square inch of the country's land since neolithic times.

Beyond Duntisbourne Rouse, we encounter some 500 acres of finely clipped turf accommodating hundreds of prancing thoroughbreds that belong to the Bathurst Estate. Karl is a horse lover and stands watching them, entranced. The Cotswolds share with Kentucky the distinction of the highest density of horses per square mile anywhere in the world. The sporting life of England is concentrated in Gloucestershire. Wherever we walk we see paddock activity, plus many horse riders on bridleways. The squirearchy still loves its horses. Private racing tracks abound, and stables and riding rings proliferate. Many young people, especially girls, are passionate about riding.

The epitome of the country's equestrian life is the national competitions. Of these, the Ascot races, such as those in the Royal Ascot meeting and the annual King George VI and Queen Elizabeth Stakes, are the most prestigious. But the ultimate event among country gentry is the Cheltenham Gold Cup race, highlight of the annual Cheltenham Festival. A key aspect of this race is the assembling of top Irish racehorses to be matched against England's finest. Horsey people of the Cotswolds flock to the festival to mingle with their peers. Cashmere, tweed, and Land Rovers rule. Dick Francis found much fodder in the Cotswolds for his equestrian crime novels.

Nothing can slow Karl down, I have found, except horses. I tug his arm to be on our way.

"Those are fine horses, John, very fine horses. I could watch them all day."

"I am sure that they are happy parading about the good Lord's pasture, Karl. I mean, of course, Lord Bathurst, who is unequivocally the terrestrial Lord in this neighbourhood. I've heard that a private helicopter is on constant standby to trundle him back and forth to London."

Karl sighs and waves his walking stick with a flourish toward his equine friends, and we trek onward.

Our view of the Frome Valley is bewitching. Far below us is a meandering stream, winding like a sinuous eel through thick woodlands, with the odd grassy rise above on which sheep graze. Fine mist hangs over patches of the river valley, while the fickle sun flirtatiously flickers and glows and then teasingly hides itself again above the patina of a feather-grey cirrocumulus cloud blanket. One expects to see a knight in full armour come charging up the slope on a warhorse. This place is truly lost in time, and I have this uneasy feeling that we are but intruders.

Lost in reverie, I am startled when three mounted riders appear as if on cue, on steeds gaily apparelled. Two men attired in bright-coloured livery, like knights of yore, flank a lady princess whose long red tresses cascade beneath her helmet onto her shoulders. No doubt they are venturing out from their castle en route to some jousting tournament. Karl and I both fall backward into the prickly bramble hedge to avoid the lead horse, which snorts and gambols his way past us down the path.

We have been cast aside like so much hoi polloi. I guess they thought we were serfs. It isn't even a bridleway, so technically it is illegal for the trio to be riding along the path. But that's okay — the sight was worth it, and it's good practice to humble ourselves even if we did have the right-of-way. In fact, as we dove for the hedge to avoid being trampled upon, I should have yelled, "Sorry! Is my body obstructing your Royal Progress?"

We dust ourselves off. Karl hunts for his walking stick, which became entangled in the brambles and blackthorn bushes when he fell into the hedge.

"Come on, John, it's all part of the adventure. Let's make tracks to our next watering hole."

The pallid sky has turned a deep indigo, and it appears we are in for a squall. The path meanders through a meadow full of wildflowers as we near Sapperton, and then it's onto a muddy bridleway uphill, through a gate where we bear "half-left," as the *Guide* enjoins, then across another field to emerge at a red telephone booth in the village.

We walk beneath ancient yews in the churchyard. Sapperton Church houses many fine tomb effigies. One of those effigies is of our friend Sir Robert Atkyns, whom we last met fighting a duel in Perrott's Brook. Atkyns had a storied career as a lawyer, judge, and Speaker of the House of Lords. He was a spirited reformer, and teamed up with Edward Coke to denounce the Court of Chancery, pleading for a return to fairer common-law principles of justice and the adoption of equity principles to favour the common man. He opposed the House of Lords acting as an appellate court. His book, *The Ancient and Present State of Gloucestershire,* became the first comprehensive history of the county.[3]

Sapperton itself is glowing with Cotswold gold. John Masefield, the Poet Laureate of England from 1930 to 1967, made the town his home base, living at nearby Pinbury Park on the Bathurst Estate from 1932 to 1940. Many in the literary establishment felt he was unworthy of his exalted position.

---

3 Atkyns's dream of the House of Lords losing its judicial role was not to be fully realized until 2009, when the Supreme Court of the United Kingdom became the highest appellate court in the land.

His range of poetry extended to Arthurian scenes, Hardy-like pastorals, sea ballads, and war drama. He was no Tennyson or Hardy, but he did give us those lines of "Sea-Fever" that most North American schoolchildren learned by heart in the latter half of the twentieth century:

I must go down to the seas again, to the lonely sea and the sky;
And all I ask is a tall ship and a star to steer her by,
And the wheel's kick and the wind's song and the white sail's shaking,
And a grey mist on the sea's face and a grey dawn breaking.

Below the village runs the two-and-a-quarter-mile tunnel of the Thames and Severn Canal. At the Bell Inn, we encounter an old collie dozing in the garden entrance. As we stand outside contemplating whether to take refreshment here, a man drives up in a Peugeot and emerges wearing a pink tie on a white shirt, pink Bermuda shorts, and long pink socks. Two elderly ladies then appear from the back seat, dressed conservatively in long mauve silk dresses, and he escorts them to the entrance, one on each arm. My smirks disappear when a burly man who is clearly the proprietor, clad in bright pink cotton slacks matched with a pink polka-dot bow tie, appears at the entrance, bows, and graciously ushers this strange trio inside.

"Karl, it looks like we're not up on the latest in Carnaby fashion — note that the men here all wear pink!"

"There are times, my friend, when I wish I was half blind instead of half deaf."

"I think we had better move along — we are both sartorial disasters."

A quarter mile down the path I stand perplexed, peering at high, wrought-iron manor gates through which the *Guide* assures us our path passes. Yet the gates are barred shut.

Help, however, is on the way. A well-groomed lady who resembles Margaret Thatcher in cream jodhpurs and black riding boots strides through the gates guiding a golden retriever on a leash. She advises us politely that the path has been rerouted through another part of her estate, as the official right-of-way passes intrusively in front of her morning breakfast window and walkers would peer in at her and her husband sipping their morning coffee. So they have donated land behind the manor house for a redirected path, but the damned sign keeps falling off the rock wall to the right of the gates. She offers to escort us through the adjacent copse. We thank her and say we are sure we can find the diversion path on our own.

"Better than setting the dogs on us, John," remarks Karl a few yards later. "I certainly wouldn't want walkers staring into *my* kitchen window while I spilled marmalade all over my face."

"Quite."

There is nothing more important to the English than their privacy. This may account for the fact that the United Kingdom has the highest rate of home ownership in Europe, from simple cottages to urban jungle flats. Jeremy Paxman notes that Continental Europeans are content to live much of their daily lives on the street: "It is the place where you eat, drink, commiserate, flirt, laugh, and pass the time of day. The English answer to the street is the back garden, in which socializing is by invitation only. Because the English dream is privacy without loneliness, everyone wants a house." At the end of the day, after finishing with her socializing, the Englishwoman likes nothing better than to go home, slam the door, and put on a pot of tea.

It is a pleasant but mucky walk through Hailey Wood. The *Guide* warns us, however, to keep away from the fenced edge near the end of the wood — it is dangerous, as an open shaft remains intact, formerly used to extract debris from the tunnel below for the building of the nearby Thames and Severn Canal. We emerge intact at the Tunnel House Inn, which the *Guide* informs us "was built to house, feed, and especially water, the navvies who dug the canal tunnel and the thirsty boatmen who used it when completed."

The tunnel was completed in 1789, and allowed boats to cross the Cotswolds from the head of the navigable Thames at Lechlade to the Severn, and thence to the eastern coast. This was the longest tunnel in Britain at the time, and was such an engineering feat that even King George III came to watch its construction. Reports indicate that the Mad King was in fine fettle, freshly released from Dr. Willis's sanatorium, which we encountered up in Greatford, Lincolnshire.

Bargemen propelled their boat through the inky blackness of the canal tunnel by means of "legging" along the sidewalls. This had to be the toughest, most eccentric way to ever move a watercraft. Two men had to lie on a plank, each placing his feet against sidewalls of the tunnel, and then crabfoot along to gain forward momentum. Sapperton Tunnel was abandoned in 1927.

The Tunnel House Inn was Poet Laureate John Betjeman's favourite watering hole. Outside hang some old, weather-beaten signs: "Craven A Will Not Affect Your Throat" and "Corston's Aerated Beverages — First for Thirst." We sample the local brew; Karl quaffs a pint of Hooky Bitter and I try the Uley Bitter. The traditional workman's fare is served, including burgers, steaks, and Gloucester Old Spot sausages — a true bangers-and-mash establishment. But one can also devour monkfish tails, goat's cheese brioche, and pig's ear. We both settle for a ploughman's lunch.

In the course of devouring our victuals, Karl overhears the term "red biddy" in conversation at another table and asks the barkeeper about it.

"You don't want any red biddy, mate," says the tall moustached barkeeper. "It might kill you."

"Why?" asks Karl. "Is it some kind of local gut rot?"

"Well, mate, it's like cheap red wine mixed with spirits — methylated spirits."

"I guess I will pass on that," Karl says with a smile.

The barkeeper winks at the two blokes next to our table, who continue to quaff their glasses of suspected red biddy.

The solicitous barkeeper does not know that Karl's stomach is so tough that he could drink paint thinner and suffer no ill effects.

8

GHOSTS, BROTHELS, *and* RAGING BULLS

Green lanes that shut out burning skies

And old crooked stiles to rest upon;

Above them hangs the maple tree,

Below grass swells a velvet hill,

And little footpaths sweet to see

Go seeking sweeter places still.

— JOHN CLARE —
"The Flitting"

CHERINGTON VILLAGE still has charm. A quaint communal pump sits on the green, with the inscription: "Let him that is athirst come." The pump is really a fountain that was fed by water drawn from an underground stream. It never ran dry, and until well into the twentieth century, most cottagers in the village drew their water from it. Now the fountain trough has become a flower bed stuffed with blue and red pansies.

The stone cottages clustered near the green are largely nineteenth century, and hence are considered modern. The shops and pub have long since shut down. My ancestors lived here as far back as the Domesday Book, compiled in 1086. In the fifteenth century, a couple of forebears migrated ten miles north to Leckhampton village, now part of Cheltenham. It was in this period of English history that the common people began to acquire surnames — chiefly by virtue of their occupation, their father's first name, or the village from which they had migrated. Hence, William moving from here to Leckhampton came to be known as William of Cherington, and eventually just William Cherington.

Karl and I amble lazily through the village on a dewy June morning. A weathered sign affixed to a cottage reads "Telephone: Telegrams may be telegraphed." At the thirteenth-century church, I gingerly open the heavy oak door and enter. It's a rather spiritual moment. As I gaze down the aisle toward the chancel, touch the ancient baptismal tub font, admire the stained glass windows, I wonder about my forebears who worshipped here so many centuries ago. What were they like? What were their hopes, their aspirations, their dreams? I deposit a few coins in a donation box. It seems so long ago that this church was built, but in the history of the Earth, it is just a millisecond.

The Way drops downhill from Cherington village to the Avening Stream, which flows into Cherington Pond. The pond is really a small lake, dug out of a marshy section of the stream in the mid-eighteenth century to facilitate boating and fishing. Today, the pond is a protected wetlands area. Here are found rare species of butterflies, dragonflies, and wild irises. At the pond's edge flourish reeds, bulrushes, and marsh marigolds. Carpets of emerald moss flourish among the trees on the upper banks.

At the far end of the pond we encounter two swans coaxing their six cygnets over a weir into the outlet stream. It was not always so peaceful in this dreamy glen. On Sunday afternoons in the 1930s, young people would congregate at the pond and play music from a record player and mobile amplifier, much as future-generation teens would brandish boom boxes and Sony Walkmans. Ice cream was sold from a motorcycle with a sidecar. Pious villagers complained that raucous sounds of revelry from the pond could be heard by them all the way up at the church during Sunday Evensong.

Just beyond Cherington Pond is the hamlet of Nag's Head. I decide to use the phone booth that I spot beside some bushes in order to line up a B&B for the following night. When I open the door, I run into cobwebs. A plastic sign that had formed part of the window clatters to the floor. Oddly, the phone actually works. I place my notebook on the counter; after I finish my call and pick it up, I find a snail securely stuck to the cover. I am so busy disengaging the slimy creature as it oozes its life juices onto my notebook that I almost step on a snake that has wriggled into the phone booth under the door — the wriggly, shiny thing actually hisses at me. I navigate past it, thrust open the door, and in my haste literally topple out into a thicket of blackberry bushes and stinging nettles — in khaki shorts. I actually yelp.

Karl is laughing so hard he doubles over.

"Having a good time, John?"

Karl says that the snake was harmless, but I am convinced that it was an adder, Britain's only poisonous snake.

I apply both hydrogen peroxide and Ozonol from my first aid kit to my nettle and bramble wounds. Life is a bitch sometimes!

We continue our jaunt toward Avening village. The stinging-nettle pain abates. My head is in a whirl after walking through the village of my ancestors. I try to remember the threads of a tale my grandfather told me under his horse chestnut tree when I was a child — about the Leckhampton Hill riots, which were precipitated by efforts of a landowner to close down the hill's popular walking trails just after 1900. My grandfather was born in Leckhampton in 1887 and grew up gazing at the famous Devil's Chimney, a weird limestone formation towering above the village on Leckhampton Hill.

The hill had been used for eons by villagers as their recreational playground — for picnics, walking, celebrations, and children's woods games. Myriad paths crisscrossed in every direction. The paths even guided children from outlying farms to and from school in the village. Leckhampton Hill, in other words, was for centuries a vital part of the warp and woof of their very lives.

Then, in 1894, Henry Dale acquired most of Leckhampton Hill. His intent was to extract gravel and limestone from the hill for commercial purposes. But Dale failed to recognize the importance of the hill in village life; he immediately began barricading trails and refused to recognize any public rights-of-way. He annoyed just about everybody — and not just the poor villagers, but even the local magistrate and chair of the district council, one G.B. Witts. In 1897, Dale built Tramway Cottage for his quarry foreman in an open space that had always been used by the villagers. Now the foreman's house occupied this common ground, and also blocked the main footpath to the hill. In 1899, Dale fenced off a twenty-six-acre parcel, as part of his Leckhampton Quarries Co. operations. Finally, in 1901, he obstructed many additional footpaths.

Leckhamptonites had had enough. In March of 1902, a gathering of villagers tore down fences beside the offensive Tramway Cottage. Four of the men involved were charged with obstruction, and promptly acquitted. On July 15, a mammoth crowd of some two thousand villagers — including my grandfather, a lad of fourteen—marched to the foot of the hill. Oddly enough, my grandfather recalled this as a festive occasion: just a couple of thousand Britons asserting their rights. Women dressed in colourful summer frocks, and men wore suits and white straw boater hats. Author David Bick writes in Old Leckhampton, "Roused to still greater excitement, the mob was led up the hill, the next stopping place being Cratchley's cottage. The occupants were ejected and fled to Dale's home. In a short time the furniture was pulled out and set alight together with the house which was afterwards razed to the ground without a stone left standing." Accounts of the events record that the police were powerless to act "where such a large and determined mob were concerned." And none were prosecuted.

My grandfather left England forever three years later at age seventeen, alone, with two shillings in his pocket. He wanted to farm, but there was little future for poor tenant farmers in England at the turn of the twentieth century, so he emigrated to Canada. But he was aware of the denouement of the Leckhampton Hill riot story. For the public regained their rights-of-way and enjoyment of the hill. Sometimes all it takes is a determined group of residents making a firm stand to protect their rights. Today, another cottage stands on the spot where Dale built his foreman's home, but instead of guarding the hill *against* the populace, it is there to protect the place for use and enjoyment *by* the community, as custodian.

THE LANE FROM Nag's Head is tree-lined and resembles a long driveway to a manor house. At lane's end, however, we find ourselves in Avening village, which is chiefly noted for the unusual history of its church.

The Church of the Holy Cross is built upon the site of an earlier Saxon church. Ancient tombs with porthole windows were uncovered near here in 1809; they have since been dated to 3000 BC. This is the only church in England ever specifically erected at the command of a queen. And it is all because of a woman scorned.

Prior to marrying William the Conqueror, Matilda of Flanders met Brittric, a young Avening noble who was Edward the Confessor's envoy to Flanders. Princess Matilda fell madly in love with the golden-haired Brittric, but he did not reciprocate her affections, returning instead to England and resuming his residence at Avening.

Matilda then married William the Conqueror, who, upon defeating King Harold in 1066 and subjugating England, was utterly ruthless with the country's Anglo-Saxon landowners. Still smarting from Brittric's rejection years before, Matilda caused William to dispossess Brittric of all his estates and throw the young man into prison, where he died. But in her later years she suffered such remorse that she ordered the Avening church built so that masses could be said for Brittric's soul. Matilda and William stayed at Brittric's residence (which of course they had appropriated) to supervise the construction. In 1080, on the day the church was consecrated, the queen gave a feast of boar's head to the workmen. Today "Pig Face Day" is celebrated on September 14 every year. A torchlight procession of villagers clad in medieval dress walks from the church with pigs' heads carried on platters. Entertainment ensues, provided by jesters, jugglers, and musicians. Then the entire village tucks into a feast of hog roast.

It is fitting that this remarkable church commissioned by a queen should have been placed in the charge of Reverend Celia Carter in 1994, when she became one of the first ordained women priests in the Church of England. One can imagine Matilda smiling with pleasure.

The climb uphill from Avening is strenuous. But we are rewarded with sweeping views of Gatcombe Park, Princess Anne's estate. Princess Anne embodies the equestrian spirit of the Cotswolds, playing host annually at Gatcombe to the Festival of British Eventing, which combines the national open, novice, and intermediate horse championships.

Down the hill and through a hedge gap, the path diverges, with a minor road that takes us to Chavenage House, an Elizabethan manor with stories to tell. There has been a manor house here since the ninth century, when an ancient Saxon Hundred Court held session on site. The estate was the location for the popular TV series *Lark Rise to Candleford,* based on Flora Thompson's nostalgic look at the English countryside at the turn of the twentieth century.

Chavenage House is considered to be one of the most haunted places in the country. Producers of horror movies such as *Dracula* and *The Ghost of Greville Lodge* film here regularly. The hauntings all stem from a visit by Oliver Cromwell's emissary Henry Ireton at Christmas in 1648. Cromwell sought to obtain the signature of Chavenage House's owner, Colonel Nathaniel Stephens, to the death warrant of King Charles I. Stephens was a key figure in the Civil War, and his support for regicide was considered important. Following an entire night of argument, Stephens reluctantly agreed and signed his consent. A few days later, his strong-minded daughter Abigail returned home from a trip and flew into a rage upon learning that Stephens had joined the regicides. She loudly and publicly cursed her father and all of his descendants. Shortly thereafter, Colonel Stephens died at home of an illness — but some say it was from his daughter's curse.

Upon the colonel's death, his body was wrapped in a shroud, at which point a fine coach drawn by four black horses silently appeared at the house entrance; the colonel's ghost rose up and glided down to the coach, which then clattered down the long driveway, ostensibly with a headless driver. When the coach reached the estate gates, it burst into flames and disappeared. Apparently, the deceased King Charles had come to collect the body of the rebel colonel who had broken his oath to serve and protect his sovereign. Every owner of Chavenage House since is said to have been collected in this manner upon his death. The current owner, David Lowsley-Williams, swears that he will make a more conventional exit from life.

Our tour of this magnificent manor house is impressive. The Great Hall is stunning, with a high ceiling, numerous pieces of artwork, and intricate wood panelling. There are over forty rooms here, all of them maintained, and several of them available for overnight guests. However, guests should not sleep in one particular room: Cromwell's bedroom, which is dark and forbidding, adorned with coarsely woven wall tapestries. A copy of the Lord Protector's portrait, entitled *Warts and All,* hangs beside the bed he slept in. Also in the room is a chilling reminder of Cromwell's legacy as a regicide — a copy of Charles I's death warrant, together with a lock of the king's hair.

Over the years, dozens of people who have slept in the Cromwell Room have complained of waking up in a cold sweat, spending a sleepless night, or worse. The current owner's grandmother felt compelled to have the bedroom exorcised, and summoned two priests — one Church of England, the other Roman Catholic — to say a blessing. This seemed to calm things down for a time. But during movie filming in the 1990s, more than one employee on the set fled the premises in terror.

Just past the estate we slog down an overgrown bridleway known as Chavenage Lane. Swallows are swooping and diving like Typhoon fighter jets. We climb a stile into a field, where a small herd of cows graze. Gingerly we make a wide berth around a mother and two calves. Just as we reach the far stile, we hear the roar of an engine, and a mud-spattered Land Rover comes barrelling across the field to stop abruptly beside us. The driver is a wrinkled, rosy-cheeked farm woman who greets us amiably.

"Saw you comin' into the field and I'm glad you stepped 'round those calves," she says, "because in the next field over last spring, one of our local farmers was killed by a cow protecting her calf when he went walking there. A darned shame, but you have to be real careful when calves are present."

She looks us over again. "If you ever need a place to stay, I do B&B back in the village, so look me up" — and she hands me a soiled card from her glove compartment. We thank her and she speeds off, clods of mud and sod spewing from her churning wheels.

Close to Tetbury, we become hopelessly lost and ultimately emerge from the woods on Cirencester Road. Almost immediately a long white building comes into view: the Trouble House Inn. The pub's signage displays a bloody hand and corpse hanging between a Cavalier and a Roundhead soldier, neither of whom is showing much love toward the other. We enter the strange building and are straightaway made welcome by the friendly publican, who studiously ignores our muddy boots. The dining alcoves are full of locals, most of them tweedily clad, several wearing their wellies. A few elderly gentlemen sit by themselves with newspapers, nursing pints. One bewhiskered Edwardian sits poring over an ancient-looking piece of vellum. The atmosphere is more London club than country pub.

I ask for a sandwich menu and the barkeeper replies, "We do gourmet only; we are really a gastropub." Karl and I both order a Guinness and look around. The Trouble House has a tumultuous history dating back to the Civil War. Despite its ancient vintage, its current name derives from trouble caused by farm labourers who rioted in protest over the mechanization of agriculture in 1830. The inn is also famous for being the site of Trouble House Halt, the only train station in England ever built solely for the purpose of servicing a pub. The publican supplied an empty beer crate to assist passengers to step up into the coaches. The rail line to the station was built in 1959 but closed only five years later. That same year Trouble House Halt was immortalized in the Flanders and Swann song "Slow Train."

The last day of the train's operation was April 4, 1964. Mourners clad in black wearing bowler hats lifted onto the train a coffin filled with empty whisky bottles. A passenger train encountered one final gesture of defiance later that same day, when its approach to Trouble House Halt was blocked by hay bales burning on the tracks. Ah, the peaceful Cotswolds!

The Cirencester Road takes us to Tetbury. This market town is famous for its Woolsack Races, held on the spring bank-holiday weekend. Stocky, tattooed men and tough, muscular women carry sacks of wool up and down the very steep Gumstool Hill. The event began in the seventeenth century as an effort by the local males to impress the ladies with their strength. The men carry sixty-pound sacks, the women thirty-five pounds. As at Hallaton, the event is followed by a merry street fair. It is no surprise that the record holders for such events are invariably members of the British Army and local rugby clubs.

Woolsack Races aside, Tetbury is a quiet, orderly stone town that reeks of old money. The usual tea and coffee shops blend with antique stores in the town centre, and tastefully painted signs swing in the breeze. I am intrigued by the town crest, which features two dolphins, since Tetbury is far from the sea. It seems a former lord of the manor was saved on a sea voyage by a pair of dolphins and wished to commemorate this event.

Prince Charles maintains his Highgrove Shop, which sells naturally grown products from his nearby estate, in a converted town brewery here. All profits go toward the prince's foundation. Cotswold chic dominates the high-street shops, with clothing brands like Moloh and Overider. Moloh has only two stores — Tetbury and London — and its women's clothes, the ultimate in British high fashion, are made exclusively in the United Kingdom.

Tetbury's Snooty Fox is a historic inn which offers a ballroom for the Duke of Beaufort's Hunt, a world-famous hunt dating to 1682. One might have thought that the Hunting Act of 2004 banning the traditional fox hunt would have dealt a death blow to this event, but not so. Hundreds of riders and spectators meet to run horses and hounds over a vast area of some 760 square miles, centring on the duke's Badminton estate. The hunt continues to be held by means of ingenious subterfuge — running out the artificial scent of a fox, for example. There are also loopholes in the act that allow "hunting . . . for the purpose of enabling a bird of prey to hunt the wild mammal." Moreover, foxes that are a proven nuisance to farmers can still be killed by means of one or two dogs cornering the fox, with the fox being immediately shot to death rather than torn apart by the hounds. This is considered more humane.

The Tetbury Women's Institute (WI) has successfully recruited Camilla, Duchess of Cornwall, as a member. This came about as a result of the 2003 box office hit *Calendar Girls*, starring Helen Mirren, which was based upon a Yorkshire WI group whose members stripped their torsos to raise money for charity. The president of the Tetbury WI, Judi Mason-Smith, states that it is unlikely that the duchess herself will be removing her clothes for a calendar, however. During the period of her clandestine affair with Charles, Camilla was frequently seen on the streets of Tetbury. At the height of the matrimonial acrimony between Diana and Charles, she retreated modestly from sight but now is fully engaged in

Cotswold life, and of course resides at nearby Highgrove with the future king.

We depart Tetbury, crossing the River Avon over a tiny stone bridge to enter Long Furlong Lane. Along the way, we pass a sliver of Highgrove. The manor house was occupied by Charles and Diana as a weekend residence from 1981 until their separation in 1992, and Princes William and Harry have spent much time here too. Prince Charles is devoted to organic gardening, which he calls "biologically sustainable farming linked to conservation." Quite the coincidence, I muse, that on this slender thread of a footpath called the Macmillan Way we should have passed through Lady Diana's ancestral home some ninety miles to the north in remote Northamptonshire and are now encountering her ex-husband's residence in Gloucestershire.

Long Furlong Lane rejoins the main Macmillan route some three miles from Tetbury. Then it's over a stile and through a gate, whereupon we see vistas of "tall and exotic trees, undulating lawns, leisurely seats, and arbours," as promised by the *Guide*. We are about to enter the crown jewel of English arboretums, known as Westonbirt. The property boasts a world-famous collection of over 16,000 trees and shrubs on 600 acres.

Sir Robert Holford created the arboretum in 1829. Holford's wealth allowed him to indulge his fantasy and scour the world for every conceivable type of plant and tree he could find. In 1956, his great-nephew transferred the vast estate to the Forestry Commission. Seventeen miles of marked paths criss-cross the arboretum.

The Silk Wood Path is the most enchanting of the forest walks. Especially interesting are the Brewer's spruces, the poetic Japanese larch, and the Corsican pines. There are some

135 species of moths and a staggering 1,268 species of fungi. The rain has become a Scotch mist, and we meander along through the trees like medieval beggars with our rucksacks holding all of our worldly possessions. As if on cue, we round a bend and are met by a band of a dozen or so medievally clad teenagers carrying swords, clubs, daggers, and bows, who are performing some re-enactment of a Robin Hood adventure.

Just before leaving the arboretum, I hear a thundering noise off to the right. I turn to catch a glimpse of half a dozen thoroughbred horses galloping past in the mist that partly obscures the Highgrove hillside, as in some George Stubbs painting. Can the prince and his equerries be far behind?

We exit the arboretum, pass through a metal gate, and cross the busy A433. We pass by two men walking four huge Russian wolfhounds, who bid us good day; I swear the dogs are as big as ponies. As we turn down a narrow, steep, recessed lane, we hear the rumble of a large vehicle, and up the steep tarmac like some ugly lobster comes a farm truck towing a gargantuan harvester machine with long, spiky, iron tentacles. There is no escape, so we press our bodies into the brambly hedgerow. As this great beast rumbles by, there are only inches to spare us from impalement.

"That was a close one," I remark, wiping the sweat.

"Just another walking hazard in Merry Old England, John," laughs Karl.

"That's twice now we've been thrown into a hedge."

"Actually, John, it's the third time — remember the pony trap up in Brampton Ash?"

In the next lane, numerous pheasants scurry in and about the copses. We observe two cocks engaged in battle; sitting demurely to one side is the female over whom the birds are presumably fighting. These are without a doubt the most regal birds in the land. The iridescent tones of their wings dazzle even in the dark lane. Each male stakes out a territory, and it is the females who come sniffing around like cougars to determine if the male would be a suitable mate. The male has a high-pitched call of *karark karark* that can be heard for over half a mile, and will flap his wings to warn other males not to tread on his territory.

Pheasant hunting is conducted with shotguns and dogs. Until the repeal of the Game Laws in 1831, it was the exclusive prerogative of the landowning class, though even then poaching was illegal. When the procuring of food for survival was the principal objective of everyday life for the populace, hunting restrictions caused the greatest social friction in rural England. Villagers believed they had a right to any rabbits, birds, fish, and hares they might catch. The poacher was often revered as a local hero. Most aggravating of all was the sheer extravagance of the landowner's hunting parties. A typical pheasant haul for an estate manor house in the eighteenth century might be some three thousand birds per year. But by 1880, some three thousand pheasants might be shot on a good day *on just one estate*. Now that's pillage.

The field path is soggy as rain begins to pelt us once again — thank God for Gore-Tex — and we cross through a kissing gate into a lane that takes us into Sherston, about as remote a little spot as one could find. (I know, I have said that before, but some of these places really are in Middle-earth.) It is definitely time to rest our bones and take refreshment, and what better spot for that than the Rattlebone Inn — especially since our B&B is only two blocks away.

The Rattlebone was named after John Rattlebone, a denizen of the village who was killed in a battle between the Saxon army and King Canute that raged for two days in 1016 in and around the village. The inn is the official headquarters of the Ancient Order of Sherston Mangold Hurlers, which is a fancy name for a lawn bowling club. The word on the street here is that Princes Harry and William had some very good times at the Rattlebone Inn during their late teen years, not to mention Charles and Camilla. This is logical, given the close proximity of Highgrove.

It's our lucky day — the Rattlebone opens early for dinner. And the place rocks. The music of the Rolling Stones, the Who, Pink Floyd, and the Beatles pulsates through the building, appealing to a wide assortment of patrons, from rock-dust-begrimed labourers to bikers to retired couples to tweed-clad aristocrats. But tonight all eyes are on the telly screen, as England faces France in an early round of the European Championship. The pub crowds erupt in a frenzy when David Beckham's free kick is headed into the French goal by Frank Lampard.

All week the English papers have been building the excitement. England is so soccer mad right now that the churches have even got into the act — cunningly inserting football similes and metaphors into their programs. A church in the Midlands will begin its program with a service titled "Life is a game of two halves," with the theme "It's not over until the final whistle blows." At another church, anger management is preached in a sermon titled "How to deal with the red card." A Baptist minister in Surrey talks about God and football with the analogy "A goalkeeper saves; God saves." And Rev. Richard Worssam, rector of a parish in Rochester, states, "There are parallels between an event like this and the act of faith. There are references to sport in the Bible. St. Paul speaks about running the race to win the crown. He also talks about taking blows like a boxer."

A stocky bloke at the bar is punching fleshy fists toward the telly, slopping his stout over the sleeve of his mate, who stares glassy-eyed at the field action. A goal is scored against England and there is a collective groan. France has tied the game. The fans don't seem to be in the mood to "take blows like a boxer." A skinny, tattooed platinum blonde sitting next to us starts shouting obscenities at the screen, her mascara running wild. Her biker boyfriend pats her shoulder and hands her a glass of gin and tonic, which she quaffs enthusiastically.

Karl shakes his head. "It's almost as bad as being at a Canucks game. Speaking of which, I must phone home and see who has won the Stanley Cup — the last I heard, the final round was tied three games apiece between Calgary and Tampa Bay."

"Karl, I've been reading my road atlas of Britain and discovered some new names. Do you know that it would be possible to spend a day visiting the villages of Booze, Brawl, and Bedlam, and then motor on the next day to Slack Head, Crackpot, and Twatt? And there's even a place up in Northumberland called 'Once Brewed.'"

"You remember how impressed the Parisians were when Whitwell in Rutland unilaterally twinned themselves with Paris, John boy? Perhaps they did it in revenge for a drubbing by France in football. Imagine the wrath if someone in Slack Head or Crackpot decided to twin themselves with Marseilles. There might be a war."

"I think if I was born in Crackpot, Karl, I would want to get the heck out of town."

Karl trundles off to the bar, where he phones home. In ten minutes, he comes back with a glass of brandy.

"You're frowning, Karl. Is everything okay on the home front?"

"It's all over, John. Tampa won the seventh game and their first Stanley Cup. I was really hoping for Calgary."

We do not tarry to watch the end of the football match. We are fagged. Karl downs his last sip of brandy and we walk home to our B&B, albeit a little unsteadily.

Before I turn out my light, I read in the paper of yet another old custom involving food — this time cheese. Five miles away, at Cooper's Hill near Brockworth, some three thousand people have assembled to watch four races of twenty people each run, roll, and plunge down a hill, chasing seven-to nine-pound Gloucester cheese containers. Participants arrived from all over the world, and twenty-one were treated by the St. John Ambulance Brigade, five for major injuries. All over some cheese barrels. The event has been held for at least two hundred years. Oh, and a streaker hurtled himself down the hill at the end, butt naked, much to the crowd's delight. Cheeky fellow! There are fewer injuries in the Indianapolis 500. Why do the English do these things? First Hallaton bottle kicking, then Tetbury woolsacks. Now this. Are they all mad?

Next morning we get an early start and follow a track beside horse stables to enter the village of Luckington. Five roads converge here, all of them minor, but they manage to slice the place up into triangular fragments. The manor house was the setting for the 1995 British television production of Jane Austen's *Pride and Prejudice*.

There is a James Bond connection with Luckington. Sir Stewart Menzies, former head of MI6 and Ian Fleming's prototype for Bond in his novels, resided in a farmhouse in the town. Ironically, right next door, from 1936 to 1939, lived Captain Robert Treeck. Treeck was secretly a high-ranking German intelligence agent. Menzies and Treeck fraternized with one another extensively, and both men participated in the Duke of Beaufort's Hunt. Treeck vanished back to Germany with his mistress, Baroness Violetta Schroeders, in 1939, whereupon his house was placed under the control of the Custodian of Enemy Property. There is something weird about two high-profile spymasters from different countries residing side by side as close friends in a remote English village.

Half the structures in Luckington are "listed buildings." Over half a million buildings in the United Kingdom are listed, a status which has serious implications for those wishing to make renovations. A listed building is a structure of special architectural or historical interest and may not be destroyed or altered without permission from a local planning authority. This means that often the only way one can build one's dream home on a plot of land is to make use of the outer walls of an old building like a barn and seek permission to turn the inside space into a residence. One is more likely to obtain permission for such a renovation than to build a new home on bare ground. The disadvantage is that one is limited to the footprint of the existing structure. Lighting also becomes an issue, since these old buildings seldom boasted large windows and the planning authority insists that the exterior be replicated. The result is that the converted vicarage, chapel, or barn can be dark and depressing unless flooded with indoor lighting.

A squishy woodland track leads toward Nettleton Mill. The last of the bluebells have wilted to a dull mauve. We have seen every kind of weather today — pelting rain, drizzle, Scotch mist, fog, and pale sunlight. In other words, typical English weather.

The entry into the wooded valley of the By Brook is truly enchanting. Here lies Castle Combe, consistently voted the most picturesque village in England. As we tramp down the steep lane to the square, we are inundated by Japanese tourists who have arrived with their colourful floral umbrellas and cameras to view this diamond of the English landscape. I feel grubby, sweaty, and unkempt alongside them.

The market cross with its water pump form the centrepiece of this classic village. This is a true "buttercross," an open-roofed enclosure that dates from the medieval period when people from neighbouring farms and villages gathered to buy and exchange butter, milk, eggs, and vegetables.

Castle Combe features on millions of postcards. Whether it's the loveliest village is subjective, but it certainly is tucked away in a dream-like glen with quaint stone buildings clustered beside a burbling stream. The church features one of the only medieval clocks still in use in England.

Castle Combe was used as a location in 1967 for the movie *Doctor Dolittle*, featuring Rex Harrison and Richard Attenborough. The filming was disastrous. First off, all of the trained animals for the production were quarantined upon entry to the UK, so they had to be replaced at huge expense. Then, shooting was continually disrupted by bad weather, and the villagers resented the director's arbitrary edicts — such as when all TV aerials had to be removed from personal residences. An artificial dam built by the producers was blown up one night by a local British Army officer, Ranulph Fiennes, using explosives he had obtained from his service, because he believed that it ruined the village ambience. The frustrated producers finally fled to St. Lucia to finish the movie.

We leave the tourists behind and exit the village along the By Brook. Then it's up a wooded slope past gnarled, vine-clad maples and a magnificent coppice of beeches, while below us we hear the swish of ducks' wings amid the *Ooo-oo* of wood pigeons and the distant call of a rooster farther down the valley.

A few scattered pollarded oak trees populate these woods. The practice of pollarding came from Normandy and used to be widespread in England. If a young tree was cut through about six feet from the ground, it would send out new shoots and form a bushy crown. Repeated pollarding created abundant supplies of small poles used for fencing, gaskets, and firewood.

At the end of the wood we descend to a stone bridge crossing the By Brook. Our landlady generously packed us a picnic lunch, and we find this an ideal spot to drop packs and grab the sandwiches. I stare at a tiny blue, paint-chipped rowboat tethered by a frayed rope to a makeshift dock. Around it swirl reflections of an oak tree with its roots literally disappearing into the water. Soft light filtered through the trees combines with the reflection to create an ethereal effect. A few molehills perforate the grassy bank. I think of Ratty in *The Wind in the Willows* taking Mole on their picnic excursion, when they hop into the rowboat on the river and sample their cold chicken sandwiches. The gentle By Brook babbles its way beneath the stone bridge on which we sit. Neither Karl nor I speak for some time, captivated as we are by this idyllic hidden riverside glen.

THE VILLAGE OF FORD lies on a small but busy stretch of the A420. We are booked at a B&B called Big Thatch, and Pat is there waiting for us. She is an attractive, vibrant lady whose first thought is for Karl's sprained ankle. She offers to massage his feet. He thanks her but demurs.

Pat's husband commands a naval vessel and is away at sea. "We don't really need the money, but you know, I get lonely and like to do B&B to meet people and have something to do."

We have a lovely meal of roast lamb and return to Big Thatch to chat and enjoy tea and biscuits with Pat before retiring. Next morning, after a delicious breakfast of croissants, fresh fruit, and strong coffee, we bid her adieu. She hugs both of us and says, "Thank you for coming into my life."

As we return to the banks of the By Brook, I reflect that wherever we walk in England, we have been amazed by the friendliness, frankness, and effusive warmth of English-women. Sure, there are the frosty, frumpy landladies of the old school who guard their central heating thermostats like a daughter's virginity. But they are hardly harridans. On the whole, I have formed the impression that many English-women are starved for attention from their menfolk and crave not only adventure but improved communication skills from the male species. That said, they always observe the proprieties.

A hazy languor pervades the fields this morning as we follow the meandering By Brook through the clover-studded fields. We see fishermen hunched on benches on the stream's bank, so motionless that one wonders if they are props placed there to create an Izaak Walton motif.

We follow a muddy path known as Weavern Lane into deep woods. Myriad mud puddles make it tough slogging. In the midst of one mass of mucky ooze I spot a pair of pink high-heeled stiletto shoes — just lying atop the mud and still shiny. We stop to ponder this. Unlike our "Tiffany site" up north, this doesn't strike us as having sinister implications.

Rather, as Karl observes, "It looks as if a fashionable lady got bogged down in the mud and decided 'to hell with it!,' then took her shoes off and carried on in her bare feet, leaving the heels behind."

"Maybe it's a practical joke, Karl. The *Guide* says we are passing through a 'Husseyhill Wood.' Is there some play on words here?"

But Karl has surged ahead and left me behind in the muck. Then the lane ends and I emerge at a stile where a sign is posted: "Beware of Bull." Beyond is a vast field of at least five hundred acres with a steep, scarped hillside above. I stand on the stile and observe that Karl is already halfway across the field. As I clamber over the stile, I hear a commotion and to my horror glance up to see a two-thousand-pound bull thumping down from the hill above, heading full tilt in Karl's direction. Karl sees him too, likely alerted by the ground shaking. But he is too far from the fence line to escape the big white brute!

There is, however, one lone oak tree standing in the field close at hand. Karl makes for this, drops his pack, and prepares to meet the enemy. Meanwhile, the bull has slowed a tad. Then he stops to stomp his feet on the ground. His massive skull shakes. He lowers his head and rubs it into the torn-up earth. He's about twenty feet now from Karl, who stands poised with his walking stick beneath the oak tree. I hear a *merrumph, merrumph* growl emanate from the beast.

The white mammoth shakes his head one last time and, with nostrils steaming and spewing out snot, he rushes Karl with his head down, chin tucked in. My heart is in my mouth. Karl stands placidly, stick raised, and then at the very last moment sidles around to the opposite side of the tree. The bull crashes into low branches, which crunch and break and dangle to the ground. The entire earth seems to tremble. The bull shakes his head, puzzled. Where is his quarry? He ambles slowly around the tree, only to have Karl reverse his body back to the other side. The bull gets worked up at this and follows Karl around the tree, crashing against the trunk again. But as he does so, Karl gets in one good thwack with his stick on the bull's nose from another side of the tree, where he has now taken up position.

The bull backs off. He stands there contemplating his phantom quarry for a few moments and then, as if to shrug, lets out a loud snort of disgust and heads lazily off, back up the scarp. Halfway up, he starts grazing, still keeping a wary eye on Karl and the tree.

By this time, I have in cowardly fashion climbed into the field and followed the lateral fence line, opposite Karl and the oak tree, ready to scramble under the fence should the bull attack again. But Karl is on the move. He is walking briskly toward the far fence line, and I jog diagonally across the field to join him, glancing nervously uphill. He is smiling, none the worse for wear, though he is covered with leaves and his Tilley hat is askew. He resembles the Green Man of English folklore.

"So what were you thinking of when the bull attacked you?"

"I just prayed like hell."

"I didn't think you were religious."

"I'm not, but sometimes you have to hedge your bets."

"A nasty brute. The warning notice was clearly posted on the stile back there, but you sure couldn't see him hidden over top of the hill."

"He's just missing his harem, John. If there are cows in the field with him and he's engrossed, he'll never bother you."

"Perhaps, but next time if there's any sign denoting a bull in a field, we take a diversionary route."

I wasn't about to test Karl's theory, as seven or eight people are killed each year in English fields by raging bulls and cows with young calves — half of them farmers, but the other half walkers. Even a minister of the Crown was recently injured by bovines while walking. Farmers are prohibited by law from allowing bulls of specified dairy breeds in fields containing public rights-of-way. Beef bulls are allowed in fields with footpaths only when accompanied by cows or heifers.

Karl is now marching well ahead, his stick clomping the turf. He exudes a jaunty Al Pacino aura of indomitability.

Historically, walking the footpaths in England was full of diverse dangers — bulls, vagabonds, and criminals being the most common. In Trollope's *The Last Chronicle of Barset*, Lily bravely exhorts her companion to enter the field footpath: "We are not helpless young ladies in these parts, nor yet timorous . . . We can walk about without being afraid of ghosts, robbers, wild bulls, young men, or gypsies. Come the field path, Grace."

We stop to rest on a bench near the By Brook. We are on the outskirts of the village of Box, near Saltbox Farm. The village name derives from the rare box tree that is indigenous to only three locations in the country, the others being Box Hill in Surrey and a spot near Dunstable. We see a number of these trees lining the path. They are short with oval leaves, greenish flower clusters, and dark grey bark. As a tree, box is not popular in England, but cuttings from it have resulted in the distinctive boxwood hedges one sees throughout the country and in North America. It is the supreme example of a wild tree being transformed into a finely wrought garden delight. The million or more boxwood hedges in the world all originate from cuttings taken from a few box trees growing in England.

While we rest, the inevitable dog walker approaches us. He is a man of about seventy, bundled up for the weather, wearing a long black raincoat, tweed hat, and bright red scarf. He is trailing behind his bulldog, who is straining at his leash to check out the two interlopers in his territory. He tells us that there are some ninety identifiable public footpaths in the vicinity. Box boasts 3,400 residents, and he finds it annoying that he no longer recognizes every soul he passes on the street. He is familiar with the Macmillan Way, especially the muddy section we have just traversed. More importantly, he is able to give us the scoop on the pink high-heel shoes.

The man advises that since the late 1980s, pairs of women's shoes have been found in this section of Macmillan Way — initially, a pair of stiletto heels fixed to the base of a tree, later replaced by a pair of pink knee-high boots, and later still by a pair of white stilettos. Apparently, the first pair was bolted so tightly to a tree that no one could remove them and they slowly disintegrated. At one point a pair of men's brogues appeared, only to be replaced by another pair of stilettos. Local walkers are baffled. Some believe there was a murder committed here and the shoes are intended to commemorate that event. Others think someone is obsessed with women's footwear. Personally, I think there is an Imelda Marcos who just tires of her manifold collection and gets her jollies putting shoes out to mystify people. Whatever — the stilettos have become part of the mystery and lore of the English country-side.

Ten minutes pass and the villager concludes his story. The bulldog tires of sniffing us out, lifts his leg by my corner of the bench, and then starts dragging his master off to greener pastures. The man smiles, says he must be off; it's ta ta, and then both man and dog disappear into the mist.

The famous Box Tunnel was built by the renowned Victorian engineer Isambard Kingdom Brunel under Box Hill. At 1.83 miles, it was the longest railway tunnel in the world at the time of its completion in 1841. Brunel was a genius who also built the longest span bridge in the world at Clifton, constructed the first ship made of iron (ss *Great Britain*), and both designed and constructed the Great Western Railway; the Box Tunnel was part of the line running from London to Bristol.

Along the main street of this village we discover an interesting stone edifice called a "blind house," a jail dating from the eighteenth century. More than a hundred of these lock-ups are still standing in England. Strategically located next to the pub, the blind house is a damp, dingy, cold place, with no windows and only tiny grilles for ventilation. It could accommodate only one or two people and was just a temporary holding pen for vagrants, brawlers, drunks, and "disreputable women." Structures like these often stood next to pillories, ducking stools, and stocks in medieval times. It must be remembered that there were no constabularies in villages or small towns until 1839, when the County Police Act was passed. So until the Victorian era, a miscreant guilty of more than a minor offence had to be transported to the nearest market town for incarceration.

"It's one step up from the stocks," Karl says with a smile. "I would sure have second thoughts about getting drunk again if I had to spend the night in that cold, dark jail."

Charles Dickens refers to the lock-up in *Barnaby Rudge*. An 1830 account of the Taunton lock-up is interesting: "A hole into which drunken and bleeding men were thrust and allowed to remain until the following day when the constable with his staff take the poor, crippled and dirty wretches before a magistrate, followed by half the boys and idle fellows of the town."

We leave Box in the mist and jog across the A365 to reach some narrow steps which lead to a path between two walls; then it's over a stile to a meadow ablaze in a riot of buttercups, purple clover, iris, and assorted other wildflowers. I turn back to gaze north from whence we came, up the delightful By Brook Valley. I am sorry to leave the stream behind.

South Wraxall is a timeless village which has the unique claim of being the first locale in England where tobacco was ever smoked. This is where Sir Walter Raleigh brought his earliest supplies of the weed from his Virginia plantations to be sampled by his friend Sir Walter Long.

As we descend into the village, the lane sinks deeper and I observe vast systems of knobby tree roots honeycombing the slope above. This deep-cut lane has all the hallmarks of antiquity. A rabbit hops across our path suddenly, only to disappear into some dark hole. This is a weird, enchanted spot — somewhere between *Alice in Wonderland* and *The Hobbit*.

These sunken lanes are known as "hollow ways." In the limestone belt it is common for continuously used tracks to wear down at the rate of two inches per century — and some tracks have been used since roughly 2000 BC. In *The Old Ways*, Robert Macfarlane asserts that "one need not be a mystic to accept that certain old paths are linear only in a simple sense."

The village is home to 320 people. The Long manor house where Raleigh visited his friend has been acquired by John Taylor, bass player with the band Duran Duran, together with his wife, Gela Nash-Taylor, founder of Juicy Couture, a high-end women's clothing brand. The clothier originally designed maternity pants. Then the brand name took off, after Gela designed a custom tracksuit for Madonna, which turned into a trend that is exploding this year after becoming popular with other celebrities. Rock stars, sheikhs, and businesswomen are the new aristocracy in the quiet backwaters of rural England.

Another blind house greets us halfway across the Avon bridge as we trudge into Bradford-on-Avon. This one was originally built as a chapel. When churchgoing tapered off, the utilitarian Victorians put the building to use as a jail.

"Jail or chapel —" Karl comments. "How ironic that this depressing, windowless structure could be so effortlessly interchanged between religion and punishment. Bah! That's because they were equally miserable for the common man."

I don't argue. But little chapels like this were common throughout Europe even during the so-called Dark Ages. One can imagine a weary wayfarer quietly entering the little chapel and finding a friar inside, sitting there with candles blazing, offering the traveller a cup of mead and a piece of fish to help him on his way.

I am impressed by several gypsy canal boats, gaily painted in purple, green, and blue. Greenery covers the decks: flowers, trellised plants, even bikes and stacked firewood. The custom of decorating canal boats dates from the 1870s, after boatmen brought their families on board to save on housing costs.

Our bones are weary — too weary for town exploration. So we point ourselves toward the side of town we believe our B&B is located. It takes us half an hour and several wrong turns, but we finally reach a rambling Victorian mansion that looks a trifle tatty. The garden is a tangle of vines, yellow-wort, and unkempt roses. A rusty wheelbarrow filled with debris sits perched precariously by a duck pond. We will call this establishment Liberty House in deference to the privacy of the owner.

Karl follows me up the path, whistling an Irish tune. I bang the big brass knocker against the stout oak door. We are greeted by a middle-aged dyed redhead who is smoking and holding a mobile phone to her ear but who smiles at us and waves her hand, her stained yellow teeth contrasting with her blood-red lipstick and blue mascara.

"Hi, we are the walkers who called for a room for tonight."

"Why, crikey, yes, you are the Americans — doing Macmillan, didn't you say on the phone?"

"Actually, we're Canadian — but yes, doing Macmillan."

"You must be achingly tired, darlings. Do come in and I will make some tea."

We shed our dirty boots at the door. She ushers us into a drawing room that is surprisingly immaculate, then resumes her cellular conversation. I sink into the burgundy leather sofa, admiring the plush Turkish carpets, fine oak sideboard, and a huge fireplace with a mantel overflowing with cloisonné objects, including incense burners and a multicoloured Ming enamel bowl. By the odour, someone has been either burning incense or smoking a joint — or both.

We have come far today, and I stretch out on the sofa, ready to purr. Then the front door opens and bangs shut as a giggling young woman dressed in a short black skirt, red blouse, and high boots breezes in, waves to us, and clomps up the winding oak staircase. The proprietress then clatters in with a silver tray holding steaming tea and biscuits. We make introductions and learn that her name is Marnie. Breakfast is at eight o'clock, and we are free to use the lounge and telly. And yes, she says, there are several good pubs just blocks away.

"I hope you gents like Earl Grey," she says with a smile.

"That will do us just fine, Marnie," I reply. As she clatters off in her high heels, I can't help thinking that the fragrance of the bergamot in the tea mingles almost too sweetly with the lingering scent of what I now know to be pot.

After a suitable repast at a crowded, noisy Bradford watering hole, we turn in early at Liberty House. I can't sleep. In the adjoining room I can hear Karl snoring through the paper-thin walls. I drift off, but awake around midnight to a noisy clomping of feet on the stairs, raucous laughter and boozy voices emanating from down the corridor. To my annoyance, there ensues continual banging and shouting throughout the night, and I don't doze off again until well after three o'clock.

In the morning, Karl and I assemble in the breakfast room promptly at eight. It is clear no one is stirring. Well, almost no one. No sooner do we sit down in the conservatory among the massive philodendrons than we hear a tap-tap on the conservatory door, which evidently leads to a walled garden. Startled, I observe a tall, swarthy young man smiling at me — and clad only in his undershorts.

I let him in.

"Thanks, mate. I'm Drew. You should just help yourself to anything in the kitchen. I doubt if anyone's up."

Karl frowns.

"Afraid Madame Marnie felt things got out of hand last night. Say, are you two blokes cooking something? I'm famished. It was bloody cold out there — Marnie just threw me out on my ear."

Karl fumbles with the toaster and searches the fridge for some eggs.

"So what was all the commotion about during the night, Drew?" I ask.

"Blimey, mate, you are foreigners. I'll be damned. Well, Marnie here, like, she runs a good 'stablishment, she does. But see, Christine, like, she's my favourite — I always ask for Christine and when Marnie said I couldn't have her last night — like I'd have to settle for Suzie — well, I blew up, you know, mate? Like it's not right — my coin is as good as the next bloke's, you see? Besides, I'm not just some ordinary punter off the street."

By this time, Karl has found some eggs and a frying pan

and soon things are sizzling, toast is popping, and the orange juice is flowing.

"So how long, ah, has this place been servicing certain local needs?" I ask.

Drew gives a start. Marnie is standing smoking in the doorway, and she looks like hell — pale with no makeup, dressed in a long, flowing, frayed Chinese silk robe.

"Drew," she says calmly, "leave these gentlemen in peace and go up and fetch your clothes. I hope you have learned your lesson."

Drew averts his eyes from us and trundles past her.

"And Drew," she shouts after him, "you are on probation. You hear, mate?"

Marnie shakes her head, her red curls falling all askew over her forehead as she pads about the kitchen in her soft pink slippers.

"Sorry about all this," she says, pulling out another cigarette. "Some blokes just get out of hand."

I quickly finish my eggs and toast, settle up with Marnie, and Karl and I tread down the path past the debris-laden wheelbarrow still teetering by the algae-covered pond. From the street, I cast a last lingering glance at Liberty House.

We take a shortcut to reach the far end of Bradford, but I am apprehensive. In the field we have to cross, there is a herd of dairy cows, amid which lolls a huge black bull.

"Come on, John, that old guy is so engrossed with his harem, he won't bother us."

I clamber over the stile. "Seems like the entire male species is well serviced in these parts, Karl."

Karl laughs and bounds forward with his customary sangfroid. He scares me by raising his walking stick as if to swat the old bull's rump as we traipse by.

9

ALFRED'S TOWER *and* STEINBECK'S QUIXOTIC QUEST

"But I don't want to go among mad people," Alice remarked.

"Oh, you can't help that," said the Cat: "we're all mad here. I'm mad. You're mad."

"How do you know I'm mad?" said Alice.

"You must be," said the Cat, "or you wouldn't have come here."

—— LEWIS CARROLL ——
Alice in Wonderland

KARL CUTS A RATHER picaresque figure this morning. He is deeply tanned, hair rather shaggy, Tilley hat misshapen. We both need haircuts. Our visages are probably making the rounds of MI5 at this moment, given our scruffy appearance and the sheer number of surveillance cameras we have seen in and around Bradford. Britain has more security cameras per capita than any other country in the world — ironic for a country that is so obsessive about the privacy of one's person, one's thoughts, and one's home.

We join the Kennet and Avon Canal towpath that forms part of the 84-mile-long National Waterway Walk that runs from Reading to Bath. A short path diverts us to view one of the largest surviving tithe barns in the kingdom. The impressive fourteenth-century structure boasts fourteen bays projecting into porches. It measures 168 by 33 feet and is unique in possessing a stone roof braced by a huge A-shaped set of wooden trusses, also known as a "cruck" support. The barn stored produce brought here from the abbey estates around Bradford by the serfs, villeins, and others who owed tribute. Tithe barns were built throughout northern Europe in the Middle Ages. A tithe represented one-tenth of a farm's produce, which had to be given to the church to help support the priests.

Just south of Bradford, we become lost and stumble onto the grounds of a dilapidated Georgian mansion surrounded by rickety outbuildings and a shabby, unkempt garden. Just as we near the entrance to the mansion on a faint field path, cars begin arriving and strangely garbed people alight — young people with tattoos, capes, and dark robes, including spike-haired punk rocker types and some goths. I nod at two angular druidesses wearing long black dresses and conical black hats. A six-foot-tall magician with dreadlocks and a nettled expression looks to be in charge, greeting the guests curtly as they straggle down the walkway to the mansion. It seems a trifle early in the day for a costume party.

Dreadlocks approaches us with an angry scowl. I point to my *Macmillan Guide* and ask him where the path might be.

"You're not coppers?" he says, frowning.

"Would cops have Canadian accents?" growls Karl, crossing his arms and placing his legs akimbo.

Dreadlocks sizes us up for another moment or two. Then he turns and motions to one of the druidesses, who struts forth, marches us perfunctorily down the driveway — and then tells us to get lost. The sweet aroma of marijuana wafts off her cape, mingling with the honeysuckle scent emanating from the tangled hedge of the driveway.

"Friendly natives," laughs Karl.

"I wouldn't want to run into any of them in a dark alley."

"Ah, they are all harmless sods — soon will be, anyway. I give them an hour before they're all completely zonked."

Twenty minutes later we reach the outskirts of Avoncliff village, a popular commencement point for scenic walks along both river and canal. The key object of interest here is the Cross Guns, said to be the most haunted pub in Wiltshire. The Blue Lady is the most commonly seen ghost, but there are others. And yes, this is all taken in dead earnest by the owner, who, after the disturbances became too frequent, called in the Dean of Salisbury to bless the pub. Staff workers swear that the hauntings continue, and that in addition to the Blue Lady, a monklike figure is sometimes seen standing close to a cellar door that opens to a tunnel leading to the nearby canal.

We pass under the Avoncliff Aqueduct, a triple-arched, 330-foot structure completed in 1801 that still ranks as one of the country's most splendid waterway edifices. It actually carries the open canal across the River Avon. It must have served as inspiration for the waterparks that kids enjoy today.

The path takes us across the River Frome on a delightful stone bridge boasting a finely hewn statue of Britannia at mid-span. The sculpted figure looks toward Iford Manor and its renowned yew topiary gardens. A few hundred yards beyond, I stand by a wire fence to take a photo of the winding river. Suddenly I feel a sharp pain in my leg and realize I have been nipped by a goose that has stretched its neck through the fence, obviously resenting my presence. Karl starts laughing and I curse.

The first goose is joined by a second one, who also wants to have a go at me. These are Chinese swan geese, a popular species as they are usually of good temperament — the golden retrievers of the geese world — but will fiercely protect their owner's property. One goose is brown-feathered and the other white, both with orange beaks.

"You're the only person I've known to be bitten by a goose while out walking," Karl chortles.

Fortunately, my jeans have absorbed most of the bite.

"Better a goose than a bull, Karl."

The River Frome is now to our immediate left as we pass a weir and enter Somerset. Waves of black clouds stack the sky menacingly to the northwest, and Karl fears that we are in for some dirty weather. The rugged castle ruins of Farleigh Hungerford loom ahead. This castle from the fourteenth century was built by Sir Thomas Hungerford, steward to the powerful John of Gaunt. It played a role in the English Civil War but fell into disrepair in the early eighteenth century, after which the locals removed most of the stones of the crumbling structure as "salvage." Only the chapel and its crypt survives.

The locked crypt here reputedly contains the finest collection of anthropomorphic lead coffins in Britain, and it is open to the public — but only on Halloween! The chapel displays one of four extant ancient paintings of St. George and the Dragon. The tomb of Sir Thomas Hungerford is impressive. But there is a feeling of unease in the air, accentuated by the storm gathering overhead.

Morbidity rules here. The blackberries, brambles, and nettles are gaining ascendancy. The Halloween ritual of opening the crypt reeks of necromancy. Though it's a beautiful setting with the Frome Valley winding below, the history of this place is replete with much violence, disease, and military conflict from the Wars of the Roses through to the Civil War. I sense bad karma.

We wander down the desolate main street of the nearby village. Ugly gargoyles adorn the church. Worst of all, the Hungerford Arms pub is closed.

"Not terribly inviting, John; all these desolate ruins — who really wants to see a bunch of half-human-, half-animal-shaped coffins anyway? Hell, there's not even tonic for a walker's parched throat. Let's keep moving. There's a wicked storm brewing."

"I thought you had your Tiger Beer from the Bradford Tithe Barn?"

"That was quaffed way back on the path."

Blazing flashes of lightning dazzle my eyes, followed by a booming clap of thunder. Then the downpour commences.

We button up the Gore-Tex and lower our heads with chins tucked into the wind — much like Karl's white bull assumed his position just before his charge. The thunderstorm lasts for a good twenty minutes as we trudge onward in the deluge, leaving Farleigh Hungerford to its coffins and ghosts. A BritRail cobra speeds past nearby, a blazing silver behemoth of metallic foam and fury that wakes us from our stupor. Modernity intrudes again moments later, when in the distance we observe the hideous hillside slash of the M5.

Karl and I emerge sodden and dripping onto a tarmac lane, which leads to a path with a hornbeam hedge running along it until Crabb House. Then we cross the Frome again via an alluring arched bridge. A World War II pillbox sits gathering moss on the opposite bank. This particular pillbox was part of a fifty-mile-long string of structures dubbed the GHQ Line, designed to slow the advance of Hitler's armies up the Frome and beyond.

Tellisford is one of the few "Thankful Villages" — those villages that lost no men in World War I. Only fifty-three civil parishes and thirty-one villages in England had all of their men who fought in the Great War return, though many of the survivors were severely wounded. Only thirteen of those thirty-one villages are considered "Doubly Thankful," meaning they experienced no military deaths in World War II either.

Our B&B for the night has been booked off trail, so we are obliged to tramp almost four miles to the village of Norton St. Philip. By now the storm has abated, the sun has come out, and all is well, except for fatigue. I am ready to drop by the time we reach our B&B. But after tea and a slice of pound cake, I take a bath, enjoy a nap, and by six-thirty am ready for dinner.

The George Inn boasts of being the oldest continuously licensed inn in England. It was originally built by monks in

1223, as living quarters for their neighbouring priory, and became a coaching inn after the dissolution of the monasteries.

Early-bird North Americans invariably find themselves sitting alone in pub dining rooms, since the English practise Continental European habits of late dining. This evening is no exception. We are alone in a vast hall, eating at a battered table that could have been used by Samuel Pepys, who stopped to dine here on June 12, 1668. The famous diarist was en route to the West Country with his wife, Elizabeth, and her maid, Deborah Willet, in tow.

Other luminaries have frequented the venerable George over the ages. The Duke of Monmouth quartered here after his defeat in 1685 at the Battle of Sedgemoor, the final act of the Monmouth Rebellion against King James II. Judge Jeffreys hanged twelve rebels at one of his Bloody Assizes, using this dining hall as a courtroom and conducting the executions immediately thereafter on the village common. The inn has also been used as a film set in three productions, *The Remains of the Day, Tom Jones,* and *Canterbury Tales,* plus two TV series, Daniel Defoe's *Moll Flanders* and Jane Austen's *Persuasion.*

Of all the pubs we have visited, this one certainly merits highest praise for ambience. Old pews surround the bar. The windows are leaded glass, the floor made of old ship's planking. Then there is the huge stone fireplace. One can easily imagine winter travellers standing in front of the roaring fire warming their hands, the windows frosted with snow, and a black dog lying there too, with the aroma of pipe smoke everywhere, as all the while a servant feeds chunks of maple and beech into the yawning, roaring fire to keep the guests toasty.

Karl and I enjoy a dinner of roast duck with cherry chutney sauce, julienne Grand Marnier sweet carrots, and mashed potatoes. I marvel at the high Tudor-style beams and wall tapestries all about us that portray knightly combat themes. A few small oak barrels hang from the ceiling beams, and numerous colourful medieval shields are displayed. I imagine Pepys sitting with his lecherous eyes peering about him, sizing up his surroundings — especially potential fleshly quarry — while his wife, Elizabeth, sits prim and proper across from him with her maid, who at the time was his secret lover.

A few months after this West Country tour, on October 25, 1668, Pepys was caught by his wife *in flagrante delicto* with Miss Willet. He expressed remorse and the maid was dismissed, but in characteristic fashion Pepys continued to pursue Miss Willet afterward. He simultaneously carried on an affair with a London singer named Mrs. Knep, who signed notes to him as "Barbary Allen," a song she sang at theatres, while he signed his notes to her under the pseudonym "Dapper Dickey."

Over trifle, our private dining hall is invaded by a noisy group of German travellers who sweep in speaking their native tongue and gesticulating wildly at the lances and swords and battle gear hanging about. Karl is amused and sits watching them, nursing his brandy. Surely, such cacophony typifies the traditional English coaching inn. There would always have been travellers from all over Europe mingling here with the natives in one clamorous hubbub. In past centuries, more French would have been spoken than German, of course. But German tourists are wild about England these days.

THE MORNING DAWNS as light and airy as fairy dust, the sky a mackerel sheet of gossamer threads. It's a long four-mile trek back to the main Macmillan. After a stiff hour's trek, we discern two miniature spires atop a church in the distance. We are at the entry point to Rode.

Inside the Church of St. Lawrence, we read about an unusual ceremony called "clipping the church," whereby the congregation forms a circle around the church on Easter Monday evening, then dances to the left and to the right, cheers lustily, sings hymns, and, finally, rushes inside. Only a few other churches in England perform this ceremony, which dates back to pagan times, and only in Rode do the people in the circle face inward, toward the church.

There is another reason Rode has a historical reputation. The town won a countrywide competition to manufacture a unique dress for King George III's Queen Charlotte, after one of its mills developed a rich blue dye that became trademarked as Royal Blue.

"And there you have it, Karl," I remark. "Church clipping and a Royal Blue dress fit for a queen."

"The only thing I don't understand is the bit about the church clipping."

"It's meant to reflect love for both the church and one another. That's why, I suppose, everyone forms a ring and holds hands. Apparently, everyone sings a song or two, like 'All Things Bright and Beautiful' and 'Morning Has Broken.'"

"Where's our next refreshment, John boy?"

"The Woolpack Inn, coming right up."

But the Woolpack is closed, and we have to suffer our thirst in silence for many miles further. On the outskirts of Beckington, we become snarled in a bevy of bowling and cricket pitches. Then we have the most terrible experience of the day — there in the distance on the motorway is the ugly plastic red and white sign of Little Chef, the British fast food chain that serves gluttonous agglomerations of over-salted, cholesterol-ridden fare to weary and unwitting motorway victims. Ugh!

We quickly scurry away from this sordid window into the outside world and dive into a copse, from which we emerge onto a lane entry to Beckington.

In 1766, Beckington was inundated by rioters, who set ablaze a mill and other buildings as part of their rage against mechanization. Fulling mills had been built along the River Frome since before the fifteenth century, and depended upon spinners and weavers working from their cottages. Now all that had changed, with the entire operation moving to large, mechanized mills. A pitched battle ensued in which one man was killed and several seriously injured.

We opt for a short walking day, as we are booked to stay at Angela Pritchard's farmhouse near the village. Angela is a warm, chatty, erudite lady who is married to Ken Pritchard, who was the navy's Director General of Supplies and Transport during the Falklands War, and was later made a Commander of the Order of the Bath for his services. She tells us over hot tea all about the Falklands conflict and how she often met the naval and soldier lads upon their return, some of them dramatically affected by combat.

Angela was named Lady Sponsor at the 1981 launch of the *Bayleaf*, an auxiliary ship of the Royal Navy. She managed to smash the champagne bottle on the first try! She tells us that the *Bayleaf* went on to see service in the Gulf War in 1991 and the Iraq invasion of 2003.[4]

---

4 I later learned that the ship was decommissioned in 2011 after sailing 1.4 million miles, and was to be cut up for scrap at a Turkish recycling plant. Angela was on hand in Portsmouth at dawn's first light on a summer morning in 2012 to watch the vessel be towed out of harbour. "It kind of feels like losing a loved one," she told reporters. "I've seen the ship come back unscathed from the Falklands and the Gulf, but now she's going to be broken apart in Turkey."

Next morning, we say our goodbyes to Angela and set forth. The hedgerows are festooned with colour — hawthorn, honeysuckle, milkwort, and red dog rose. Chaffinches are singing, rabbits dart across the path, and all is right with the world. I twirl my stick and experience a real joie de vivre.

A mile down the path we encounter signs warning walkers that the resident Highland cattle are neurotic creatures and should be avoided. The path has been altered by the farmer, winding to the left, whereas both the *Guide* and intuition tell me it should be to the right. We plunge through a copse of firs for ten minutes and decide it's hopeless, then crash through heavy undergrowth, with brambles, nettles, and burdocks having their way with my legs — terribly so, as I am wearing shorts today. Stung, welted, and covered with burdocks, we finally emerge into a field, where a herd of steers approaches at speed. We wiggle beneath a barbed-wire fence to escape their clutches. Below I spy the Frome Valley, dark and mysterious.

Nothing looks familiar. Damn those Highland cattle!

"Not often that we get lost," offers Karl.

"We're not lost! As Tolkien once said, 'All who wander are not lost.'"

"John . . . face it, we are lost, and you damn well know it!"

I know better than to argue with Karl, so I just stand there and pick a few burdock burrs off his back. Then he laughs.

Our male egos bruised more than our bodies, we walk across a field immersed in purple thistles and by good luck stumble upon a path that leads us back to the Macmillan. Half an hour later we straggle into Buckland Dinham.

At about this point I reflect on our situation: that despite all of the manifold delights of our adventure, one must also consider the hazards and travail — ravaged feet; inclement weather; wading through field after field of wet, thigh-high rapeseed; avoiding charging bulls and other bovines; boggy bridleways; dangerous horse encounters; near-death experiences on busy roads, not to mention pony carts and tractors; scratched and punctured skin from brambles and nettles; crime scenes; ploughed-up, muddy fields; attacks by canines and geese; getting lost in driving rain; and encountering the odd dodgy character. So, please, do not take a long-distance walk in England lightly. Still, I love it.

I find burdock burrs still clinging to my shorts. These prickly, sticky balls are found worldwide. In England, dandelion mixed with burdock constitutes a soft drink associated with the hedgerow mead that was consumed during medieval times. The burdock root has even been used as a bittering agent in beer. Its greatest usefulness, however, was as inspiration for a Swiss inventor named George de Mestral. George was walking his dog one day in the 1940s when he became curious about the burrs that clung to his pet's fur. He studied them with his microscope and realized that a synthetic approach could mimic Nature's method of causing seeds to disperse through "stickiness." The result after ten years of effort was Velcro, the "zipperless zipper."

The village bulletin board advertises a weekly yoga class. The local inn is hosting a charity curry night. A chalk sign proclaims "Ladies Film Night," which sounds a tad racy. Are only ladies allowed? Do they look at male strippers? Chick flicks? This village is a far cry from Flora Thompson's Candleford.

Near Great Elm, Karl and I decide to take a *Guide*-recommended diversion to Mells, where there is reputed to be great refreshment at the Talbot Inn. Not far along we reach a crossroads called Mary's Grave, the origin of which name is based upon one of four alleged scenarios:

1. a young woman in 1850 murdered by a jealous wife from Great Elm is buried here;

2. a gypsy caravan containing a gypsy queen was cremated here;

3. a suicide named Mary is buried here; or

4. a highwayman who disguised himself as a woman, was tried by Judge Jeffreys, and was hanged at the Old White Horse Inn is buried here. (This is my personal favourite.)

There used to be a stone etched with a cross at the presumed site of Mary's grave, but this vanished in 1998 when a new road was built. It must have been a wild, violent place around here, as there is a Murder Combe and a Dead Woman Bottom en route as well.

Mells is well worth the visit. This unspoiled village tucked away from main roads has three notable features: a tall, withered palm tree; a fascinating graveyard; and a fifteenth-century coaching inn — The Talbot Inn free house. I marvel at the great hall of the Talbot, whose matching oak doors lead to a cobbled courtyard cluttered with beer barrels where village fete events are staged in the summer. There is even a "tithe barn sitting room" with a Sunday cinema. The inn proper is a labyrinth of obscure passageways. We take a pint and a sandwich in the Coach House Grill Room, where the food is still grilled over a charcoal and wood fire as in medieval times.

Upscale inns like the Talbot cater to everyone from country rectors to the Rolling Stones. Coaching inns were specially equipped for stabling the teams of horses used for stagecoaches. Their heyday ran from 1650 to 1850, after which time they were converted to country pubs or inns with limited accommodation. The courtyard cobbles of the Talbot conjure up visions of steaming, stamping horses.

In *The English Inn,* Thomas Burke quotes one seasoned nineteenth-century traveller's impressions of coaching inns:

Inns of good dimension and repute . . . where portly sirloins, huge rounds of beef, hams of inviting complexion, fowls, supportable even after those of dainty London, spitch-cocked eels, and compotes of wine-sours, were evermore forthcoming on demand.

What home-brewed — what home-baked — what cream cheese — what snow-white linen — what airy chambers — and what a jolly-faced old gentleman, and comely old gentlewoman, to bid you welcome. It was a pleasure to arrive — a pain to depart.

A glowing tribute, but I just don't know about those spitch-cocked eels.

Mells Manor was owned by the Horner family for centuries, and is associated with the nursery rhyme "Little Jack Horner." The story involves the Abbot of Glastonbury, Richard Whiting, who held title deeds to twelve manorial estates and who, in resisting King Henry VIII's order to destroy all the monasteries, decided to bribe the king by handing over the deeds to those other estates — in return for the king sparing Glastonbury Abbey. Whiting's steward was Thomas Horner, who set about the bribery mission by secreting the twelve title deeds in a large Christmas pie so as to avoid being robbed of same while travelling to Westminster.

Horner double-crossed the abbot, so the king learned in advance of the plot to save the abbey. In a strange twist of fate, Horner then sat on a jury that found his own abbot guilty of treason. Whiting was hanged, drawn, and quartered on Glastonbury Tor, and Horner was rewarded with the title to Mells

Manor, the "plum" of the twelve estates. (The king obtained title to the remaining properties.) Hence the nursery rhyme:

Little Jack Horner
Sat in the corner,
Eating a Christmas pie;
He put in his thumb,
And pulled out a plum,
And said, "What a good boy am I!"

Subsequent generations of the Horner family have protested that the manor was properly purchased by Thomas Horner, but the rhyme has been used by satirists over the centuries to ridicule politicians and sycophants who get fat on the public purse.

Before leaving Mells, we visit the churchyard and discover the gravestone of Siegfried Sassoon, the famous poet. The simple headstone is surrounded by miniature crosses stuck into the grass. Sassoon was one of the first prominent anti-war activists in modern history. He served in the trenches on the Western Front and experienced their horrors. In time he became a thorn in the side of the Establishment, using satire in his poems to attack the "patriotic pretensions" of those who believed in war being necessary and honourable. Even before World War I Sassoon is said to have written, "France was a lady, Russia was a bear, and performing in the county cricket team was much more important than either of them." Yet he enlisted and was awarded the Military Cross for gallantry in rescuing countless soldiers from death. He later threw his Military Cross into a river.

"And he was damned right," muses Karl as we slowly walk away from the grave.

"I thought you were a fan of Attila the Hun, Karl."

"Not on your life. Oh, I would have gladly fought in World War II — I just missed it — and my brother was badly injured and captured at Arnhem by the Jerries, but that Great War was pure genocide. Certain generals on both sides should have been hanged for ordering such senseless slaughter."

We retrace our steps back to the main Macmillan path. We enjoy the peace of a deeply wooded coomb, then slog wet pastures in the rain, inch through a kissing gate, and find a tree-lined driveway. The lovely Nunney Brook now runs beside us, and we follow it to the next village.

Nunney is dominated in its centre by a castle that is modelled on the Bastille. It was erected in 1373 as a fortified residence, not a military stronghold. During the English Civil War, it was defended for the Crown, but a few Roundhead cannon blasts breached one wall. The castle fell, and its interior was gutted by Cromwell's soldiers.

The castle lay in shambles until the 1900s, when the rubble was removed and the structure partly restored. It was auctioned off in 1950 for six hundred pounds to one Rob Walker, of the Johnnie Walker whisky dynasty. We wander about the castle ruins; there is no one about but the pigeons that mass on the towers. The place is well maintained, surrounded by manicured clipped grass and a quiet brook.

At the George Inn, one can always enjoy a pint of refreshment and a pound of local gossip. The beam holding up the sign at the entrance was used in the seventeenth century to hang the condemned. At that time the inn doubled as a courthouse for judges travelling the circuit. Occasionally, says the barkeeper, one can hear the sound of taut ropes and creaking from outside, as the bodies of the criminals sway in the wind from the beam — which beam, by the way, is actually "listed" as a legally protected heritage structure.

A local ghost story concerns the lane between Nunney and Frome, which is haunted by a phantom hitchhiker. The ghost wears a sports jacket and trousers and takes great pleasure in fetching lifts from motorists, then vanishing before their eyes. Several motorists over the years have filed reports with the local police. Karl just shakes his head in disbelief.

"I think the whole country is haunted," he says with a smile.

I reflect that despite Karl always charging ahead of me on the trail, we are getting along just fine — both of us stubborn and blunt in our own ways. In her book *The Cruel Way*, Ella Maillart discusses the trials and tensions of travelling with a companion in terms of a *vie à deux*, but our drama consists more of a good-natured joshing from time to time — and no argument between us can maintain ill humour in the face of a good steak and ale pie, a bottle of red wine, and a sticky toffee pudding at the end of the day.

In fact, I have never seen Karl so mellow. I know his sprained ankle is bothering him, but he shrugs it off, and now walks with a kind of half-smile. At first I thought it was by way of cynical reaction to untoward events, but not so. He seems genuinely amused by everything, taking it all in stride. Thich Nhat Hanh writes that the Buddha always walked with a half-smile: "The half-smile is the fruit of your awareness that you are here, alive, walking. At the same time, it nurtures more peace and joy within you." I never thought that I would be thinking of Karl and the Buddha at the same time!

"So, John, how many days until we get to the coast at Abbotsbury?"

"At least another five, or six if we stay an extra night at Cadbury."

"That long?"

"Emerson once said that life is about the journey, not the destination. Don't tell me you just can't wait to get back to the rat race?"

"I'm torn, John. This has been great fun, and in some ways I wish it could go on and on. But I need to get back to the business and see the family."

But his mind has drifted off and now he is thinking again about poor Tiffany. "Do you think it's too early for us to call the Oakham police again?" he says.

"Yes, I do, Karl. And don't expect a whole lot. After all, there was no immediate report of a missing person. I'd be surprised if they were to conduct DNA tests on the clothing unless they had cause to believe it might match that of a reported missing person."

After refreshment, we wander the Nunney streets, where ducks waddle about freely. The path from here ascends a steep ridge toward the great woodlands of eastern Somerset, culminating in King Alfred's Tower. We plod up the escarpment. Near the tower we enter dense woods. Round a bend, however, our lovely path suddenly turns into an ugly-looking commercial gravel road, with a sign posted: "Logging in Progress; No Public Access."

"Bloody hell, no public access!" sputters Karl as he marches onward. His mellow half-smile has vanished.

Just then a walrus-moustached walker dressed in a faded tweed coat approaches us from the opposite direction and stops to say that the Forestry Commission is doing some clear-cutting ahead of us and it is they who have placed the signs on the path, one of which he has just torn down. He is a calm, unflappable fellow in his seventies, who gesticulates toward the hillside with his black cherry walking stick, quite rightly pointing out that Macmillan Way "is open to the public and that is that."

"That's the spirit," cries Karl with his familiar panache. "Tally ho, then!"

When we round the next bend in the trail we immediately spot the rectangular Forestry Commission sign the tweedy gentleman has torn down, lying to the side of the path — and with alacrity add our own boot prints to it. A chainsaw wails loud and shrill as we pass through a coppice and encounter two forestry workers standing by a yarder. They must have seen the blood in Karl's eye, for they just smile and make no attempt to stop us.

"Another blow struck for freedom to walk, Karl."

"Bloody bastards," he growls. "I've managed lumber camps all my life and have never tried to bar access to a public trail. Course, it's not those workers' fault — it's their bloody bureaucratic masters who think they are so high and mighty they can close off a public right-of-way."

Eleanor Farjeon, biographer of Edward Thomas, recalls how she used to walk with Thomas on the footpaths and one day accompanied a group of walkers from Thomas's cottage on a mission to tear down and burn a private sign warning off walkers from a traditional path. "May the fumes suffocate Squire Trevor-Battye, arch-enemy of ancient Rights of Way," she wrote exultantly after the fiery deed was done. The experience inspired her to write a children's story, *Elsie Piddock Skips in Her Sleep,* about how a new lord of the manor closed footpaths where generations of children had always skipped at the new moon. The English take their walking rights seriously, with the same enthusiasm with which Americans defend their rights to own guns. NRA — meet the Ramblers!

Suddenly the tall finger of Alfred's Tower projects on a hillside above us. It is now very muggy and we are sweating like pigs. We finally arrive at the base of the tower, parched and out of breath. The folly was erected in 1772 as a dual memorial: to commemorate the conclusion of the Seven Years War, just finished, and to celebrate the Battle of Ethandun, Alfred's decisive victory over the Vikings in 878, in which the Danish army under Guthrum was vanquished. As a result, the West of England, or Wessex, was left to be governed by the Anglo-Saxons, and the eastern portions of the country became the Danelaw. The tower stands near Egbert's Stone, where Alfred rallied his Saxons to battle.

We pay the entrance fee at the kiosk and purchase a couple of bottled waters.

The tower is 161 feet high, and there are 205 steps up a tiny, winding dark stone staircase, at the top of which sits a platform on a crenellated parapet. We are rewarded with incredible views across Somerset. I can discern in the distance Glastonbury Tor and the ancient town of Glastonbury. On our way down we note a point where the tile becomes darker, demarcating rebuilding that occurred in 1986 to repair the damage caused when an American warplane accidentally crashed into the tower in 1944, killing all aboard.

A recommended diversion of two miles to Stourhead Garden is well worth the effort. One follows open woodlands down to a lake and then into the village of Stourton. The Garden was opened in 1740 and comprises 2,650 acres. The setting is dominated by Grecian follies — little temples, romantic grottoes, and, the pièce de résistance, a reproduction of the Parthenon. The ninety-minute walk round the lake is a memorable experience and should not be rushed. It is so quiet and peaceful here that I find myself holding my breath, wanting to take in every bird's twitter, every leaf's movement in the breeze that gently whispers across the lake.

We trudge the two miles back to Macmillan. I am dehydrated and hot. At the tower I purchase another bottle of water and drink deeply. The trail is wide and pleasant south of here. This was a major trackway in the Middle Ages, used by drovers herding cattle to London markets.

Soon I am peering through the gateway to Redlynch Park. This was the seat of Charles Fox, leader in Parliament of the Whigs, who opposed King George III's going to war against the American colonies. Fox was an enlightened reformer who persuaded Parliament to pledge itself to ending the slave trade. It would have amused him to learn that his estate was used in World War II to house the 3rd Armored Division of the U.S. Army preparatory to the D-Day invasion. Remnants of the command bunker are still visible at the park entrance, where hangs a plaque from the Americans thanking the local Brits for their hospitality. And so the wheel of history turns.

Redlynch was also the home of John and Elaine Steinbeck for nine months in 1959, when the noted author rented Discove Cottage. The cottage was crude. Steinbeck had the landlord furnish a refrigerator, which he named "His Majesty's Voice," stating "It must be his late majesty because it stutters." He chopped wood, grew veggies in a garden, and whittled wood carvings from old oak. On March 30, 1959, he wrote, "The peace I have dreamed about is here, a real thing, thick as a stone and feelable and something for your hands . . . Meanwhile I can't describe the joy. In the mornings I get up early to have a time to listen to the birds. It's a busy time for them. Sometimes for over an hour I do nothing but look and listen and out of this comes a luxury of rest and peace and something I can only describe as in-ness."

Steinbeck used his time in and around Redlynch and neighbouring Bruton to familiarize himself with the Arthurian landscape of Somerset. He yearned to produce a modern version of the Arthurian story based upon Malory's fifteenth-century *Le Morte d'Arthur*. Steinbeck became a familiar sight on the streets of Bruton, where he frequented the pubs and the post office. He engaged a local typist, to whom he dictated the beginning of his manuscript.

John Steinbeck was completely overwhelmed by the landscape. He writes, "The other night I discovered that fifty feet from our house, you can see St. Michael's Tor at Glastonbury. Elaine didn't believe it until I showed her and she is so delighted. It makes the house so much richer to have the Tor in sight. Am I in any way getting over to you the sense of wonder, the almost breathless thing? There is no question that there is magic and all kinds of magic."

Sadly, Steinbeck died in 1968 after only partially completing the manuscript for his planned magnum opus, which was published posthumously in 1976 as *The Acts and Deeds of King Arthur and His Noble Knights*.

The Leland Trail overlaps our Macmillan route for seventeen miles to South Cadbury. The trail is named after John Leland, an erudite scholar who became chaplain to Henry VIII. The king commissioned Leland to perform an inventory of all books and manuscripts in the religious houses of the realm. This was important in view of the impending destruction by that same king of most of those monasteries. Leland's work led to many valuable manuscripts being preserved.

Leland also authored a major work, *The Itinerary*, in which he recorded the key antiquaries, artifacts, and geography of the kingdom. He toured the West Country in 1542. Leland became a learned advocate for the notion that the hill fort at South Cadbury was in fact the legendary Camelot of King Arthur.

Bruton joins with other towns in the West of England that have become chic and trendy. A large Congregational chapel fallen into disrepair on High Street is being renovated into a country hotel with an in-house bakery. The plan is for the building to contain a piazza where the community will come together, particularly for arts and crafts events. Its name: "At the Chapel."

A small country town, Bruton has it all — a superb parish church, a Gothic almshouse, a narrow packhorse bridge, Augustinian abbey relics, and three ancient public schools: King's School, the Bruton School for Girls, and Sexey's School, a boarding academy.

On a packhorse bridge I stop to peer down at the coppery water of the River Brue, where lie medieval stepping stones forming a "giant's causeway" across the stream. A few minutes later in town, hordes of teenagers clad in smart navy blue blazers pass us on the sidewalk, laughing and playing with their mobiles. Sexey's takes children aged eleven to eighteen, and was founded in 1891. It is named after Hugh Sexey, who was Royal Auditor to both Elizabeth I and James I and left a fortune for the benefit of Bruton's educational needs. Sexey's was described recently by the Secretary of State for Education as "one of the most outstanding schools in the country."

"Ah, Karl, we're not supposed to ogle here — those girls are young enough to be your grandchildren."

"They do look gorgeous in their uniforms, John. And the boys too are so smartly dressed. Why can't we do that in Canada?"

"We do, at the private schools. But don't forget those private-school kids have a reputation for mischief equal to kids from any public school."

"Perhaps, but they sure as hell look smarter dressed than the baggy-panted, mop-haired kids you see on our streets these days. By the way, I could use a Guinness about now."

"You will have to wait, I'm afraid, until Castle Cary."

We leave the streets of Bruton behind, pass the oddly named Quaperlake Lane, and trundle up Trendle Hill. A dark track called Solomon's Lane leads to huddled farm buildings denoting the outskirts of Higher Ansford. This village was the home of the famous diarist James Woodforde.

Woodforde was vicar of Castle Cary Church and rode his horse to town to give sermons. He was a keen observer of town and country life, and his *Diary of a Country Parson* is a classic. He was not your archetype churchman of strict and sober demeanour. His entry for January 1, 1767, records the revelry on New Year's night: "I read Prayers this morning at C. Cary Church being New Year's Day. I dined, supped and spent the evening till 10 o'clock at Parsonage, and after . . . I spent the whole night and part of the morning till 4 o'clock a dancing, on account of Mr. James Clarke's apprenticeship being expired. A great deal of company was there indeed . . . We had a very good band of musick, 2 violins and a Base Viol. We were excessive merry and gay there indeed."

Parson Woodforde had his eye on a local maiden for several years, but despite his boisterous, outspoken demeanour, he never mustered the courage to propose to Mary Donne (whom he liked from first meeting, when he wrote, "Miss Mary Donne is a very genteel, pretty young Lady and very agreeable with a most pleasing Voice abt. 21 Yrs. very tasty and very fashionable in dress"), and lived out his life a bachelor. He also enjoyed a good table, as extracts from his diary, such as this, relate: "We had for Dinner to day one Fowl boiled and Piggs face, a Couple of Rabbitts smothered with Onions, a Piece of rost Beef and some Grape Tarts."

Not all the parishioners were sober, respectful Christians. Woodforde records in his diary a sermon he preached at Castle Cary in 1770 that was interrupted by an uncouth individual: "Whilst I was preaching one Thos. Speed of Gallhampton came into the Church quite drunk and crazy and made a noise in the Church, called the Singers a Pack of Whoresbirds and gave me a nod or two in the pulpit."

One wonders what Woodforde would have thought of today's byline in *The Telegraph* informing us that the rector of nearby Bath Abbey has just been defrocked after being found guilty of extramarital sexual affairs with not one but *three* different women, and attempting an affair with a fourth!

We see nary a soul in Lower Ansford. But Karl stops abruptly ahead of me and points with his walking stick to a strange sculpture atop the crenellated wall of a manor house. I look up in disbelief. Clearly visible is the stone figure of a man bent over, clutching his bare buttocks and mooning. A copper weathervane is mounted on top of it.

"What do you suppose *that* is all about?" laughs Karl.

"The owner definitely wanted to make a statement, Karl; but I doubt if his neighbours appreciated that sculpture — and I am certain Vicar Woodforde would have frowned at it as he rode by."

"Is it that old?"

"Well, the architecture is part Tudor, part Georgian, it seems. So it's a reasonable bet that the sculpture was present in Woodforde's era."

Mooning, or exposing one's butt to the enemy, has been practised since ancient times, and in England since at least

1743. In the Siege of Constantinople in 1204, Greek defenders mooned the Crusaders. Hundreds of Norman soldiers mooned English archers at the Battle of Crécy in 1346. And in June of 2000, a mass mooning was orchestrated in front of Buckingham Palace by the Movement Against the Monarchy.

Charles II hid in a house in Lower Ansford on September 16, 1651, while being pursued by Cromwell's troops after his defeat at the Battle of Worcester. His escape route through England is commemorated by the long-distance Monarch's Way path. From time to time our Macmillan footpath overlaps with it as we wend steadily southwestward toward the English Channel.

Beyond slumbering Ansford, we turn down a rutted track with overhanging trees, eventually emerging into the Ansford Road approach to Castle Cary. Our B&B for the night is south of town.

If the blind house in Box was dreary, the lock-up here is pathetic. Picture a round stone erection with a dome on top, all barely large enough to hold one man. This aptly named Pepper Pot resembles a poor Hobbit's hovel. It was built in 1779 at a cost of twenty-three pounds. The structure is said to have inspired the shape of the British police helmet, and that's exactly what comes to mind. It sits in the only parking lot I have noticed in the entire town, perhaps to remind motorists that if they overstay their allotted hours, they stand to pay more than just a small fine. Daniel Defoe dubbed this the most impressive structure in Castle Cary.

I have no luck in finding a bookshop that is open. The quaint store in Castle Cary looks intriguing, but there is no light on inside. I check with the antique vendor next door, who says the bookshop owner has gone on a walking tour to Scotland. Karl laughs and says I have enough books already.

Another year, in Arundel, I diverted especially to visit a venerable bookshop, only to find a sign on the door advising that the owner had gone fishing. On yet another visit, I almost struck out with my favourite shop in Dorchester, where the owner had posted this sign: "Proprietor has lost his keys — shop will open when keys located." I waited around and a short, balding man eventually appeared with keys in hand and let me in. In the course of chatting with him, I discovered that he had formerly been a film editor, and he avidly recalled working on a television edition of the CBC's *This Hour Has Seven Days.*

Despite the Pepper Pot's pall, Castle Cary exudes a relaxed air of charm and sophistication, and I love the museum that sits in the centre of town, with its vast plaza of stonework out front where people lounge about on benches. The building itself is a mini Areopagus — classical and stately, with pointed windows, casements, and majestic pillars.

Across the road from the museum sits another George Inn. It was here that Somerset cudgel battles took place in 1769 and 1771 to mark the anniversaries of George III's coronation. These were bloodthirsty contests between two strong men who each tried to break open his opponent's head. Contestants and bystanders recited the words "Keep up your butt and God preserve your eyesight." Inn landlords organized the affairs and dragged them out over two or three days to maximize drinking profits. The contest ended in victory for one man either when blood began to flow above the neck or when a man cried "Hold!" This brutal activity was also called "backswords." A tempered variant of the sport still exists in Chipping Campden, where "Cotswold Olympics" shin-kicking contests are held. Two contestants kick each other viciously until one party relents.

Castle Cary is the hometown of Douglas Macmillan, after whom the Way is named. Across from the Methodist chapel we find Ochiltree House, where Macmillan lived. Fittingly, the Macmillan clan's motto is "I learn to succour the distressed."

Macmillan never recovered from his father's slow, agonizing death from cancer in 1911. He was aghast at the ignorance of the disease and at the absence of medical and community support for cancer patients. Determined to help alleviate cancer suffering, he founded the Society for the Prevention and Relief of Cancer, now known as Macmillan Cancer Support.

Macmillan believed that cancer patients should be able to remain in their own homes even in the late stages of the disease. His society was a game-changer. Today Macmillan Cancer Support collects 150 million pounds a year and employs some 2,000 nurses and 300 doctors in Britain. Every second shop in England seems to have a donation box for Macmillan, and its influence has even spread to North America. I witnessed my law partner dying of cancer, yet he remained of good cheer until the end, while remaining in his home overlooking the ocean, surrounded by family and friends.

Castle Cary is the jumping-off point for Macmillan Way West, a 102-mile walking path created as part of the Macmillan system in 2001. It is now feasible to walk 346 miles from Boston to Barnstaple — from east coast to west — omitting the southern leg to the Channel. Last year, Karl and I sampled a slice of Macmillan West over two days as part of our general reconnaissance for a long-distance walk. The Way West passes through the Levels, a low, marshy area of meadowland resulting from the convergence of eight rivers that meander toward the sea. King Alfred famously burned the cakes he was tending while hiding in the Levels from marauding Vikings.

2003 DIARY FLASHBACK: *We commenced at the Pepper Pot, from which one descends swiftly to a series of pleasant meadows. Here we encountered several rare red roe buck deer jumping about. The route parallels the meandering River Cary for a stretch. The meadow grasses were full of wildflowers, through which we caught glimpses of darting hares, or "jackrabbits." These creatures differ from rabbits by virtue of their longer bodies, floppy ears, and burrowing habits. Hares grow so large in East Anglia that they are called "fen donkeys."*

At Somerton Church we opened the heavy oak door for a peek inside, only to stumble upon a full wedding rehearsal. A beautiful young girl was singing "Ave Maria" to an accompanying organ. We sat respectfully in a back pew and soaked it up.

From Somerton, the route follows the River Yeo. Here we ran into serious trouble. We had about fifteen fields to pass through, with the River Yeo on one side and a deep canal on the other. The weather turned inclement. Driving rain slashed our faces — it was "chucking it down," as the English say. Each field held between twenty and thirty steers. And I tell you, they were rabid. Usually when you enter a field, a herd of bullocks will approach you and you yell and wave your walking stick and they back off. These animals did not back off. They kept coming, eyes red, mouths foaming. It was like a nightmare, with the lancing chill of the rain and the charging herds of steers — Stephen King's Christine *is not half so terrifying as those mad brutes chasing you! We kept getting pushed farther down the slope of one field, and I glanced toward the river as a possible escape route. But Karl can't swim. We were in a desperate pickle.*

As we clambered wearily over stile after stile into each succeeding field, the aggressiveness of the steers intensified, until in the last field they were wholly bent on running us down. We yelled and screamed with all our might, but they kept coming in a raging fury, and we knew that we were about to be trampled to death. Somehow we reached the far fence but were not going to make it to the stile, so we crawled

under the low-hung barbed-wire fence and bloodied ourselves.
The herd charged after us and careened past, and then the lead
four or five steers crashed into both stile and fence and rolled over
and over down the hillside, covered in blood, into the river below,
taking most of the stile and fence with them. Karl and I just lay
there panting.

"That last bit ought to have taken the bollocks off some of the
bullocks," Karl deadpanned.

When we reached our B&B at Huish Episcopi, the proprietress
looked at us as if we were a pair of wet weasels, for we were sodden
and bleeding and bruised; but a good cup of tea soon sorted us out.
In a quiet conversation with a farmer that evening at the local
pub, we gleaned — without any incriminating admissions — that
because of the recent foot-and-mouth disease epidemics, many
farmers were injecting their cattle with hormonal drugs that
supposedly made their animals more resistant to disease but had
the unfortunate side effect of "perhaps making them a tad more
aggressive." You think?

AT CASTLE CARY, we are fortunate enough to book into a
wonderful stone manor-house B&B on the town's outskirts.
Jenny, the owner, even offers to cook us a roast beef dinner.
This suits us just fine. Karl heads immediately for the soaking
tub, while I update my journal. The day has been long and
tedious, and we have overdone it with an eighteen-mile walk
that included the climb up Alfred's Tower and a ramble to
Stourhead Gardens and back.

Jenny is an effervescent widow in her late seventies. She
is both refined and compassionate, and makes sure we have
plenty of heat for our rooms — a welcome change from the
norm! Jenny is also dying of cancer, yet keeps in good spirits.

Promptly at seven, she raps on my door and announces
that dinner is ready, and would I please let Karl know? I will

indeed, but have to rap hard on his bathroom door to distract him from his tub ablutions, as I hear him singing amid a cacophony of splashes and thumps. He reminds me of Churchill, who used to behave like a walrus in his bathtub.

"It's time for dinner, Karl!"

No response. I rap harder. Finally the splashing stops.

"Karl, roast beef in five minutes!"

"Ask her if she has Shiraz and plum brandy; I'll be down shortly!"

We relax over a scrumptious meal of roast beef, Yorkshire pudding, creamed cauliflower, and mashed potatoes lathered in rich black gravy. Dessert consists of homemade trifle. And yes, there is a choice bottle of Barossa Valley Australian Shiraz, but Karl will have to settle for sherry for his nightcap.

Jenny's joy lately has been anticipating a visit from her long-lost nephew in the United States, whom she wants badly to see. She has no children. The nephew had not stayed in touch since leaving England for America years ago, but recently he noticed her website advertising her B&B and contacted her by email. He is now scheduled to come over and visit her in the summer. She says she hopes to live long enough for his visit, as her cancer, which had been in long remission, has now recurred and she has decided to refuse chemotherapy and radiation. But she does not dwell on this, and is immensely cheerful at our candlelit dinner, saying she enjoys the company of many friends. Moreover, the Macmillan Cancer Relief nurses are of immense benefit.

"And are you both enjoying your walk?"

"Yes indeed," I say. "It's a very different world we see along the Macmillan Way. So much history! A little arduous, mind you, when it starts raining and the wind blows across those muddy fields."

"Ah, yes, I expect so. A different world for those of us too, John, who have dwelt here all our lives. People in the town now often commute to London or work out of their homes. Not like the old days — why, I walk down High Street now and hardly know anyone!"

Jenny serves strong Colombian coffee with the trifle, and life is good.

Before I turn out my light, I reflect that Douglas Macmillan would be very pleased to know that Jenny is able to continue living in good spirits in her own home despite her body being ravaged by cancer.

10

CADBURY CAMELOT

On either side the river lie

Long fields of barley and of rye,

That clothe the wold and meet the sky;

And thro' the field the road runs by

To many-tower'd Camelot;

And up and down the people go,

Gazing where the lilies blow

Round an island there below,

The island of Shalott.

— ALFRED LORD TENNYSON —
"The Lady of Shalott"

THE FIRST COMMUTERS TO London are gathered at the Castle Cary train station early this morning, most of them carrying laptops. Nearby, a cappuccino board beckons patrons into the Old Bakehouse Coffee Shop. Strong espresso tweaks my nostrils. Needful Things Interiors boasts of its fine silk curtains; Pantry by the Pond offers delicatessen delights such as paella, port tagine, and cream cheese roulades; Maya Boutique offers ladies' clothes, including Scottish cashmere. Sophisticated town meets country here. Expensive SUVs mingle with Mitsubishi pickup trucks on the town's main street. No kitsch, please.

I ponder why women like Jenny do B&B and conclude that there are two main types: those women who crave human company, and those who are needful of money. Jenny is evidently of the former category, and I so admire her pluck and her graciousness toward travellers in the face of such a difficult disease.

The ascent up Lodge Hill from Castle Cary is invigorating. We pass the earthworks of the old castle and gain a sweeping view of the Mendips, the Quantocks, the Somerset Levels, and Glastonbury Tor. Three huge crosses stand on the brow of the hill. An empty bench overlooks the town below. Here we stop to catch our breath. A plaque on the bench commemorates one Jack Sweet, who died in 1995 and loved to walk here.

We say hello to a friendly man and his collie, who approach us. The fellow is dressed in a long, plain beige raincoat, clutches a yellow polka-dot umbrella, and wants to chat about the fine view and such. But Karl is in no mood to talk. He is on a mission, impatient to bury his little plastic capsule containing a note to his children and some coins. Having dug up his daughter's cache at the Yorkshire abbey, it's now his turn to bury some treasure.

The man with the collie tells us a story about Jack Sweet, informing us that the man hanged himself in 1995 after some involvement with the hard drug trade — a morbid tale for sure.

"Something doesn't quite fit here," I say. "It's not normal for plaques to be erected to honour criminals, least of all those involved in the shady underworld of drug trafficking."

"Ah, mate, this Jack Sweet was the darling of the ladies and could sweet-talk his way out of any dilemma. No jail cell ever held him for long. Mind you, he only went to jail on minor charges like break and enter, but he was known to be dealing the hard stuff. Then he seems to have gotten on the wrong side of the big blokes running a local gang, and decided to hang himself. Of course, some people maintain it wasn't suicide."

Karl fidgets about, trying to get the man to leave so he can dig his hole by the bench and bury his treasure cache.

"Come along, Webster." The man finally decides to leave, since for several minutes he has only received guttural responses from the two rude North Americans. Webster reluctantly follows. Then Karl begins to dig furiously like a mole, dirt flying in all directions.

Alas, he should have waited for Webster to wander out of sight. His digging provokes Webster into thinking there must indeed be something interesting underground, and the dog comes bounding back, barking furiously, very excited. His owner calls him back, to no avail.

Karl freezes as Webster nuzzles him and peers into his hole. Could there be a mole or a rabbit down there? The dog pokes his nose into the hole.

"Go away, mutt!" Karl shouts and resumes digging, this time with a corkscrew because the earth has become too hard for his spoon and he must loosen up the soil. It does the trick, and soon Karl is scooping out the earth so furiously that the collie's tail wags faster and faster as he excitedly anticipates a rabbit emerging from below. Finally, the exasperated dog owner arrives and yanks Webster's collar, staring in disbelief at Karl and his hole.

I just stand there leaning on my walking stick. "He's burying treasure, that's all."

"Of course, and I'm the man in the moon. So sorry about all this, chaps. Come along now, Webster."

The owner leashes Webster and drags him off, both man and dog casting backward glances at Karl on his knees. Even a couple of kestrels swoop and dive overhead, eyeing these weird human antics with curiosity.

A few moments later, Karl finishes with his treasure caching and we resume the trek southward. The route winds gradually downhill to the Levels, where the walking is flat and comfortable. The Levels are composed of marine clay layers plus peaty moors that rise in the inland areas. Neolithic people laid the world's oldest timber road, known as the Sweet Track, over the Levels in 3800 BC. The lowlands are bounded by rises of land such as the Mendip Hills, islands of high land like Glastonbury itself, and, finally, the southern hills such as Cadbury Castle, which lead into Dorset.

We are approaching a climactic point of the Macmillan Way. About two miles from Castle Cary, the path crosses the River Cam. Here the stream babbles and sings through bright yellow willows. Goldfinches dart about. A couple of boys stand on the banks dipping nets into the stream. I stop to ask the tousle-haired lads what they are trying to catch, and one of them shows me the contents of his net — dozens of wriggly worm-like creatures known as "elvers," or baby eels. A large grey heron suddenly squawks and flaps itself heavily into a nearby elm tree.

We are truly in the West Country now — that magical, sought-after realm of walkers, holidayers, and adventurers that encompasses the counties of Devon, Dorset, Somerset, and Cornwall. As Susan Toth notes in *My Love Affair with England,* the West of the country is often associated with "myth, legend, and the land of faeries." The western horizon has enchanted and obsessed people since time immemorial. It was not only the search for discovery of new lands to the west that gripped the imagination of the ancients. The daily dipping of the sun below the horizon was also of great concern. Would it return? Hawaiians still celebrate the traditional blowing on the conch shell, or *Pu,* at sunset, to celebrate the sun's passing and to give thanks, *mahalo,* for its daily return.

In *The Lord of the Rings,* Bilbo, Frodo, and Gandalf all depart for the West, with Frodo dreaming of white shores and "beyond them a far green country under a swift sunrise." This powerfully evokes the mythology of ancient Britain. Tennyson recalls the Greek enchantment with the Western horizon in his poem "Ulysses," where the wanderer on his perpetual quest, his odyssey, remains true to his purpose. The concluding lines of this poem have always inspired me. I once recited them when emceeing the retirement dinner of a well-known Canadian member of Parliament who was terminally ill:

To sail beyond the sunset, and the baths
Of all the western stars, until I die.
It may be that the gulfs will wash us down:
It may be we shall touch the Happy Isles,
And see the great Achilles, whom we knew.
Tho' much is taken, much abides; and tho'
We are not now that strength which in old days
Moved earth and heaven, that which we are, we are;
One equal temper of heroic hearts,
Made weak by time and fate, but strong in will
To strive, to seek, to find, and not to yield.

Thus it is appropriate that the West Country be the land of dreams and fairies and myth. Often paradise is imagined as a valley. C.S. Lewis grew up imagining that a picture hanging in his home depicted a verdant heaven, when in fact it was a painting of the Golden Valley in Herefordshire. Lewis modelled his Narnia after this idyllic scene.

In the biographical film *Shadowlands*, Lewis agrees to Joy's suggestion that they take a holiday and track down this Golden Valley, which Lewis has never visited. When they find it, the valley is resplendent, with green meadows and a winding brook bathed in sunshine. Their Arcadian experience is a highlight of the film, with Joy and Lewis walking through fields, holding hands and laughing like lovers do. However, clouds inevitably appear, rain begins to fall, and the Narnia landscape darkens — both literally and metaphorically — with the imminent end of Joy's remission from cancer and her subsequent death.

In my own recurrent dream, Arcadia is a deep, wide valley with a meandering stream, emerald fields, and little copses spread hither and thither. The faint outline of low blue hills appears like a mirage in the distance. I am walking slowly, wending with the stream; I hear the occasional humming of bees on clover and the splashing of trout. The path beckons me onward, and I must follow. The sky turns crimson toward the horizon. But in the dream, the sun never goes down and I keep walking toward the sunset, the landscape about me bathed in shafts of golden light.

The portal into the world of Camelot is a sterile concrete viaduct over the A303. The vehicles whizz along far below like ants rushing in straight lines to and from their nests. We halt to inspect Chapel Cross Cottage, with its little thatched chapel that John Leland noted when he passed through here in the sixteenth century: "I turned flat west by a little chapelle," he wrote in his diary. Long before we reach the village of South Cadbury, we spot the wooded scarp of the high hill astride it called Cadbury Castle — or, colloquially, Cadbury Camelot.

A mile beyond, the massive earthworks of Cadbury Castle loom directly above us. The village of South Cadbury lies at the very foot of the hill fort, with the Red Lion Inn close by. The word Cadbury comes from Cada's Fort, the ancient, high hill fort that has so intrigued archaeologists and Arthurian New Agers.

Arthurian lore comes to us principally from writers of the medieval period. Of these, Thomas Malory is the best known. He wrote *Le Morte d'Arthur* based upon a combination of folk tradition and chivalry, the latter being all the rage in Western Europe in the Middle Ages. Prior to that, Geoffrey of Monmouth, in his *History of the Kings of Britain,* refers to a King Arthur with his principal court in Caerleon-on-Usk. Arthur was reputedly born at Tintagel in Cornwall, a windswept, towering, impregnable fortress on a sea cliff. Shakespeare refers to Arthur's seat as being Camelot in *King Lear,* as does Tennyson in *Idylls of the King.*

Not to be overlooked is the persistent local tradition of Arthur and Camelot that has been passed on by successive generations. John Leland wrote of the site in 1542 thus: "At the very south ende of the chirch of South-Cadbyri standith Camallate, sumtyme a famose toun or castelle, apon a very torre or hille, wonderfully enstrengtheid of nature . . . In the upper parte of the coppe of the hille be 4. diches or trenches, and a balky waulle of yerth betwixt every one of them . . . Much gold, sylver and coper of the Romaine coynes hath be found ther yn plouing . . . The people can telle nothing ther but that they have hard say that Arture much resortid to Camallaet." William Stukeley visited Cadbury in 1723, and described the hill fort: "Camelot is a noted place; it is a noble fortification of the Romans placed on the north end of a ridge of hills separated from the rest by nature; and for the most part solid rock, very steep and high: there are three or four ditches quite round, sometimes more; the area within is twenty acres at least, rising in the middle . . . There is a higher angle of ground within, ditched about, where they say was King Arthur's palace . . . the country people all refer to stories of him."

Leslie Alcock describes the epic archaeological digs he oversaw at Cadbury in the 1960s in his book *By South Cadbury Is That Camelot*. He notes that "Cadbury Castle has few equals among British hillforts for the number, complexity, and above all the towering steepness of its defences. Leland's description, as we now see, was by no means over-dramatic."

So what about King Arthur? Is he just a myth, or something more? What we do know is that there lived a real warrior leader who fought and won many battles against the Saxon invaders, including at Badon and Camlann. The dates of those battles remain fluid; however, there is some evidence that they occurred in AD 490 and 499, respectively. Alcock and some other commentators believe that Arthur was the successor of the Romano-British general Ambrosius Aurelianus, who was a major leader by 437. This would fit in nicely with the refortification of Cadbury Camelot, which according to carbon-dating analysis was effected in the 470s.

Whether Arthur was the real name of this inspiring chieftain and whether he was truly a king or just a leading warrior are still debated. However, we do know that such a chieftain would have required a high, defensible hill fort in southwest England, that the hill fort must be surrounded by fertile fields and a good source of water, and that the location should not only be defensible but strategically situated in relation to the sea, Cornwall, and travel routes generally. Cadbury Castle meets all of these criteria.

Archaeological interest in the Cadbury site was revived during the twentieth century after numerous shards of pottery and other artifacts were ploughed up by farmers. These artifacts were associated in time with similar objects found at Tintagel and elsewhere in Cornwall. Alcock's excavations in the sixties revealed three fascinating aspects of Cadbury Castle. Firstly, it is now known that this hill fort was continuously occupied from neolithic times — by first the Celts, then the Romans, and finally the Saxons. Secondly, Alcock established that the hillfort defences were massively reconstructed in the 470s, in the largest engineering project of the period in Britain. This may have been where the Romano-Celts made their last stand against the marauding Saxons.

The capstone to all of this, and the key discovery of Alcock's archaeological team, is the Great Hall, a massive room that dominated the hill and "was the principal building — the feasting hall, in fact — of the Arthurian stronghold."

Based on what we know of the prevailing hierarchy, this is consistent with the presence of either a king or a supreme warrior leader. The hall has been carbon-dated to between AD 470 and AD 580 — precisely the time period in which the Romano-Celts were fighting their final desperate battles against the Saxons. Judging by its location, its Great Hall, and its history as the highest, most defensible hill fort in the region, Cadbury Castle was probably *the* key stronghold from which the West Country was defended in the late fifth and early sixth centuries.

No historian or archaeologist has rationally refuted Alcock's findings. However, Alcock himself admitted later in life that there is still no real evidence that a king or leader named Arthur ever lived, nor that any home base equivalent to the Camelot of legend ever existed. That said, given the strategic importance of Cadbury Castle, there is little doubt that the Saxons could not have extended their grip to include western England without capturing Cadbury Castle — and Alcock's excavations indicate that a major battle ultimately spelled the demise of the hilltop fortress.

Historian Michael Wood is adamant that Arthur was likely not a high king but rather the leading warrior chieftain of the day. Yet Wood recognizes that this does not derogate the myth or the historical consciousness of the British people. "The figure of Arthur," he writes, "remains, as it always will, a symbol of British history; the living bond between the Britons and the English Spirit."

The "once and future king" written about by Malory lives on in the hearts of Britons and people the world over, judging by the number of Hollywood films, books, and Arthurian societies which continue to flourish. As we have seen, it was not enough for even John Steinbeck that he author some of the most successful novels ever produced about American life. He regarded his career as unfinished until he produced a modern rendering of Malory's epic. And it was to Somerset and Cadbury Castle that he looked for the inspiration for his proposed tome.

THE CLIMB UP Cadbury Castle by the prescribed route commences at South Cadbury. Woods surround the lower flanks, with patches of grazing land perforated by rabbit holes and badger setts. The layers of earthen ramparts are visible at various levels. The lane we climb is deep rutted, muddy, and lined by pink campions. The hill is five hundred feet high, with four main defensive perimeters. At the top is a sloping, grassy field. There was never a stone castle here, but rather wooden walls, ramparts, and a massive gate at the main entrance facing the southwest, above Sutton Montis village.

Within the hill fort walls would have stood the Great Hall and many buildings housing arms, food, and animals. Habitation would have been limited to the chieftain (or king), his household, and his leading warriors and their retinues. Most of the common folk lived below in villages clustered about the hill near the River Cam.

In the great hollowed bowl beneath the hill lay the storybook fields that would have supplied the castle community with grain and other crops; there are two springs in the hill, the most famous being King Arthur's Well, which has been located on a path near the church in Sutton Montis. According to legend, once a year at midnight the thundering hooves of Arthur and his knights' horses can be heard as the entourage travels down from Camelot to drink water from this well.

The view at the summit is breathtaking. The sun is setting and the fields below are backdropped to the northwest by the pillar of Glastonbury Tor, appearing as some distant phallic symbol, its dark image projecting defiant against a rising cuticle moon. Far to the northeast I discern the silhouette of Alfred's Tower, standing guard over Wessex. And I am here at Cadbury Camelot — Arthur's centre of operations in resisting the Saxons. It is at this moment that I simply sit down on a rampart, overwhelmed by emotion, and weep. Karl turns away, embarrassed.

Later, I discover that I am in good company in my brief emotional meltdown. John Steinbeck describes his own experience standing atop Cadbury Castle on April 30, 1959: "Yesterday something wonderful. It was a golden day and the apple blossoms are out and for the first time I climbed up to Cadbury-Camelot. I don't think I remember an impact like that. Could see from the Bristol Channel to the tops of the Mendip Hills and all the little villages. Glastonbury Tor and Alfred's Tower on the other side . . . I walked all around the upper wall. And I don't know what I felt but it was a lot — like those slow hot bubbles of molten rock in a volcano, a gentle rumbling earthquake of the Spirit. I'll go back at night and in the rain, but this was noble gold even to use Tennyson's phrase — mystic-wonderful. Made the hairs prickle on the back of the neck." Then Steinbeck broke down.

One reason why myths remain powerful in culture is that they often contain many kernels of truth. They just won't go away. For example, as hard as Anglo-Saxon writers from Bede onward have tried to ignore the evidence of early Celtic Christianity in Britain, it just won't wash. Historians now accept that many Britons had been converted to Christianity well before the Roman legions began to withdraw in 410. In fact, Britain sent three bishops to the Catholic Council of Arles in 314. It was the departure of the legions and the arrival of the pagan Angles and Saxons that set back the faith. The latter pushed the native Britons farther and farther to the western fringes, into Cornwall and Wales.

St. Augustine of Canterbury landed in Kent in 597 and converted the Saxon King Æthelbert. Over the next century, the entire hierarchy of Anglo-Saxon rulers was brought into the Christian fold. It took a century or more for the Celtic bishops to be vanquished by the overwhelming forces of Roman Catholicism as directed from Canterbury. But Rome recognized the importance of gaining the loyalty of the Romano-British inhabitants and so ordered construction of the largest abbey and monastery in Britain — at Glastonbury.

Glastonbury was and remains the spiritual centre of Britain, notwithstanding the formal designation of Canterbury as the seat of Anglicanism. Glastonbury is associated with both Druidism and Celtic Christianity. As the mecca of New Agers, Wiccans, and assorted hippie types over the years, Glastonbury now extends its appeal to a much broader cross-section of the population who find spiritual nourishment, mystery, and wonder in this ancient Isle of Avalon.

On Wearyall Hill in Glastonbury stands a thorn tree native only to Israel and Lebanon. There is also one standing on the abbey grounds. Of course, these offshoots of older trees could have been planted in Glastonbury at a much later date than the first century AD. But the tradition of Joseph of Arimathea having landed here upon the Isle of Avalon shortly after the crucifixion is a powerful folk legend that has endured through every century. As a trader and merchant, Joseph would have certainly known of, if not participated in, the trade of the Phoenicians with Cornwall for the precious tin and iron found there. Associated with this is the theme expounded by William Blake, whose most famous poem evokes the possibility that Joseph of Arimathea brought Jesus to Britain as a young boy on one of his voyages as a merchant to these parts: "And did those feet in ancient time / Walk upon England's mountains green . . ."

As a warrior king, Arthur would have been well aware of the spiritual importance of Glastonbury, and the mythical tradition of he and his queen being buried at Glastonbury is also credible. Even so, Arthur appears on the historical landscape as a noble zephyr, ever ethereal. It is fitting that the largest music festival in Britain is now held annually at Glastonbury, attracting hundreds of thousands of people and such luminaries as the Rolling Stones and Sir Paul McCartney. Perhaps they are coming home to their roots.

WE ARE STAYING two nights at Parsonage Farm, a B&B at the foot of Cadbury Castle run by John and Elizabeth Kerton. Just across the lane is the twelfth-century Sutton Montis church, which stands on a much older site believed to have been a Saxon place of worship. The church embodies the spirit and mythology of the region. A lovely and unique stained glass window commemorates the history and landscape, with the River Cam, tilled fields, Cadbury Camelot, and Glastonbury Tor all celebrated.

To the west of the church is a sublime orchard which leads to Queen Camel village a couple of miles distant. In late afternoon, I go for a walk in this orchard, just aimlessly pottering along and enjoying the fragrance of the late apple blossoms, until I become deliciously lost in a distant field. On my return walk, a kind villager appears in her garden and offers me refreshment.

Jean is a retired widow. We sit chatting in her solarium sipping elderflower cordial — cold, fizzy, and refreshing, its aroma mingling with the ripe apple blossoms. Ambrosia for the soul.

Jean at one time lived on Salt Spring Island, near Vancouver. She and her husband had retired back to Somerset, and she enjoys reminiscing about her years living on the west coast of Canada.

"Such vastness," she sighs.

I thank Jean and rejoin Karl at Parsonage Farm. Another lodger is staying here — a short, slight German named Bruno, a seventy-year-old former civil servant from Bonn. Bruno is determined to learn English before dying, so he has enrolled in a grammar school in Somerset that caters to immigrants, though he has no intention of moving to England. He practises his English on us. We like him. He wears a beret — appearing more French than Teutonic — and swings a neat cherry-red walking stick. He displays much joie de vivre.

But it so happens that on our first night at the Kertons, Bruno asks us where to go for dinner. I have to think quickly. We were looking forward to the brassy hospitality down the road at the Red Lion Inn, within easy walking distance. The proprietor there, however, is implacably — nay, violently — anti-German, and would surely cause a scene. So I try to divert Bruno off to the pub at Corton Denham. Alternatively, I suggest, if he doesn't mind the drive, the Mitre at Sandford Orcas serves a fine meal.

"But where you go to eat?" he queries.

"Uh, there's this hole down in South Cadbury, and we are likely going to just have a beer or two."

"Why not eat?"

"Bruno, it's more of a bar. Trust me: for food, go elsewhere."

He shrugs, and I feel badly because he likely thinks we just don't want to dine with him, when that is just not the case. But he takes it in his stride and clambers into his Volkswagen and says he will try the Mitre.

We sup at the Red Lion in South Cadbury. Al, the feisty, ex-British Marine publican, says he is thinking about changing the name of the inn to the Camelot — but thinking even more about retirement. He regales us with stories of the Korean War. As noted, he is fiercely anti-German and also anti-French, and will not stock their wines, but fortunately he has good Australian Shiraz. Once he has finished excoriating the French and the Germans, he moves on to voice acerbic thoughts about the EU, the Chunnel, welfare bums, and Germans again.

"Beer and skittles are on tap tonight at the inn," he says. "It'll be a hell of a ruckus."

"So, Al, what is skittles all about?" I enquire.[5]

Al shouts at his dog, Charley, who has his paws up on the bar stool, to lie down.

"Like bowling for you North Americans," he says. "Hard to explain much more, and the rules vary throughout England. But it's going to be a hell of a ruckus tonight, mates, a hell of a ruckus," he repeats.

We sit at our table sipping Shiraz and observing the locals coming in for a pint or two. Above our table hangs a tacky charcoal sketch of a dusky nude woman. Charley has now worked his way under our table. Al, seeing this, interrupts his customers at the bar by barking at the old mutt, "Charley, get out of there! Charley!" The dog finally moves.

Al personally delivers the plates, piping hot. "There, lovies. Enjoy."

One doesn't get this kind of personal service in most pubs, least of all from the proprietor. But then, there are only three tables in the entire place. Al's wife does the cooking.

---

5 Regarding skittles, I have learned that in Somerset there are six players per side, and the balls are made from apple wood. This is a popular indoor pub game that dates to 3300 BC in Egypt. It shares an ancestry with lawn bowling. The skittles themselves resemble small bowling pins.

We have both ordered steak and kidney pie. It burns the mouth but tastes delicious. We watch as village children come in from time to time to buy chocolate bars and Smarties. Al treats them all with smiles and warmth. A local farmer sits at the bar watching the soccer match on the tiny telly mounted on the ceiling.

"I saw a beautiful fox on the road today, Allen," the farmer says.

Rejoins Al, "Was it dead?"

Two dogs start to muck about at the bar, but our Charley stays out of the fray. The farmer at the bar suddenly cheers as his team scores a goal.

"You're not wearing your Roman ring," Karl says abruptly.

"I know; I put it on last night and had horrible nightmares of monsters and Black Riders and gladiators, all spattered with gore. So I took it off about three in the morning."

"Sounds to me like your brain cells got King Arthur mixed up with *Lord of the Rings*."

Later in the evening at Parsonage Farm, we sit in the kitchen with John and Elizabeth Kerton. John is of medium build, taciturn, and enjoys his tea with a few wedges of cheese and apples. His faithful collie lies by his side. There is no central heating in this fifteenth-century farmhouse, but we are dry and cozy in our rooms. The kitchen woodstove provides ample warmth this fine June evening. "But blankets and water bottles are needed for the chilly nights," explains Elizabeth.

Elizabeth is a wonderfully erudite, well-groomed lady who is concerned about the decline of village life, vandalism, and farm succession. Almost all the cottages in the village now have burglar alarms installed, she advises. John cuts some apples with the paring knife and nods. Through the open window we can hear the family's favourite horse kicking and snorting in his stall. John's eyes roam toward his fields, around and up the slopes of Cadbury Castle. A true country-man always keeps farm and weather within sight and hearing.

John and Elizabeth are kind and thoughtful pillars of the community and stalwart stewards of the land, quietly carrying on with the spirit of yeomanry and service that has defined country people throughout English history. They have allowed archaeological excavations on their farm property, on and around which have been located Iron Age foundations of a group of neolithic huts. Romano-British artifacts have also recently been found in an area that likely served as an approach to the main southwest gateway to Camelot.

John weighs in on the subject of badgers — creatures every-one wants to hate — by writing a Letter to the Editor in response to the movement to cull the badger population of the country:

It may seem peculiar but if I am wearing my farming cap I would certainly not like our badgers culled. Nobody could possibly have more badgers than we have on Parsonage Farm . . . As far as we can tell they don't have any TB . . . One can only presume that we are breeding and exporting clean badgers in some quantity and if they were culled, in would come infected ones . . . If I am wearing my green ecological, conservation hat, I would certainly support a cull. We have always had two large setts on the farm and in the old days that number of badgers was sustainable . . . The farm is all old pasture and cider orchards. No artificial fertilisers are used and no tractor spraying, and because of the sheep, no grass is cut until early July.

Until about twenty-five or thirty years ago the farm was teeming with wildlife — plovers, skylarks, pippits, wild English partridge and wild pheasants, also plenty of hares and hedgehogs. Now as far as ground nesting birds and ground game, the farm is the epitome of The Silent Spring.

Somerset is known for its dairy production, apple orchards, and cider. A folk ritual is practised here called the "Apple Wassail." Wassailing dates to the pagan era. It typically involves a wassail queen leading a procession to the oldest and most fruitful tree in the orchard. She dips a piece of toast in mulled cider, which is placed in the tree boughs to draw favourable spirits. More mulled cider is poured round the base of the tree, which, when combined with the noise of sticks banged together, scares away evil spirits. The tree is then serenaded by the crowd.

Country apple festivals are held in Somerset and Dorset to promote local apple varieties and make the public more aware of the importance of conserving orchards. These liquid events invariably highlight three periods of English history: Merrie Olde England, where locals portray medieval times by dressing in tight green jerkins, playing fiddles, and waving around pig bladders; the era of *Mansfield Park* refinement, with women wearing muslin dresses being driven around in elegant horse-drawn carriages; and the modern era, with everyone joking around on tractors, baling oats, and quaffing cider to a bevy of off-key fiddlers. Morris dancers and one or two flutists round out the program.

OUR SECOND DAY at Cadbury is spent relaxing and puttering about the lower reaches of Cadbury Castle. In the evening, we again dine at the Red Lion. On our way back to our B&B, we ascend the hill fort for a final visit.

I sit overlooking the sweep of the Somerset Levels atop the highest rampart, dreaming of Camelot and wishing I could have watched Leslie Alcock and his keen archaeologists dig up the grounds and uncover the king's Great Hall. I can see Glastonbury Tor to the northwest and, immediately below, the quiet village of Sutton Montis, with Parsonage Farm, the precious little church on the lane, cute cottages, and the lovely apple orchard winding away toward Queen Camel like some Avalonian garden. Overhead can be heard the drone of a small plane. The plane looks military; it comes closer, circles briefly, then dips its wings and buzzes off like a hummingbird toward Yeovilton's Royal Naval Air Base.

In the mind's eye, thick dust is billowing, as a knight canters up the main entrance from the fields below to enter Camelot and report to his warrior king on the latest incursions of the Saxon hordes. And is that the Lady of Shalott and Sir Lancelot standing furtively in the shadows of the Great Hall?

The idyllic scene is complemented by a huge amphitheatre of quilted fields bounded by high rolling hills to the south with cattle and sheep grazing as mere dots on the hillsides. Glaciers long ago rounded out this landscape into hill and hollow and coomb. Neolithic hunters eventually arrived, followed by Celts, who began to farm and gradually refined the smooth hills by adding a patina of velvety green furrowed fields. It seems a thousand miles from urbanity here, yet the nearby A303 can take you to London in two hours.

Of all the places I have been in the world, few move me as much as the summit of Cadbury Castle. New Agers have made much of theories about ley lines around Glastonbury and Cadbury, but one does not need to study astrology to feel the power and magnetism of this fascinating place.

Karl is obviously moved as well.

"I can certainly see why a warrior leader would choose this spot to defend the West Country from the Saxons," he muses.

Then, after a long pause, Karl turns to me. "This alone was worth the walk, John."

At that moment I know that he has felt the same frisson of excitement I have felt, the very charged atmosphere of Cadbury Camelot.

11

RALEIGH PASSION *and* HARDY HAUNTS

It is not our part to master all the tides of the world,

but to do what is in us for the succour of those years wherein

we are set, uprooting the evil in the fields that we know, so

that those who live after may have clean earth to till.

—— J.R.R. TOLKIEN ——
The Lord of the Rings

THE CLIMB OUT OF South Cadbury follows the crest of Corton Ridge for over a mile. Karl and I pause to look back north. Cadbury Camelot is directly across from us now, as the apex of a triangle. Glastonbury Tor is faintly visible to the northwest, and to the northeast I can see the silhouetted finger of Alfred's Tower. As I ponder the enormous significance of this historic triangle for one last time, a writhing steel snake in the guise of a high-speed train passes far below us near Queen Camel. I hear the church bells ringing in Sutton Montis, then the familiar *Ooo-oo* of a wood pigeon. I know that there is something wonderful here, something to be cherished.

The moment is broken by bracing wind gusts, lashing us on this exposed ridge. Waves of fierce, ugly black nimbus clouds approach from the northwest. The nefarious antics of English weather.

"Dirty weather coming, John," warns Karl. "Best we hunker down and fortify ourselves."

We scramble for Corton Denham, a Lilliputian village hidden in a high, remote corner of Somerset. Solace awaits at the Queens Arms, a hospitable free house known for its fine local ciders and sumptuous accommodation. On this high ridge winding down from the Dorset border one is in a virtual fairyland. A lovely parish church nestles into a coomb. Horses, paddocks, and sheep cluster the steep hill upward to the sky like on some *Black Beauty* movie set.

The pub is busy inside. We know we are welcome because of the friendly sign out front: "We like dogs and muddy boots." So we each order a pint of local cider. Sitting next to us is a family, the father dressed in a tweed sports jacket, jeans, Italian silk shirt, and wellies. Perhaps this is the new attire of the squirearchy — or, more likely, the affluent Londoner down to his cottage for the weekend. Through the back window of the pub I admire a wattle fence decorated by a low lavender hedge.

Refreshed, we don jackets and Tilley hats but have to huddle in the doorway for several minutes to avoid a passing squall. Our route takes us to the village of Sandford Orcas along a narrow lane now slick from the downpour. Cool rain lashes our faces in alternating sheets and splatters.

Sandford Orcas dozes in a copse just inside Dorset. The unusual name originates from a ford here with a sandy bottom — hence "Sandford"; the "Orcas" derives from the Norman Orescuilz family, who were given the village manor by William the Conqueror. The current manor house was built in Tudor times from Ham Hill oolitic stone — and is one of the most haunted places in England.

A team from the Paraphysical Laboratory concluded in 1966 that the house held five separate ghosts. One of them is thought to be the spectre of a depraved footman who was known to rape the young maids of the house. This phantom targets only virgin girls. As part of the Lab's investigations, two allegedly virgin women volunteered to spend a night in a bedroom. Next morning they emerged from the locked room in a terrified state and independently described a seven-foot-tall man dressed in Georgian costume.

I don't know about the ghost, but I am accosted by an angry, rotund gardener who yells and gesticulates at me to go away when I approach the grounds with my camera, repeatedly telling me that the garden is closed. I am simply trying to photograph the manor house framed by the lovely terraced gardens and topiary. My dander up, I yell back at him, "Being England, sir, I expect nothing less!" which leaves him rather nonplussed, likely more befuddled by my accent than by the cheeky purport of my riposte. Perhaps if I had resembled a medieval knight he might have been friendlier. (A fellow walker, Jonathan Greatorex of Stamford, passed through here recently on Macmillan and related how he felt an "out of body experience" when approaching the manor house, suddenly imagining he was a knight returning from a Crusade.)

Squalls lash us, so we stop for a bite at the Mitre Inn. Unfortunately, our ploughman's repast is spoiled by the inane chatter of a henpecked husband being berated by his wife over his refusal to purchase a new bed — I feel like opening my wallet to help the poor bloke just to terminate the tiresome conversation. Then at the bar a disgruntled stonemason complains to the proprietor that his work that week has not been properly appreciated by the homeowner — "Not at all, sir," the stocky lad moans, "not at all." The publican commiserates in gentle, cooing tones. The lad gratefully accepts another cider.

On the road again, the capricious clouds part and we are treated to a cerulean blue sky, but with a stiff breeze. Just past the pub we stop to chat with a thatching crew who are refurbishing a stone cottage.

"I love thatched cottages, Karl."

"They may look quaint," Karl says gruffly, "but they are dirty and impossible to maintain."

We have had this argument before.

The use of thatch for roofs dates to the Bronze Age in England. The materials used vary from sedge, flax, and broom to mere grass and straw. Neolithic hut-circles were often roofed with reeds spread over brushwood laid between the poles. The roofers here are using wheat straw. It is estimated that some 250 roofs in England today still have base layers of thatch that were placed over 500 years ago.

Victorians moved away from thatch in favour of tile roofs. Thatch was a symbol of poverty and was condemned as a fire hazard. But today there is a real revival of the "old ways," and the swank businessman and his wife from the city demand that their West Country cottage be thatch-roofed. It is now considered chic.

At the south end of the village we encounter a lady in her garden cheerfully digging turf with an undersized spade. Overhead, her parrot sits in a dovecote-style cage, rudely talking back to her. She looks up at us, wipes her brow, and all three of us suddenly laugh. Then the parrot laughs. I admire her sea of electric blue cornflowers, clumps of hollyhocks, peonies, and lavender. We chat for several minutes and she offers us tea. We demur, thank her, and cross over a stile to enter a hidden coomb.

I relax and catch my breath in a hollow before the final ascent of the hill, enjoying a scene reminiscent of Hardy's *Far from the Madding Crowd*. Below me a shepherd walks through a narrow valley, herding sheep with the help of his collie. He is dressed in a tattered old wool coat, patched pants, and wellies. Surely I am in another century? I finally climb and crawl my way up the draw, through a spinney. I am looking for Karl's back but instead come face to face with two ruddy-cheeked golfers who are hunting in the brush for a ball. Below me to the south sprawls the historic market town of Sherborne. I was oblivious to the approach of urbanity; the golfers in turn are oblivious to the scene of the shepherd and his flock just below in the valley to the north. Parallel universes.

The sunken roads, enclosed gardens, and high hedgerows give England a three-dimensional look. It is unreal how a country smaller than Oregon appears so gargantuan when sliced up into so many little compartments. Indeed, landscape gardeners have long employed the tactic of creating mini-arboretums, nooks, and bowers so as to enhance the perception of size. Another clever device is the insertion of a "ha-ha" — a low hedge or fence unseen from the home — which gives the illusion of one's property extending to vast fields beyond. Add to this the English propensity to build mazes, and you have a fascinating rural landscape.

Karl is waiting for me in front of the clubhouse. Just beyond this point we enter narrow lanes with recently clipped hedgerows. From time to time on this section of the route from Cadbury into Dorset we encounter hedgerow trimmers, who are pruning the vines, yews, and hawthorn to promote denser growth. The laying of a new hedge must be done in late fall or winter. Branches are intertwined, and it is considered an ancient art to do it properly. The most popular trees for hedge-laying are hawthorn, blackthorn, and hazel. A top binding must be laid to keep it all together, and for this layer willow and hazel are favoured.

In Slavonic languages, *zhivy plod* means "living fence," that is, a hedge. The word *hedge* comes from the Old English *hecke,* or "enclosure." Indeed, the Enclosure movement resulted in thousands of miles of hedges being constructed in order to fence in animals and eliminate the common areas previously available to the peasantry. William Wordsworth lovingly referred to thick hedgerows as "little lines / Of sportive wood run wild." George Eliot viewed the hedge as indissolubly tied to the personality of the countryside. In *The Mill on the Floss* she wrote, "We could never have loved the earth as well if we had had no childhood in it . . . These familiar flowers, these well-remembered bird-notes, this sky with its fitful brightness, these furrowed and grassy fields, each with a sort of personality given to it by the capricious hedgerows — such things as these are the mother tongue of our imagination."

As woodland areas decreased, the hedgerows became increasingly vital to sustain insects, birds, and small animals. The hawthorn, for example, attracts a variety of insects, including beetles and caterpillars, which most songbirds rely on in turn as a food supply. Hawthorn leaves were used for centuries by the peasantry for tea, and the flowers, like the elderberry, were used for making wine. Elderberry leaves are still used by some folk for lotions and ointments.

Hedges help with erosion and block wind far more efficiently than walls or fences. It is estimated that in southern England, as many as one fifth of all surviving hedgerows date from Saxon times. The hedgerow is, like the church and the castle ruins, an ancient yet living monument of the past. Together, hedgerows and cottage gardens represent England's greatest green resource.

The movement toward corporate-style agriculture began at the end of the nineteenth century and continued until very recently. The enormous enlargement of fields has led to a huge loss of hedgerows. There remain some 236,000 miles of hedges in England and Wales — a huge extent, but still less than half the total in 1945. Now hedgerows are being planted throughout the land to replenish green corridors. The 500,000 acres of hedges estimated to be extant in Britain in 1968 represent twice the area of all the country's nature reserves.

On the outskirts of Sherborne we tool around a corner and come to a halt beside what I can only describe as "trailer-park gardens" — all these ticky-tacky aluminum trailers sitting in a row, nestled into a wooded hill, surrounded by a flowing landscape of Japanese maples, honeysuckle, peonies, St. John's wort, irises, wild roses, poppies, cornflowers, sunflowers, lavender, and yellow celandines which so overwhelms the humble appearance of the abodes that for a moment I want to live in this paradise. What a rich panoply of colour and scents! Bees are humming, butterflies flitting. I see a small, bent-over, grizzled figure clad in a plaid shirt tending with love a little herb garden he has planted to the side of his trailer. A calico cat sits calmly beside him.

"More garden than I saw in half of northern France," Karl says with a smile. "Of course, the Dutch wouldn't allow such random growth. Have you ever seen their rows of tulips?"

"Yes, and I find them far too regimented, though you probably love the neatness."

"How far away did you say our next drink was?"

"Not far — the George Inn of Sherborne coming right up."

"Why are there so many George Inns in this country?"

"That would have something to do with there having been six English kings named George."

"Better get the move on, John — there's dirty weather approaching again."

But I still stand transfixed gazing at the trailer-park gardens. For I realize that across the road is another feature of this unique spot: the huge abandoned rock quarry that at one time supplied much of the stone for Sherborne's buildings. The trailer park, I now see, was also part of the former quarry, and this otherwise ugly bowl, surrounded on both sides by towering rock scarps, has been reclaimed as a park — with paths, benches, and flowering trees. Instead of becoming a rundown, grungy trailer park, it has been transformed into an environment of living beauty and joy. It reminds me of a mini version of Butchart Gardens, near Victoria in British Columbia, one of the most popular attractions of western Canada, which is an arboretum established out of the hollows and detritus of a vast gravel pit.

The love of the English for gardening is well known, but how far back in time villagers enjoyed gardens is *not* known. The landed gentry have always boasted arboretums, orangeries, and well-manicured landscapes. After common fields were eliminated by Enclosure, villagers lobbied for yards and gardens of their own, abutting their cottages. Victorian legislators eventually agreed, believing that gardening would keep men away from the pubs. An eighth of an acre was considered adequate, enabling the villager to keep some chickens and a pig, plus grow potatoes and other vegetables and herbs used as medicines. If room could not be found in the village, then allotments were created in a spare field — and indeed there is a revival of allotments today, as we have seen en route.

A side effect of the Enclosure Acts, therefore, was the eventual sprouting of gardens everywhere, many of them walled. The cottagers, in a way, were mimicking the landed gentry, whose vast gardens had evolved into status symbols. A walled cottage garden became the Englishman's place of quietude, no matter how humble his dwelling. The first such gardens were purely utilitarian, catering to cultivation of veggies, herbs, and fruits.

Flora Thompson has written of the herb patch in the cottage garden, "stocked with thyme and parsley and sage for cooking, rosemary to flavour the homemade lard, lavender to scent the best clothes, and peppermint, camomile, tansy, balm and rue for physic." The rural English love their herbs and readily identify with the lyrics of the ballad "Scarborough Fair," a song memorably covered by Simon & Garfunkel but which derives from the medieval period.

The idea of flower beds originated with monasteries. William of Orange later brought to the throne of England a passion for flowers. This added impetus to the idea of an "aesthetical garden," especially when he imported bulbs from Holland and thereby created a trend. The garden also became a palliative for the annihilation of the ancient forests. Edward Thomas noted that the English sought to recreate their ideal country of the past in their gardens "as in a graven image." The Green Man, that Celtic guardian of the woods and its mysteries, has been replaced, notes A.A. Gill, by the fictional Puck: "hobbit of the garden; the sprite of the window box and the hanging basket."

The 1911 children's novel by Frances Hodgson Burnett, *The Secret Garden*, centres upon the magical, therapeutic qualities of the walled garden attached to the home of Colin, a little lame boy who secretly spends part of every day there, getting stronger and stronger until eventually he gets up from his wheelchair and walks — to the utter astonishment of his overbearing father, who has written him off as a cripple. The hallmark English imagery of hidden doors leading to magical places is present when Mary finds a key that turns the lock of a door, and suddenly finds herself standing inside Colin's secret Eden. This imagery is key to understanding the secret world of the countryside in English literature. The wardrobe closet of C.S. Lewis in *The Chronicles of Narnia* is another portal to that idyllic "other world." In *The Lord of the Rings*, Tolkien also refers to the journey of adventure along the road "out from the door where it began."

The last half mile, plunging down rain-soaked lanes with cars streaming past our eyeballs, is unpleasant, as the rain is driving at us now in droplets the size of paintball pellets. Fortunately, the George Inn lies on the upper outskirts of town. We stamp our wet boots and enter to a hubbub of men standing and mingling at the bar. One chatty bloke greets us cheerily.

"Rather dickie out, yes?"

"Indeed," I respond. I try to slither a tad closer to the huge fireplace that's roaring and crackling its flaming warmth like an angry lion. We find a table next to eight English bankers on a walking trip. They explain that they like to go from pub to pub quaffing the local brew; all are in their twenties or thirties. Each year they walk a different part of England, at about eight or nine miles a day. We chat it up and they become a little subdued upon learning that seventy-four-year-old Karl has just walked over three hundred miles.

I replenish Karl's Guinness with a half pint and order another lager. The talk at the bar turns to the hot topic of the day — the great Gold Hill brothel scandal. Sherborne has a virtual twin in Shaftesbury, which lies a few miles to the east; both are ancient market towns that sit perched on hills bordering Thomas Hardy's Blackmore Vale. Gold Hill is a steep lane leading down from the edge of Shaftesbury to the Vale, adorned by picturesque, multi-hued cottages. It is a favourite photo stop for tourists, a scene rendered familiar to Brits by the now classic TV commercial for Hovis bread that features a delivery boy pushing a bike with a basketful of baked goods up the cobbled street.

But alas, it seems that Gold Hill these days is appealing to more than just tourists snapping their photos. The press reports that a retired army major set up his wife as a hooker on the internet. Police became interested in a website that offered the "cultured, gentle and sensuous services of Jilly, a woman who loves to be borrowed and shared." When police burst into the major's picturesque cottage on Gold Hill to arrest Jilly and her hubby, their timing could not have been better, for she was halfway through a rather sensual massage. As the Hooker on the Hill, Jilly may be a joke right now, but in this quiet, conservative corner of rural England, the community is not so forgiving. The press report quotes local resident Janet Bardy, sipping coffee at the Café Rose, her shaggy dog Max at her feet, asking, "What did she do for 500 pounds a night?"

Karl shakes his head in amusement at all this.

"So maybe, John boy, our Liberty House experience was no isolated phenomenon. Besides, wasn't that Thomas Hardy a bit of a horny bastard?"

"It's all about being discreet, Karl. Marnie up in Bradford flies under the radar. This part of Dorset is a conservative, stricter part of rural England — you just can't sell yourself blatantly as some online English Rosie, sensuous and wicked, because here you stick out like a sore thumb. Besides, town officials no doubt think it's bad for tourism. Thomas Hardy country is supposed to be quaint, not racy."

That said, British society has moved toward the European model of a liberal approach toward sex and morality, closer to the libertarian approach of the eighteenth century than to Victorian prudishness. When someone handed me a mainstream British newspaper the first time I travelled here, I thought I had been given pornography, but it was just *The Sun* with its topless Page 3 girls. And I have hastily skipped through breast-filled sections of other English papers in embarrassed, furtive fashion at coffeehouses — only to glance over my shoulder to see a wispy, white-haired old dear in a lavender and cream jacquard dress sipping tea, unabashedly enjoying both the stories and the skin show.

We rise to leave, our backpacks now reasonably dry. It is hard to disengage from this noisy yet convivial chatter and the warmth of the fire to face the fierce rain outside. Before we reach the door, a man and woman, both in full riding costume, sweep through the entrance with a retinue of wet equestrian types behind them, much like royalty. This must be the local squire and his wife, because the publican and his assistant both rush out from the bar to bob, bow, and curtsey.

Sherborne is a mad jumble of narrow, twisting streets. Cheap Street careens downhill and is lined with lichen-dappled, ochre stone shops full of Dorset knobs, fresh-baked scones, creamy blue vinney cheeses, sticky honeys, and succulent hams. The shops cater to all wallets, from a Diva accessory store associated with Castro clothing to an Oxfam bookstore full of earthy intellectuals. I count eleven coffeehouses, including Caffe Baglioni, Kafe Fontana, and Costa Coffee. One guidebook advises that "if the town were a woman she would be a popular socialite who relished the envy she generates in everyone else. She has an impressive aristocratic pedigree spanning hundreds of years, and exudes a refined sense of style."

The town attained affluence from the wool industry, later becoming a manufacturing hub for lace, gloves, and buttons. Famous residents have included Sir Walter Raleigh, John Le Carré, Cecil Day-Lewis, Alan Turing, and Sophie Kinsella. Hardy often frequented the town, and he references Sherborne Abbey and the town's marketplace in his novel *The Woodlanders*.

Dominating the town is Sherborne Abbey, which has been a Saxon cathedral, a Benedictine abbey, and a parish church throughout its chequered history. Henry VIII would have demolished it at the Dissolution if the townspeople hadn't clamoured to make it their parish church. I note the expansive Perpendicular Gothic windows, ornate pinnacles above the gargoyles, and decorated flying buttresses. The abbey's bells hold the distinction of possessing the heaviest peal of eight bells in the world.

Light penetrates the abbey interior through enormous clerestories, illuminating the decorous vaulted ceilings. Crested heraldic symbols and painted flowers line the walls, and stained glass windows everywhere overwhelm the senses — a fabulous display that must be credited to those busy beavers, the Victorians. Both Henry VIII and Cromwell's Puritans viewed colour as being idolatrous, and their minions destroyed a large percentage of the stained glass windows in England. But the Victorians believed in restoration, and built and fitted some eighty thousand stained glass windows into churches across the land during the nineteenth century.

Two of King Alfred's brothers, both of whom became kings — Æthelbald and Æthelbert — are buried in the abbey. Sir Walter and Lady Raleigh attended services in the Leweston Chapel when Raleigh was not abroad or imprisoned in the Tower of London. Lady Raleigh introduced to Sherborne Castle, the Raleigh home, a flower known as clove pink, which still grows on the castle grounds and is known as Lady Betty's Pink. Clove pink flowers are still cut on special occasions and placed in Leweston Chapel as a reminder of the good old days of the First Elizabethan Age when chivalry abounded, adventure lurked, and poetry ruled.

Sherborne's Pack Monday Fair is an important civic event that dates to medieval times. It is held in October and is preceded on the weekend by much festivity. Traditionally, the fair opened at midnight on Sunday with a noisy parade through town making "rough music." People in Sherborne complained in Henry VIII's era that labourers used their "riotous expenses and unlawful games to the great trouble and inquieting of the inhabitants next thereto adjoining." In 1962 and 1963, hooliganism added to the noise problem, and in 1964 the chief constable of Dorset turned up with a hundred police officers and suppressed the traditional procession.

The nature of such fairs had begun to change in the second half of the nineteenth century, when the focus shifted from food and animal displays to entertainment spectacles. In Thomas Hardy's *The Mayor of Casterbridge*, the pens where horses and sheep had formerly been exhibited had disappeared; yet dense crowds poured over the fairgrounds, including "journeymen out for a holiday, a stray soldier or two home on furlough, village shopkeepers . . . among the peep-shows, toy stands, waxworks, inspired monsters, thimble-riggers, nick-nack vendors, and readers of Fate." The fair is still held — minus the midnight procession.

A highlight of any visit here is Sherborne Castle. The old castle was built in the twelfth century by the Bishop of Salisbury. Queen Elizabeth granted it by lease to Sir Walter Raleigh in 1592. Raleigh loved it with a passion, calling the entire town of Sherborne "fortune's fold." He updated the castle and also converted the nearby hunting lodge into a turreted manor house now known as the New Castle.

Raleigh was a swashbuckling adventurer, sea captain, soldier, explorer, and courtier. He stood six feet tall, with a full beard, dark black hair, and a sword always at the ready. Queen Elizabeth found him dashing and gallant with his quick wit and demeanour, and flirted, teased, and toyed with him for over ten years. Raleigh in turn was fascinated with Elizabeth. Using a ring she gave him, he once etched in a window pane at court the words "Fain would I climb, yet fear I to fall." The queen noticed this and famously responded, to complete the couplet, "If thy heart fails thee, climb not at all." Raleigh publicly referred to the queen as a "chaste moon goddess."

Raleigh was given the right to colonize North America on behalf of the Crown and attempted two settlements on Roanoke Island, naming the newfound territory "Virginia" in honour of his queen. His daring exploits complemented his colonization attempts, including a bold raid on Cádiz, Spain, where he was wounded. He competed with Sir Francis Drake for being the most gallant figure of the Elizabethan era, but Drake was more single-minded and successful in his endeavours, concentrating on plunder, adventure, and exploration. Raleigh got involved in everything — politics, plunder, colonization, tobacco cultivation, poetry, and social climbing. In modern parlance, he "overextended himself."

In 1596, Raleigh composed his poem "The Nymph's Reply to the Shepherd," in playful response to Christopher Marlowe's "The Passionate Shepherd to His Love." The first stanza is well known to high school students:

If all the world and love were young,
And truth on every shepherd's tongue,
These pretty pleasures might me move
To live with thee and be thy love.

Alas, Raleigh may have worshipped Queen Elizabeth as a "chaste moon goddess," but he compromised himself by secretly marrying one of his queen's maids of honour, Bess Throckmorton, with whom he fathered a child — not necessarily in that order. Elizabeth was furious when she discovered the secret marriage, and threw both Raleigh and Bess into the Tower of London. She relented after a few months and allowed the couple to return to Sherborne Castle, but upon her death, Raleigh was again imprisoned in the Tower, this time by King James I, who believed Raleigh had been involved in a plot to depose him. Here the gallant knight languished for thirteen years. Finally, in 1616, the king offered Raleigh a chance to redeem himself by sailing to search for his famous El Dorado in South America. But the aged adventurer failed to find any gold for the royal coffers, and in the process offended the king by plundering a Spanish outpost, riling up Spain when the king could ill afford another war. To both appease the Spanish and remove a thorn in his side, the king had Raleigh beheaded in 1618.

ON THE GROUNDS OVERLOOKING a tranquil lake, I sit on Raleigh's Seat, a stone bench where the old courtier used to smoke his pipe with his newly minted Virginia tobacco, contemplating the peaceful setting. It was while he was sitting on this very seat one day that a passing servant unfamiliar with pipe smoke threw the entire contents of his water pitcher over Sir Walter's head, thinking his master's beard was on fire. Raleigh took his dousing with good humour. In the castle museum, one can view a pipe he was given by a Virginia tribe. The ghost of Raleigh has often been seen walking about the grounds, dressed in Elizabethan court attire. The ghost strolls about through the trees until reaching this seat, whereupon he mournfully stares across his grounds. He is seen most frequently around the anniversary of his death, on September 29 of each year.

Karl is anxious to move on, and so we leave Raleigh's ghost behind at his favourite bench and turn southward. The rain has ceased. Birdsong bursts forth as we dance down the pavement of Sherborne's Half Moon Street by the railway station.

Then it's over the busy A352 and through muddy fields, with a kissing gate and a group of ponies to greet us on the other side. The sun is peeking through an oyster-shell sky as we enter Honeycombe Wood. Bulbarrow Hill is seen on the distant skyline, some eleven miles to the southeast. Crossing a ditch, Karl slips on the narrow plank and retwists the same ankle that is already sprained. Too late do I read the *Guide*'s caution that "between two stiles is a deep ditch bridged by single sleeper, which may sometimes be concealed by dense undergrowth."

We arrive at our farmhouse B&B in Lillington. No one answers the front door, but I hear sounds of life inside. I try entering a gate to the garden back of the house — big mistake. No fewer than six Jack Russell terriers come tearing around a corner and rush me, barking furiously. I manage to back off and close the gate just in time. Then a heavily made-up, frumpy, middle-aged lady opens the front door and demands to know who we are and why have we upset her dogs. Not a good start to a B&B relationship.

I manage to convince her that despite our seedy appearances, we are not vagrants but in fact the Macmillan Way walkers who have booked her home for the night. My accent convinces her. She ushers us into the house and points to our room . . . which measures about eight by ten feet and contains two short single beds and about fifteen dolls. That's right, dolls — in the corners, on the dressing table, in windowsills, even in the ensuite, lining the tub. Myriad dolls, of all sizes, shapes, and genders. And that's just for starters. The rest of the house is crammed full of dolls as well, some of them so realistic that it feels like their eyes are following us and it's hard to distinguish between dolls and living folk. I experience a creepy feeling like in a Hitchcock movie, where you just know that one of these dolls is either going to attack you or keel over dead. There are bodies here, for sure.

We are offered tea in the garden by the Doll House Lady. Her husband, Roger, is already sitting at tea outside on a lounge. The Jack Russells are nowhere in sight. Roger is sixty-ish, unshaven, and completely obsessed with birds.

"Do you hear that wren?" he asks me in a gentle, melliflu-ous voice.

"No," I replied. "Er, at least I didn't recognize it as such."

"Walking all those miles, you two gentlemen must have seen and heard so many birds!"

"Well, yes."

"Have you heard a nightingale yet?"

"I don't think so."

"And you won't, there's nary a one left in these parts. Rooks, robins, and finches, with a few wrens — seems that's about all we get in Dorset now; and as it is, I have to keep the damned cat from going after them. I have a good mind to declaw the little killer."

I catch a fleeting glimpse of a black feline in the grass. So does Roger, and he calls out to his cat: "Bert, Bert, come here now and stop stalking that wren. It's time for bed."

"Roger," I say, "you have quite the farm here. Have you ever dug up any artifacts from the past?"

"Artifacts?"

"Why, yes. I've read that human habitation in this part of Dorset goes back to the Romans, and of course there was Neolithic Man and the Celts. I would love to have a metal detector here."

"Good God, man, are you insane?" he says. "Why would I disturb the good earth for such relics?"

I leave it there and ask when the pub opens.

"The pub? Don't rightly know. Don't even know if there is one."

With that, Roger sighs and heaves his bulk out of the lawn chair, calling for Bert. "I'd best take him inside, as he's about to cause a ruckus with that wren."

Alas, Roger is right: there is no pub in Lillington. So Karl and I take a taxi back to Sherborne to dine at the George, enjoy fish pie washed down with a Yellow Tail Chardonnay, and return via the same cab to the Doll House for an early turn-in. I also buy a paper to catch up on current events.

The Telegraph reports this week that the 80,000-strong Royal Society for the Prevention of Cruelty to Animals is trying to force the Queen to step down as patron of the charity because of her support for hunting. The militant members also want to drop the "Royal" from the charity's name. A leading RSPCA member, David Mawson, a vegan chef from Catford in southeast London, says that Her Majesty should be removed because "she battered a pheasant to death recently." Several militant candidates for the RSPCA board belong to the League Against Cruel Sports, Compassion in World Farming, the British Union for the Abolition of Vivisection, and People for the Ethical Treatment of Animals. All vehemently oppose fox hunting, though one is left to speculate on whether they would allow a farmer to defend his chickens from the depredations of a fox by shooting one *in flagrante delicto*.

The press also reports of the controversial hearings at Sherborne, where Madonna is battling with the Countryside Agency against the opening of her 1,130-acre Wiltshire estate to walkers under the new "right to roam" legislation. The singer has referred to Ramblers fighting the case against her as "Satan's Children." She and her film director husband, Guy Ritchie, run a commercial sporting business on the estate, based on bird hunting. Madonna claims that her privacy would be compromised and that there is a question of safety for walkers with all the shooting that goes on.

Next morning we make an early exit from the Doll House and visit the village church and graveyard. Many of the grave inscriptions reflect the piety of parishioners who fervently believed in the raising of the dead at the Second Coming, particularly stones from the seventeenth century, when Puritanism was flourishing. One of the funniest tombstone inscriptions I've ever read in England was found in a church-yard in Bury St. Edmunds: "Here lies Jonathan Yeast — pardon him for not rising."

We tramp along country lanes and bridleways on this fine misty morning, with nary a care in the world, though I am still worried about Karl's ankle, which is slowing him down to a pace that keeps him only slightly ahead of me on the trail. Three miles out of Lillington we pass a recycling site and emerge into Brierley Hay, a hamlet on the outskirts of Yetminster. It resembles Forest Lawn on a slow day.

Yetminster is a large village of a thousand people on the River Wriggle. Many of the buildings are seventeenth cen-tury, the houses built of honey-coloured limestone standing in neat rows. Yetminster Fair is one of the oldest in Dorset, dating from the thirteenth century. It is held in July and often culminates in a performance by the Yetties, a famous five-piece folk group from the village that has performed throughout the world since 1961. They have recorded forty-five albums, including two songs using Thomas Hardy's own fiddle and other Hardy family instruments. The genre they perform is described as "Scrumpy and Western," though they have remained true to their Dorset roots by performing many old English ballads.

A unique feature of Yetminster is the eccentricity of the church bells. Six times a day these chime out the hour and then play the national anthem. It really is rather quaint. A painted sign at the church entrance cautions, "The swallows are nesting above. Please keep the inner door closed so they won't get trapped in the church. Thank you."

We are in real Thomas Hardy country now. We observe many dog roses in the hedgerows. The dog rose is the national flower, made famous during the Wars of the Roses, when the rose was chosen by Henry Tudor as a symbol of unity. It is one of over a hundred species of wild rose found in Britain, and grows up to ten feet as a bush. The fruits, or "hips," of wild roses are so rich in vitamin C that the government collected 2.5 million bottles of rose-hip syrup during World War II to bolster the health of Britons, the equivalent in vitamin content of 25 million oranges.

The mist continues to envelop us and gives a mysterious gothic feel to the landscape. The Way now winds toward Melbury Park. The *Guide* enjoins us to follow the path to the edge of Chetnole Withy Bed (no, it's not someone's bed — it's a wood, a copse) and warns that if you don't head across a field directly to the single oak standing beside the wood, you will lose your way. We spot the oak and enter Melbury Park. A large herd of deer graze near the path, unconcerned by our intrusion. The current owner of the park and nearby Melbury House is Lady Theresa Fox-Strangways. She also happens to be High Sheriff of Dorset and Master of the Cattistock Hunt.

"I wouldn't want to be caught poaching one of her deer," remarks Karl. "She sounds formidable."

Such is the fame and influence of the ancient Melbury family that a fictional Lord Melbury stars in the 1975 pilot episode of the popular series *Fawlty Towers*. In it, John Cleese's

Basil Fawlty fawns over the sophisticated Lord Melbury and scorns his other guests in the dining room. He accidentally knocks the lord off his chair onto the floor while browbeating a family to move from their table to allow Melbury to sit there. Basil is at his sycophantic best in imploring the lord to allow him to make it up to him after the unfortunate incident. Melbury obliges by asking Basil if he would cash a small cheque for a hundred pounds. Basil asks obsequiously if that is sufficient, and is aghast when the lord ups the amount to two hundred. Basil honours the cheque, which of course bounces, as the man is actually a fraud artist.

Melbury Osmond is a photographer's dream, full of thatched cottages and charm. It is also the cherished home of Thomas Hardy's mother, Jemima. The village appears as Little Hintock in *The Woodlanders*. Jemima was a former maidservant and cook, but she loved reading and encouraged her son to read the classics in Latin. Her childhood cottage sits next to the church. Inside the church we find displayed a framed copy of her marriage certificate, presumably intended to silence wagging tongues as to Hardy's legitimacy.

Geologically, this village is interesting in that it possesses a mixture of limestone and clay that produces a special polish known as "Melbury marble." Melbury Osmond was historically important for the manufacture of plated buckles, horn buttons, and dowels. Button making was once Dorset's number-one cottage industry. Hundreds of craftsmen engaged in "doing buttony." This trade was dealt a severe blow in 1851 when a Danish button machine was displayed at the Great Exhibition in London. Machine production soon replaced handicraft work, leading to great poverty and distress throughout Blackmore Vale. Attempts to revive the trade have been partially successful, with production of a specialized button known as the Cartwheel. But the old models, such as High Tops, Birds' Eyes, Mites, and Honeycombs, have all vanished.

There is a long-standing folk tradition in Melbury involving Satan. A grotesque apparition known as the Dorset Ooser still appears at cottage doors every Christmas. Its head is carved from wood, with staring eyes, matted hair, a wide maw of a mouth with yellow teeth, and a huge pair of bull's horns. It is carried on a short pole by a man who hides his head under a long cloak. "Ooser" is apparently a corruption of "Worst One" — meaning the Devil. Thomas Hardy recorded the lyrics of folk songs about the Dorset Ooser sung by pranksters who accompany the figure door to door.

Every village and town in Dorset has memories of the occupation during World War II by Allied troops, especially hordes of Americans. Dorset was particularly important to preparations for Operation Overlord, the code name for the invasion of Normandy, as the practice exercises for landing craft and scaling cliffs were conducted along the coast here. The American troops tended to swagger, wowing the children in particular. Diana Mitchell grew up in Melbury and remembers: "When the war times came we had Americans in Melbury Park and I used to swing on my front gate waiting for the Yanks to throw sweets to me. I was too young for the nylons. On Sundays we would go to watch them playing basketball in the park."

We wade through a raging stream inundating the paved roadway at a ford. Melbury Park stretches for about three more miles south of Melbury Osmond, and we eventually emerge onto a minor road by a triangular green at the entry to Evershot, the second-highest village in Dorset, at 700 feet above sea level. The mist clears and we are bathed in warm sunshine.

I hear the sprightly tones of fiddles, and we shortly encounter a bustle of activity along the main street. Evershot is holding a spring fair. Stalls line the road, full of books, clothes, and crafts. A wide variety of local produce is on sale, from homemade jellies to walking sticks, rugs, and assorted baked goods. A talented carpenter has carved some unusual miniature tables that look like they must cater to Hobbits, with angled maple poles supporting flat tops that are finely crafted with dowels.

For the first time on our journey we observe people in shorts, which is not typical English attire. The onset of warmer weather this week has moved *The Telegraph* to comment on the poor taste Englishmen display in dressing for the sun: "One of the benefits of colder weather is that it encourages men to cover up — thus disguising their anatomical imperfections. However, the summer seems to take them by surprise and without preparing the rest of us . . . Otherwise normal and ostensibly respectable people take to the streets in states of near undress. They can be seen in wardrobes seemingly scavenged from long-neglected cupboards and corners of the attic: shapeless shorts, elderly polo shirts stretched over paunches, or untucked business shirts worn like peasant smocks, their stocky, pasty legs ending in shabby deck shoes or sandals from which poke calloused toes." Well, men's exposed legs did not seem particularly grotesque in Evershot, though I will admit to detecting a certain chalky, pasty whiteness that confirms these particular blokes did not holiday in Spain last winter.

We enjoy the street music and linger to take pleasure in the dancers, then pop over to ogle the antique cars at the Acorn Inn. They are interesting, but not half so much as the inn itself. Thomas Hardy used Evershot as his key setting in *Tess of the D'Urbervilles*. He called the village Evershead, and the

Acorn Inn became the Sow and Acorn. Tess stops for tea in the village on her way to Emminster, the fictional representation of Beaminster, making "a halt . . . and breakfasted . . . not at the Sow and Acorn, for she avoided inns, but at a cottage by the church."

The River Frome has its source in springs located beside the village church, proudly marked by villagers as St. John's Well. This little river is only thirty miles long but is the major chalk stream in southwest England. Formerly a favourite fishing haunt, the river's salmon runs have declined from 4,000 fish in 1988 to only 750 in the year of our walk. The decline of Atlantic salmon is a serious problem on both sides of the pond.

In Evershot, as elsewhere along our journey, the footpaths tend to converge at the church because people came from so many directions on a Sunday to attend services — which were compulsory until the modern era. Flora Thompson writes of this in *Lark Rise to Candleford:* "Ding-dong, ding-dong, went the bells of the village church in Lark Rise, and when they heard them, the hamlet churchgoers hurried across fields and over stiles, for the Parish Clerk was always threatening to lock the church door when the bells stopped."

It is hard for us today to understand how pervasive the church was in the life of the common folk in centuries past. On one hand was the lord, succeeded later by the more benign squire; to the former one paid tribute in the form of labour or tax, while to the latter one gave deference. The church represented the other half of the equation, demanding its tithes — and enforcing morality by means of the ecclesiastical court, commonly known as the "Bawdy Court." Although the church's power to impose penalties was legally questionable, few ever challenged its authority since most penalties were in the nature of humiliation of the miscreant, who was publicly called to account. Church offences ranged from poor service attendance, failing to pay tithes, and swearing in church to more serious moral offences such as prostitution, fornication, and fathering a child out of wedlock. The line between the jurisdiction of the civil and religious courts was frequently blurry until statute law clarified matters in the nineteenth century.

The interior of Anglican churches underwent a change in appearance during Thomas Hardy's lifetime. Box pews disappeared and were replaced by rows of bench pews, facing an altar with a decorative cloth rather than a plain table covered with linen. Tiles replaced stone flags underfoot, which made the interior more colourful. But perhaps the two biggest changes to church interiors were the replacement of plain with stained glass windows and the introduction of the organ.

Village orchestras usually comprised performers who, as described in Thomas Hardy's "A Few Crusted Characters," could play a jig better than a hymn and frequently became drunk during church service. It was embarrassing to the vicar when the orchestra broke out into a dance tune. The organ lent a new air of respectability to proceedings.

Yet it was too late to rescue Anglicanism from its lackadaisical, class-driven ways. The proliferation of Baptist and Methodist chapels throughout the country attested to the increasing democratization of society. The squire, his family, tenant farmers, and some of the very poor still patronized the parish church, but the dissenting parson attracted other tenants, shopkeepers, tradesmen, and independent labourers. The parson was typically less educated or wealthy than his Anglican counterpart, but the villagers tended to think of him as "one of us." Of course, an ever-increasing segment of the population failed to attend church at all.

Evershot reeks of Hardy's influence. In 1893, Hardy was still practising his hand as an architect, designing a wing of the village mansion known as Dower House that year. This was the last project he took on before turning to writing full-time. One imagines him traipsing through Dorset to gain inspiration. He was a keen observer of the countryside. "Every village," he wrote, "has its idiosyncrasy, its constitution."

Hardy's famous home lies some ten miles from Evershot in Upper Bockhampton. The Hardy Cottage is visited by thousands of tourists each year. It still holds its charm, boasting an expansive front garden brimming with flowers. The structure is of cob and thatch construction. A clump of walking sticks hewn from local limbs sits in the entrance hall, as if waiting for the master's touch.

Opinion is still divided on Hardy's significance in English literature. There is no doubting his descriptive powers, yet his constant themes of romantic but unrequited love, the tragic endings to his characters' liaisons, and his vivid drawing of assertive female personalities have caused many literary commentators to assert that he was a misogynist, while others maintain he was ahead of his time and was advancing the cause of women's rights.

Hardy more than any other nineteenth-century novelist reflected the influence of landscape and setting in the human condition — that sense of place. He was passionate about Dorset, using features of many towns and villages of the shire in his novels. The tithe barn in Cerne Abbas is the model for the great barn in *Far from the Madding Crowd,* the novel in which Troy spends the night on the parish church porch in Puddletown — the real name of which used to be Piddletown, but this offended Victorian sensibilities, so was legally changed; think "spotted dick."

Hardy was raised as a boy in Puddletown. Perhaps the rough-and-tumble ways of fellow villagers affected his attitude toward religion and society in later years. An old ditty from his town was sung by residents during his era:

Into church
Out of Church,
Into Cat,
Out of Cat,
Into Piddle.

The "Cat" was the Old Catt Inn, and the Piddle was the river into which the slops from that inn were delivered. Hardy understood the hypocrisy of his fellow Victorians who paid the utmost attention to the proprieties of outward appearances — such as attending church — before they decamped to the local inn.

Thomas Hardy represents the pastoral life with deft realism, much like other prominent English authors, such as Jane Austen, the Brontës, and George Eliot. Even if one cannot live the country life, there is always the imagination. And this is where *Winnie the Pooh, The Wind in the Willows, Peter Rabbit, Watership Down, The Chronicles of Narnia, Alice in Wonderland,* King Arthur, and Robin Hood continue to capture the collective English consciousness. Nostalgia rules. The most endearing parts of *The Lord of the Rings* on the screen for English viewers are the scenes of the Shire.

The philosopher Roger Scruton maintains that the English still search for their lost childhood, which always lies in the enchanted countryside. The Englishman never truly grows up. He plasters his walls with hunting and fishing scenes. He wants to play horsey with his children; to imagine that he can walk at any time into a labyrinthine Arcadia of rabbit holes and streams, downs and wolds, perhaps shoot a couple of colourful pheasants, and visit a quaint pub that has sat in unspoiled countryside for five hundred years, where he can quaff the local ciders and ales. Walking along the Macmillan Way, one can almost believe that this rural idyll is the true reality and the M1 is just an aberration.

12

THE DORSET GIANT, MAIDEN NEWTON, *and* CHESIL BEACH

The Road goes ever on and on

Out from the door where it began.

Now far ahead the Road has gone,

Let others follow it who can!

Let them a journey new begin,

But I at last with weary feet

Will turn towards the lighted inn,

My evening-rest and sleep to meet.

— J.R.R. TOLKIEN —
The Lord of the Rings

THE WEATHER CONTINUES balmy. Lazy herringbone cirrus formations gild a diaphanous sky. The path winds downhill from our lofty Evershot perch atop of Dorset as we head steadily southward toward the Channel. We encounter an electric fence running through a stile; the cover has torn, exposing the bare wire. Karl nimbly pops over the stile — sprained ankle and all — while I wrestle with my pack and finally jump over, landing heavily on my side. I have always had a fear of electric shocks. Just ahead, we enter a wet spinney.

We emerge from the spinney into the remote hamlet of Chantmarle. The word is Norman French for "blackbird's song." The one impressive set of buildings is Chantmarle Manor, an imposing stone edifice which housed the Dorset Police Training College from 1951 until 1995. Local lore has it that for many years at the beginning of the eighteenth century, a ghost was heard in the Great Hall shouting out the words, "Search for Wat Perkins!" This occurred on the same night every year. Later, workmen digging in a ditch on the property discovered a headless skeleton. An investigation ensued, and a widow named Kit Whistle, who lived at a nearby cottage, confessed to murdering a Scottish peddler twenty-two years earlier. She had placed the man's head beneath her cottage hearthstone and buried the rest of the corpse in said ditch. After her arrest, the ghost was never heard from again.

Dorset is a treasure chest of superstitions, folklore, and wild tales. Western society has yet to come to grips with the extent to which magic and sorcery played a role in daily life even after countries such as England became officially Christian. For instance, every Dorset village had its own "conjurer," who, much like a shaman, was a fellow of good reputation thought to possess some limited supernatural power that he exercised for the common good. He was also reputed to be able to cure certain illnesses. Thomas Hardy refers to such a Wessex character in his story "The Withered Arm."

WE AMBLE DOWN green lanes to the rustle of hedge life and birdsong. The path eventually veers left through a silage area to enter the village of Cattistock.

I stop to peruse a village bulletin board, where a letter is posted from the lieutenant commander of a Royal Navy frigate, who promises to update villagers on NATO naval exercises. He plans to berth his vessel at Weymouth soon so that villagers have the opportunity of getting reacquainted with the ship. The ship's name is HMS *Cattistock*. We recall Pat up in Ford and Angela in Beckington, both of whose husbands served with the Royal Navy.

Like other villages in Dorset, Cattistock was at the heart of the World War II D-Day effort. The village also served as an important detention area for prisoners of war. First an Italian and then a German prisoner-of-war camp were established here, both providing agricultural labourers for local farms that were desperate for field workers. Over 150 Germans were billeted at the farms where they laboured.

Cattistock is home to yet another local tradition involving food and sporting competition, this one known as "knob throwing." The Dorset knob is a hard, dry savoury biscuit made only in the west of the county, at Bridport, baked three times over from bread dough containing extra sugar and butter. It is named after local knob buttons. Dorset knobs were a favourite delight of Thomas Hardy, who ate them for dessert with Stilton cheese. Locals claim it is Dorset's most famous export. *The Telegraph* describes the knob as "the most obscure edible object produced in Britain today."

The Knob Festival occurs on the first Sunday in May, and the main event involves competitors trying to throw a knob the farthest distance. The rules provide that the contestant must keep both feet on terra firma and throw the knob toward a marked area. The longest distance a knob has been thrown is 26.1 metres. Additional fun events include knob painting, a knob and spoon race, guessing the weight of the Big Knob, knob darts, and a knob pyramid.

We leave Cattistock to its knob-throwing delights. The Way now follows the River Frome. Mallards, teals, and white swans are all teeming on this stretch of the stream. Our path takes us through a large copse full of willow, beech, ash, hazel, and alder, from which we emerge to walk under an old railway arch, eventually stepping into a large field recently cut for barley.

Karl is dragging his doubly sprained ankle, but I still find it difficult to keep stride with him. He eagerly anticipates reaching our destination at Abbotsbury and dipping his ravaged feet into the English Channel. When I finally catch up with him around noon, I find to my surprise that he has snagged a couple of new walking companions: Marcia and Wynn, two Rambler ladies at least his age or older. Both women walk in shorts. Marcia is tall and gangly, with short white hair and calves of muscled knots resembling contoured road maps. Wynn is petite, well tanned, and toned; she carries the Ordnance Survey map in a plastic case dangling from her neck.

The three of them are wetting their whistles from water bottles beneath a clump of oak trees at the side of the path. Marcia explains that they walk British footpaths in Rambler outings and on their own, and together they have trekked all of the Pennine Way, much of the South West Coast Path, and the North Downs Way. They are currently planning a major walking trip in Luxembourg. When I refer to the footpaths as "trails," Wynn grimaces and chastises me, objecting that the word "trail" is an Americanism creeping into Britain; she insists that I call "a path a path." She turns to Karl and produces from her knapsack some ointment, which she proceeds to spread on his sprained ankle. She then wraps his foot in athletic tape. Finally, she applies a small brace.

"You absolutely must take care of this, Karl."

Karl just smiles wistfully and basks in the attention.

After a few more pleasantries, Marcia and Wynn wish us cheerio and lope off down the path. A couple of hours later we turn into a friendly inn for refreshment. I know these two ladies are in residence for the night because I recognize their freshly washed wet socks waving in the breeze, hanging from a second-floor window ledge, drying in the pallid sun.

"Energetic gals," smiles Karl.

"They certainly took a shine to you."

"They are Good Samaritans. Most walkers are decent sorts."

"Did you see Marcia's thigh muscles?"

"They're pros, John. They could keep pace even with our friend Colin from Derbyshire."

We are nearing Maiden Newton, where we have booked two nights' accommodation at the Chalk & Cheese pub.

Maiden Newton was dubbed "Chalk-Newton" by Hardy in *Tess of the D'Urbervilles,* and our inn is where Tess is harassed by some young blokes as she eats breakfast. To ward off any further unwelcome attention from these or any other aggressive males, she heads into a field, tears her dress, cuts off her eyebrows, and covers up her hair.

In the inn's dining room this evening we meet Bill, an eighty-two-year-old widower from Southampton who is staying at the Chalk & Cheese because this is where he and his wife came for many years to enjoy their annual vacations. She died very recently. He has his black Labrador dog with him, and both he and the dog are as gentle as lambs. Bill is blue-eyed and cheerful, despite having everything to be angry at the world about. His wife is gone and he is battling throat cancer. He tells us that since the doctors removed a significant portion of his larynx, his voice has been rather high-pitched and faint, and he apologizes if he sounds shrill. Bill says that he spent his working life in the mines of Yorkshire as an electrician and is just glad to be alive. When he learns that we are walking the Macmillan Way, he talks about the wild roses and holly blooming gloriously in the hedgerows.

"Wonderful, innit?" he says.

Later on in the night, through the thin wall that separates our rooms, I hear him rasping and sucking for air. Poor Bill.

Maiden Newton has been occupied for thousands of years. On Hogscliffe Hill, excavations have unearthed an Iron Age cluster of dwellings built over twenty-six acres. Above the railway embankment one can still see long lynchet rows characteristic of the strip farming used by the Celts and Saxons. Round shot from muskets was found in the Norman doorway of the church of St. Mary's, fired by Cromwell's men during the Civil War. Interesting paintings are etched onto the north wall inside. These include a man blowing a horn, a lady wearing a fourteenth-century head covering, a snarling dog, and a dog with a bone. So dogs already played an important part in English culture ten centuries ago — they even made it to the inner areas of churches.[6]

During World War II, Maiden Newton was of prime importance to the Allied cause. The village was on the main rail line from Bristol to Weymouth, and was also the junction of a line that ran to Bridport and West Bay, connecting troops from the interior with the naval exercises on the coast. In the weeks preceding D-Day, thousands of tanks, troops, and trucks streamed via these rail connections for loading onto the invasion ships.

Every two years, during a weekend in late June, "Maiden Newton at War" re-enacts wartime Britain on the eve of D-Day. Genuine military vehicles from the war, a few surviving

---

6 Regarding dogs in English culture: In 2014, a British company called Woof & Brew launched a range of herbal teas for canines. The tea costs up to $22 for twenty-two tea bags and is now sold at more than three hundred stores in the United Kingdom. Many cafés and tea shops carry the brew so that owners may offer tea to their pets at table while sipping their own tea or coffee beverages.

veterans, and enthusiastic volunteers combine to put on a realistic performance, the highlight of which is a pitched battle between assaulting Allied troops and German soldiers, with jeeps, tanks, half-tracks, and fighter aircraft all involved. Gunfire, smoke, and artillery explosions make this an unusual event for the quiet village. One wonders, of course, what passing German tourists think of it all.

Being so close to the famed Cerne Abbas Giant, Karl and I decide to walk the short four miles off trail to observe this artifact. The Giant is a 180-foot-high man carved on a steep hill in foot-wide chalky trenches. In one hand he holds a huge club, and his virility is in no doubt, given his forty-foot-long erect penis and scrotum. His outline served in past centuries as a warning to would-be invaders that Dorset people are not easily intimidated. He was widely believed to aid in fertility, and many couples desiring a child over the centuries have spent a night sleeping beside the Giant "to ensure a healthy birth." As recently as the late twentieth century, young women were known to leave their knickers with the Giant for good luck.

It is amazing that the Victorians didn't plough the Giant under, given their hyper-sensitive attitudes toward sex. So why did they let this chimerical monstrosity on the hillside survive intact? All I can think of is that they feared an insurrection by the locals if they dared to touch it. Indeed, why didn't Cromwell and his Puritans destroy it during the Civil War? Cromwell ruined enough churches, and regarded even market crosses as blasphemous. Victorian mothers were so embarrassed by the Giant that they told their children he was a "tailor with a large pair of scissors in his lap." During the 1930s, local schoolchildren recited a rhyme:

The giant he looks over us

A-doing of our work

He must be very chilly

'Cos he hasn't got a shirt!

John Steinbeck and his wife, Elaine, visited the Giant in the summer of 1959, and Elaine commented, "I think they put him there to scare the tar out of passing ladies."

On May 1 of each year, Wessex Morris dancers "bring in the May" at Cerne Abbas by performing fertility rites around the Giant, followed by festivities in the village itself. Bringing in the May is an ancient custom in England. In the twelfth century, the Bishop of Lincoln chastised his clergymen for participating with common folk heading into the forest, picking flowers and greenery, and decorating their homes to welcome in the season. Later clergymen railed that virgins were defiled in the course of "a-maying" festivities. The maypole was banned by Cromwell, then revived by Charles II. The Victorians dumbed down the tradition by turning it into a children's custom. Children were encouraged to make a spring garland, travel around the neighbourhood, and ask for money, much like kids do on Halloween in North America.

Scudding clouds sweep over the Giant as we dawdle down the steep slope. We have time to explore today, so we hike the two miles south to Godmanstone, where we visit the Smith's Arms, reputed to be the smallest pub in England. We are not disappointed. The tiny structure is made of stone with thatch, and the front is only eleven feet wide, with just one, Hobbit-sized dining room. The building is 600 years old and used to be a smithy. When Charles II rode through the village and stopped to have his horse attended to, he asked the black-smith for a drink and was appalled to learn that the smith had no licence, so he granted him one forthwith, and it has been licensed ever since. It also offers the usual pub services: shove ha'penny, darts, table skittles, and a variety of lunches. A terrace outside is where we have to eat as part of the overflow — in fact, this is where most of the customers sit, good weather or bad.

THE SIX-MILE TREK back to Maiden Newton is miserable. Rain lashes our faces, and cars speed by dangerously on the narrow twisting road, splashing us as we dart to nonexistent verges. I look back at one point when I hear thunder, and catch a brief lightning flash on the hillside illuminating the Cerne Giant's head. Karl just presses ahead with vigorous strides. When we finally arrive at the Chalk & Cheese, we are as drenched as otters, and I am ready for a hot bath and lasagna. There is no sign of Bill.

At dinner, we talk in low tones about the walk and how it will soon be over.

"So Karl, at some point in life does one opt for a safe harbour as opposed to ongoing adventure?"

Karl contemplates me with a frown and downs some more Shiraz.

"I don't believe in safe harbours. Once you decide to pack it in with your work, your wanderings, or your hobbies, you go to pot — physically and mentally. You have to keep going. As George Burns used to say, 'Use it or lose it.' And there is no Nirvana; even quaint places have problems."

My mind focuses for a moment on an apple orchard in Somerset and a small cottage with a garden and a little picket gate with a sign reading "The Shire." In *Watership Down*, a group of rabbits search for a safe haven. Ratty advises in *The Wind in the Willows*: "Beyond the Wild Wood is the wild world" — and he's never going there. Yet even though the outer world is too much with us, most of us feel the need to press on into it. Frodo and Bilbo press on when convinced there is danger to their precious shire and a greater good to be achieved.

The storm is still raging outside and the entire inn shakes with a couple of rolling peals of thunder. Rain spatters the smoky leaded glass windows. A St. Bernard lazily shifts his position in front of the blazing fireplace.

I don't believe in safe harbours, Karl said.

I join Karl for an after-dinner brandy. Then I stumble up to bed. Through the wall, I hear Bill rasping and coughing.

Before turning out my lamp I read the latest press report on Madonna's battle to keep her estate closed to walkers. The planning inspector in Sherborne has just ruled that only 130 acres of Madonna's 1,130-acre tract will become accessible as "open country" under right to roam legislation, not 350 acres. Both sides in the dispute seem happy with this decision.[7]

Bill is now talking to someone, although I can't hear the words distinctly. Then I realize that he is quietly praying.

The second story to catch my eye in the newspaper is the conviction and sentencing of two brothers who have systematically abused a gypsy family, which is an offence under the provisions of the Race Relations Act. "Neil Shepherd, 41, a crossword compiler, and his brother Martin, 36, a psychology student, called the family 'scum' and 'vermin' as they drove past their camp beside the A350 at Blandford, Dorset," reports *The Telegraph*. A crossword compiler? A thirty-six-year-old psychology student? The family in question qualify

---

7 Madonna and Guy Ritchie have since divorced, and Madonna has given up her life on an English manor.

as travellers, and like the Romany, are a specified protected minority group under the law. These are the first convictions involving racially motivated behaviour against the traveller community.

The thunderstorm continues through the night. When Karl and I assemble for an early breakfast in the dining room, I notice streams of water cascading down the village street.

"We may want to wait for this storm to abate, Karl. I don't fancy stepping out into that maelstrom."

"Weather's supposed to improve by mid-morning, John. Let's go. We have to get to the coast."

Before we leave I need to call our B&B at Abbotsbury — our final destination — because we will be arriving a day earlier than expected, and I have booked rooms only for the following night. So after breakfast I use the pay phone at the Chalk & Cheese to ring up the establishment.

"Hello, it's Mr. Cherrington here, and we have a booking to stay at Farley Lodge for the fifteenth of June, and I'd like to book an additional night now for the fourteenth, as we are going to arrive a day early. You see, we are walking the Macmillan Way."

"What, you want to change your booking, sir?"

"No, I'd like to book one extra night, please."

"What is your name, sir?"

"Cherrington."

"I will have to check the booking sheet, sir." The pay phone beeps to prompt me for more coins.

"Are you there, sir?"

"Yes, I'm here."

"I am sorry, sir, but I must check out some guests. Could you call back in twenty minutes?"

"Uh, sure."

Twenty minutes later . . . "Hello, Farley Lodge."

"Yes, it's Mr. Cherrington again."

"Yes, sir."

"Can you confirm my booking now?"

"Confirm, sir?"

"Yes."

"You wanted the fourteenth of June, you said?"

"Yes, but I'm booked for the fifteenth already and would like the same room for both nights."

"I was going to check and see if we had you down for the fifteenth, sir."

"Yes, you were." The pay phone beeps for more coins.

Silence; then I hear a rustling of paper.

Finally, a gushing torrent: "Oh, sir, sir!" the woman cries. "Why, I've located you in the book! It's Mr. Cherrington, correct?"

Can orgasm be far behind?

"Uh, that's great."

"You're booked for Room 7, sir."

"Okay."

"Yes, sir, it's a twin room."

"I know that."

Silence again.

"So, ma'am, how about the fourteenth, then — am I booked for the extra night as well?"

"Oh, right, you'd now like the fourteenth, wouldn't you. Do you still want the fifteenth, sir?"

"Look, how many times do I have to tell you — I want the fourteenth *and* the fifteenth. Twin room — okay?"

"Sorry, sir, you don't have to get angry. I am doing the very best I can."

The phone beeps for more coins.

"Please, ma'am, please just tell me that we are now booked for the fourteenth and the fifteenth."

"Well, it would seem fine, sir, but I will of course need your credit card number to hold the room for both nights."

"But you already have my Visa number from my earlier booking!"

"Sorry, sir, it is not showing up—" The phone connection cuts out, as I have run out of coins.

After obtaining more change at the pub, I return to do battle.

"Farley Lodge."

"It's me again, Mr. Cherrington. I'm sorry that we were cut off."

"Well, sir, you didn't have to hang up on me like that!"

"Please! I didn't hang up — can't you see that I'm in a phone booth on the Macmillan Way and it cuts off when I run out of coins . . ."

"I see, sir."

"Yes, quite. Now here is my Visa number—"

"Sir, I'm afraid you cannot have the same room for the fourteenth as the fifteenth, as your Room 7 has been previously booked by another party. Do you want a different room for the fourteenth?"

"Please God! Yes, of course I do. I am so sorry for all of this."

Indeed, it was all my fault. As the learned Anglo-Afghan writer Idries Shah — himself a naturalized Englishman — observes, "It is normal practice in England not to answer anything directly. Standard practice too, is not to ask direct questions: it is considered aggressive to assume that the other person can, should or will answer at all. The correct form if compelled to approach another for help, is to start with 'Excuse me, I wonder whether . . .'" And this clearly had been my sin. Instead of charging ahead and boldly demanding my rights, as one does in North America, I should have delicately asked the lady to pardon my behaviour and requested her — nay, begged her — to perhaps accommodate us, if at all possible, without undue inconvenience to her, the staff, or other guests, with a room for both nights. One learns, but slowly.

Karl laughs at my *Fawlty Towers* encounter.

"We've dallied long enough, John. Time to heft packs."

Just as we prepare to embark, Bill rattles down the stairs and into the dining room. His dog follows at his heel.

"I am afraid we have to be on our way, Bill," I say.

"Oh dear, nine o'clock already; why, I must have overslept!" His dog looks up at me accusingly, as if I am leaving him and his master in the lurch, alone at the breakfast table.

Then Bill embraces Karl and me both, and wishes us a safe journey.

"Cheers, Bill. Take care of yourself," I say.

He waves from his window seat as we pass by, and we wave back with our walking sticks. I can see his blue eyes twinkling, though. A good, kind man, undaunted by life's cruel twists.

"Poor chap," says Karl. "All alone with just his dog."

I muse over the fact that we embraced one another on departing without even knowing each other's last names. I think of Pat at Big Thatch, who also hugged us both.

The rain has finally ceased. Our route follows a wide track out of Maiden Newton, with the landscape rapidly changing to wide, flowing uplands of grass crops interspersed with little copses.

It is a steep hike to reach a bridleway that merges with the Dorset Jubilee Trail, a 90-mile regional path. Ahead are great views, with the 72-foot-high Hardy Monument clearly visible to our left. This high landmark that so proudly adorns the hill commemorates not Thomas Hardy but rather Captain Thomas Masterman Hardy, to whom Nelson, as he lay dying at Trafalgar, whispered, "Kiss me, Hardy." When Nelson expired, Captain Hardy commanded the return to England of the surviving fleet.

England has been and continues to be defined by the sea. The ocean facilitated the empire, proving that a small land mass was irrelevant provided that a nation could establish a strong navy and a strong trading regimen. The Battle of Trafalgar was the decisive sea battle, forcing Napoleon to abandon his attempts to conquer England, the Middle East, and other environs, and marked the beginning of the end of his rule. Captain Hardy went on to become a rear admiral and later, in 1830, First Lord of the Admiralty. The Hardy Monument was erected in 1844 to both commemorate his achievements and serve as a navigational aid for shipping. The tower is octagonal and resembles a spyglass, with the corners representing the eight points of the compass.

From this high point I marvel at the Dorset Downs and the picturesque patchwork fields, much like scenes from children's stories — the curves so graceful, the fields tidy and neat, the villages all quiet and ordered, with no sprawl. Thomas Hardy's Valley of the Black Vale lies glimmering like a pearl to the east.

The *Guide* advises to "walk down a pleasant sunken lane with, in high summer, many butterflies and the scent of camomile. Beware of deep ruts in tract." Well, those deep ruts are filled with water this morning after the storm, and it requires some occasional balancing acts to avoid them. Still, the capricious sun is appearing now and then from under a cirrus blanket. Cattle and sheep dot the steep hillsides; pheasants strut; curlews, rooks, and magpies circle and squawk about; and from this neolithic ridgeway, one is very much on top of the world.

Myriad round-barrowed neolithic burial chambers abound. The key one is a Bronze Age site known as the Kingston Russell Stone Circle, comprising eighteen low stones. It can scarcely be coincidence that this circle exists precisely at a point where no fewer than five public footpaths converge. No one can convince me that ancient man had no appreciation for art and aesthetics. At the highest point of White Hill, we have incredible views over Abbotsbury to the Channel, including the long line of Chesil Beach with the lagoons of the Fleet, and even the peninsula of Portland Bill beyond to the east. The sea at last!

The last three miles of the Way take us steeply downhill at first, over freshly trimmed fields still wet from the thunderstorm. Then the path descends sharply into a large ravine, where we follow a stream bed. The *Guide* cautions here, "Despair not if things seem jungly, as path suddenly emerges into pleasant, small grassy water-meadows." Yeah, right.

Just over a mile from Abbotsbury, we become hopelessly lost in the swamps. All about us are tentacle-like branches with lichens, ivy, moss, bracken, and fungus — a tangled primeval soup. We are immersed in Tolkien's Mirkwood! Karl halts and peers in dismay at the tangled morass of marshy woods ahead.

"Do you know where you are going?"

"No, Karl, and I don't see any footpath; we've been following some fox trail."

"We can't be far from a road; hell, it's only a couple of miles to the Channel!"

Karl pulls out his compass and we straggle through the quagmire in a southerly direction, getting muddier and wetter by the minute as we traverse boggy patches. At one point my boots sink up to the ankles in quicksand and I have to grab a vine maple branch to pull free.

We finally emerge from Mirkwood up a tiny dirt lane, and from here manage to reconnect with the Macmillan on a hillock beside some startled ewes, where we stand catching our breath. I hear a loud noise above and look up to see an enormous military helicopter hovering above us like some silver dragonfly contemplating its insect prey. After a long few seconds, it finally moves on toward the Channel, only to be followed by a second copter that zooms down to have a look at us. It reminds me of that opening scene in Hitchcock's *North by Northwest*. I yell to Karl that we are being targeted.

"Don't pay any attention, John — they're just practising their rocket launcher settings for Afghanistan."

I AGAIN REFLECT that in England there prevails an acute awareness of the sacrifices made in two world wars. The annual re-enactment of battles staged by Maiden Newton is another reminder of those sacrifices. There is quite a dichotomy between rural and urban collective memories in this regard. It is the hinterland that stores the memories; and it is in the hinterland where the military maintain a constant presence. In the Cotswolds, we watched as vast numbers of military transport planes droned by to land at some nondescript airfield near Cheltenham. Military bases lie discreetly hidden in the countryside and there are mysterious comings and goings at all hours of the night. The Royal Navy too is omnipresent — in the Channel, the Irish Sea, and the North Sea — probing, patrolling, protecting the shores. England may not be the great power it once was, but its compact fighting force seems very much at the ready.

One more stile and we are through a field and across the main street of Abbotsbury. This village of five hundred inhabitants very much caters to tourists. Our B&B can wait, as we are on a mission to dip our feet in the English Channel to complete our Macmillan walk. We limp by the Abbotsbury Tithe Barn, touted as the largest thatched building in the world. The final leg before we reach the sea is a climb up Chapel Hill. The path is covered with sheep shit. No matter — at the summit stands St. Catherine's Chapel.

The chapel belonged to a Benedictine abbey established by King Cnut a few years before the Norman invasion. The abbey has disappeared, and only the tithe barn and this chapel remain. The structure is constructed of ochre-tinted limestone, with a parapet, turret, and heavy buttresses. The abbey monks used the chapel as a retreat. After the Dissolution in 1539, it became a navigational aid and shrine. The dedication of this chapel to St. Catherine is interesting. St. Catherine was a high-born and scholarly Christian lady of ancient Alexandria. After torture on a wheel, she was beheaded during the persecutions of the Emperor Maximus in 290. She was widely venerated in the Middle Ages and considered the patron saint of spinsters. This is why women seeking husbands came here and recited the following prayer, which we find inscribed inside the chapel:

A husband, St. Catherine;
A handsome one, St. Catherine;
A rich one, St. Catherine;
A nice one, St. Catherine;
And soon, St. Catherine!

Below us stretches the long curving wedge of Chesil Beach. The sun is waning in the west. An approaching wall of fog from the Channel heightens the contrast and drama. The English have a saying when conditions for boating are inclement in the English Channel: "A pity — now the Continent will be cut off."

KARL LIMPS one last painful mile from St. Catherine's Chapel toward Chesil Beach. With his bad ankle, he is leaning heavily on his walking stick. Herring gulls swoop and squawk overhead. The tide is out. Fog is rolling in.

Our boots crunch the billions of rounded stones and pebbles that comprise the beach. Flotsam and jetsam abound: a dinghy's painter line, a rowboat panel, yellow rope, green netting. There is also the unsightly detritus of holidayers and weekenders: empty water bottles, popsicle sticks, cigarette packages, an old shotgun shell, nappies, a Nivea Care bottle, Styrofoam coffee cups, a small plastic Bombay Gin bottle, a battered toothpaste tube. Flanking the beach is a flowery meadow area intersected by sand dunes reminiscent of *Summer of '42*.

I shiver a little as we stumble our way over the rocks to the grey water. Winter storms here can be ferocious. Villagers say that one can determine the sea conditions and pending weather from listening to the drawing sounds of the pebbles on Chesil Beach in the evening.

Karl is now quietly doffing his boots and socks. He limps forward to plant his toes in the cold sea water. I follow with the same ritual. Then, as we stand there, the mist unexpectedly parts and we glimpse the grey outline of a British destroyer slowly knifing its way through the fog, appearing like a ghostly mirage before our eyes. The realm, I muse, is ever protected by the Royal Navy.

It is a poignant moment. I stuff my pockets with a few of the ubiquitous flints and cherts glistening on the beach. We then begin a slow trek back to the B&B in the village. Neither of us has said a word on Chesil Beach.

KARL IS STILL PENSIVE as we dig into a fish pie at a village pub. From a corner near the massive stone fireplace, a fiddler entertains us with stirring Irish ballads. When the red-faced fellow puts down his instrument, the mellow jazz of John Coltrane kicks in from the overhead speakers. The pub is all one could wish for — fine spirits, ale, and food; copious rows of pump handles; brass vessels hanging on medieval walls; a roaring log fire; good music; and only a few quiet patrons lingering over their ale and port.

"Karl, you ought to get that ankle looked at soon. It looks painful."

Karl ignores the remark. "It's good to be alive," he replies instead. "I feel privileged to have tramped all those miles — and could do it again."

Aside from the achievement of his conquering Macmillan Way physically, it is clear that the walk has altered Karl in other ways. He talks fervently of history, of culture, of different ways of seeing things. He even intends to pick up the complete works of Thomas Hardy. This was a personal mission for him as much as for me. He seems ageless — a compact, rugged character with a generous heart who still loves challenge and adventure.

Yet it is not exactly an evening of sybaritic delight, as both of us soon become immersed in our own thoughts. I calculate that we have walked about 365 miles, including the diversions. Not a great physical feat — the famed Land's End to John o' Groats walk is 1,200 miles. Moreover, we have taken some twenty-six days in leisurely fashion, whereas Colin of

Derbyshire surely completed Macmillan in just under two weeks. Yet it has been a profoundly moving and humbling experience.

We linger over dinner, then Karl orders his usual cherry brandy nightcap. Five minutes later, he ambles up to the bar and returns with two foaming pints of Guinness.

"Don't be so sombre, John boy. We did it — the whole bloody Macmillan Way. And it's therefore time for one last pint."

"To the walk!" he roars. We clink glasses.

"And to Cadbury Castle," I intone. Karl raises his glass again, then pauses. Loreena McKennitt's soft Celtic voice is purring "The Lady of Shalott" overhead.

"Say what's in your heart, John," he says, his blue eyes twinkling. "To Camelot," he adds spiritedly, and we clink glasses a second time.

I am lost in reverie for a few moments. The magic is broken when Karl suddenly raises the subject of Tiffany again. Should we be getting in touch with the Oakham police to see if they have made any progress on the case?

"Karl, I promise that I will contact the constabulary by email upon return to Canada, and follow up on it. That's all we can do."[8]

He frowns and downs the last dregs of his brew.

---

[8] As for the mysterious Tiffany, the police never got back to us, but on March 13, 2009, a jury found London cab driver John Worboys guilty of drugging and sexually assaulting twelve women in his cab. He is suspected of having assaulted more than one hundred women between 2002 and 2007 in London and environs. Seventy-one women have come forward to make complaints against him. Although it is only speculation that Tiffany was one of his victims, the timeline certainly fits. There is of course also the possibility of more than one taxi-cab rapist at large. Tiffany may be simply one more unreported runaway whose fate will never be known.

AFTERWORD

EVERY DAY OF our walk we discovered powerful vestiges of
the past: neolithic megaliths; Celtic resistance to Romans;
Roman villas and roads; King Arthur and Camelot; Saxon
chapels; Viking names and traditions from the Danelaw;
Norman churches and architecture; the ravages of civil war —
Parliament against King; village pride and medieval customs,
such as fairs and athletic competitions; Victorian achievements like Brunel's railways and canals; countryside change,
ruin, resistance, and resilience; the painful scars of two world
wars. From ancient barrows to World War II bunkers, every era
was represented. We even followed the Jurassic belt of rock
that has so defined central England — reminder of a geological
age of cataclysm that ushered in life, teeming and abundant,
much of it embedded in Cotswold stone.

Along the length of a slender footpath we encountered
an astonishing array of historical figures: Queen Boadicea,
King Arthur, King Alfred, King John, Sir Walter Raleigh,
Samuel Pepys, Charles I, Oliver Cromwell, Charles II, George III,
Alexander Pope, John Dryden, Jane Austen, Thomas Hardy,

Isambard Kingdom Brunel, Siegfried Sassoon, Edward Thomas, John Steinbeck, Ralph Vaughan Williams, Princess Diana, Camilla, and Prince Charles, all of whom are part of the historical tapestry of Macmillan Way — not to mention countless lesser luminaries such as Parson Woodforde, Queen Matilda, George Washington's ancestors, John Cotton, Charles Fox, John Masefield, J.B. Priestley, and Stewart Menzies.

Along the Way, we met warm, generous people, many of whom opened their homes and hearts to us and who were careful to never give offence. And everywhere on our journey we found a quiet acceptance of life by England's rural residents — plus a certain reticence, a hesitation to be too critical of others, and a reluctance to wave the flag.

We discovered an astonishing independence of thought and defiance of authority: bottle kicking at Hallaton; the sauciness of Whitwell villagers twinning their flyspeck hamlet with Paris; the rebellious Banbury folk with their Lady Godiva statue and Hobby Horse Festival debaucheries; Morris dancing run amok; the gypsies of Stow carrying on the tradition of a horse fair in defiance of court orders; woolsack-racing madness in Tetbury; Yetties in Dorset maintaining folk-song tradition; the fierce protection by villagers of the Cerne Abbas Giant; a Castle Combe resident blowing up an artificial dam that spoiled the look of the village; and the civil disobedience of Rutlanders in demanding their separate little county. Not to mention country marches on Westminster to protest the fox-hunting ban, fights against culling of animals — whether they be badgers or hedgehogs — and countryside Ramblers policing the public's right to walk the footpaths. It's live and let live — but don't dare interfere with our privacy, our wildlife, our green spaces, or our country customs.

THE ENGLISH FOOTPATH is symbolic of the resistance of the English to change but also a symbol of enshrined liberty in the eyes of the common folk. Sovereigns and governments come and go. The Industrial Revolution despoiled much of the landscape; the Enclosure movement barred access to vast areas of tillable soil. But the inherent right of passage represented by the footpath lives on — and will be fiercely defended by Ramblers and others who regard this as a sacred entitlement, the legacy of every citizen. The hills, the fields, the wolds, the moors — all are part of the land over which free people may roam, mainly on legal footpaths, green lanes, and bridleways.

The footpath restores, energizes, and connects with some things lost. It is a tunnel to the past and a link to the future. Myriad spidery footpath networks underpin the nation, the gossamer acting like glue, embedding the very history of the land into the consciousness of a people. In a fast-paced world of change, it is vital that a people remain grounded, so that amid the clash and clang of metal on the highway, the buzz of electronics, the swoosh of a jet fighter overhead, the peace of the path will always be there for contemplation and solace. And the path will remain in one's memory forever.

In *Nineteen Eighty-Four*, George Orwell's hero, Winston, yearns for a landscape he dubs the Golden Country. The Golden Country can be reached by a footpath through a lovely park-like countryside. It is here that Winston is able to meet with his lover, Julia, beyond the watchful eyes of the state and its ubiquitous telescreens. As Kim Taplin notes in *The English Path*, "If we want the Golden Country to exist outside the imagination, we must keep the paths to it open."

Some walking days are arduous, though one never remembers the icy rain; the slogging through muddy fields where the path disappears; the scrapes, the bruises, and the blisters and sprains. The joy of each day's discovery outweighs all of that. Robert Louis Stevenson writes in his essay "Walking Tours" that at the end of the walk you might question yourself as to whether you have been the "wisest philosopher or the most egregious of donkeys . . . but at least you have had a fine moment, and looked down upon all the kingdoms of the earth."

The path also resonates in another way. In *The Lord of the Rings,* Tolkien writes that "Bilbo used to say there was only one Road; that it was like a great river: its springs were at every doorstep, and every path was its tributary." But the road and the path also represent the cohesion of all life, since even the tiniest footpath in the shire leads to distant and often sinister places. It is often comfier to stay in one's willowed brook or shire, but the wider world awaits, to be explored, tasted, and perhaps improved. And it is the footpath that represents the way out. So the Macmillan Way is very special. It unlocks doors. And for me, it also proves the truth of the adage *Solvitur ambulando* — you can sort it out by walking.

ACKNOWLEDGMENTS

A number of people contributed to make this book possible.

First, many thanks to my literary agent, Robert Mackwood, who never lost faith in the project.

My chief editor, Scott Steedman, worked indefatigably to improve the manuscript, and it was fun working with him. I will forgive Scott for favouring soccer over hockey. Stephanie Fysh, my copy editor, showed thorough and often piercing insight into textual matters. She is a true professional.

Thanks to the entire publishing team: Chris Labonté has assembled a talented group, including my ever helpful managing editor, Lara Smith; media savvy Mark Redmayne, who coached me into learning some of the finer points of social media; and book designer Natalie Olsen.

Thanks to Peter Titchmarsh, who facilitated the creation of the Macmillan Way, despite many obstacles from recalcitrant landowners.

My friend and walking companion Dave Green provided valuable insights on the manuscript and my thanks to him also for his impressions of English rural life.

To Karl Yzerman, surely the Al Pacino of long-distance walkers, my heartfelt thanks for so many enjoyable hours of rural walking adventures. Karl was the inspiration for this book.

Last but not least, thanks to my wife, Dee, who as always provided valuable critiques of the manuscript and encouraged me along the way.

CHAPTER NOTES

Quotations from the *Guide* are from Peter Titchmarsh, *The Macmillan Way: The 290-Mile Coast-to-Coast Path from Boston to Abbotsbury* (Ipswich, UK: The Macmillan Way Association, 2003).

INTRODUCTION

"That village, so often near a Roman road, is sometimes clearly a Saxon hamlet": H.V. Morton, *In Search of England* (London, 1927).

"For all the drawbacks of rural life and its tough and uncompromising history": Joanna Trollope, "The country we love," *The Telegraph* (March 1, 1998), reprinted in *The Hedgerows Heaped with May: The Telegraph Book of the Countryside*, edited by Stephen Moss (London, 2012).

"These by-paths . . . admit the wayfarer into the very heart of rural life, and yet do not burden him": Nathaniel Hawthorne, "Leamington Spa," in *Our Old Home* (Boston, 1883).

"right of . . . thoroughfare on his land for every vagabond": George Eliot, *The Mill on the Floss* (Edinburgh and London, 1860).

CHAPTER ONE

"There are certain things that happen at nature reserves": in "Amorous birdwatchers get back to nature," *The Telegraph* (August 6, 2009), reprinted in *The Hedgerows Heaped with May*.

"Realism; fatalism; phlegm. To live in the Fens is to receive strong doses of reality": Graham Swift, *Waterland* (London, 1983).

In fact, the great drainage schemes of the eighteenth century: Marion Shoard, in her book *The Theft of the Countryside* (London, 1980), argues that with the removal of trees, bushes, and hedgerows over the centuries of reclamation schemes, the Lincolnshire Fens are now "just a production line for food products."

"a cluster of lavatory brushes in the sky": Sir Bernard Ingham, quoted by Robert Bedlow in "Sir Bernard takes a tilt at windmills," *The Hedgerows Heaped with May*.

"Badger hates society, and invitations, and dinner, and all that sort of thing": Kenneth Grahame, *The Wind in the Willows* (London, 1908).

"I can only teach you two things — to dig, and to love your home": T.H. White, *The Once and Future King* (London, 1958).

"little water vole": Stella Gibbons, *Cold Comfort Farm* (London, 1932).

"Feather-footed through the plashy fens passes the questing vole": Evelyn Waugh, *Scoop* (London, 1938).

"Every British animal has its cheerleaders": Sarah Lyall, *The Anglo Files* (New York, 2008).

"read it and reread it": in Alison Flood, "First edition of *The Wind in the Willows* sells for £32,400," *The Guardian* (March 24, 2010).

"I am nervous; I am not ill, but I am nervous": King George III, quoted by Frances Burney in her court journal for 1788, published after her death as *The Diary and Letters of Madame D'Arblay*.

"men who are ceaselessly battered by the wind and rain": Pierre Daninos, "Contradictions" (1957), reprinted in *In a Fog: The Humorists' Guide to England*, edited by Robert Wechsler (Highland Park, NJ, 1989).

CHAPTER TWO

"Few other peoples lavished so much money on charity as the British": Ben Wilson, *The Making of Victorian Values* (London, 2007).

"There are few things which give such a feeling of the prosperity of the country": William Howitt, *The Rural Life of England* (London, 1838).

The spirit of the Celts was epitomized by this brave woman: Tacitus, *The Annals* (AD 110–120), translated by Alfred John Church and William Jackson Brodribb (London, 1888).

"In the course of a day's walk, you see, there is much variance in the mood": Robert Louis Stevenson, "Walking tours," *The Cornhill Magazine* (1876) and *Virginibus Puerisque, and Other Papers* (London, 1881), available at grammar.about.com/od/classicessays/a/walkingtouressay_2htm.

"If you see something along the way that you want to touch with your mindfulness": Thich Nhat Hanh, *The Long Road Turns to Joy* (New York, 1996).

"white narrow roads rutted by hooves and cartwheels, innocent of oil or petrol": Laurie Lee, *Cider with Rosie* (London, 1959).

CHAPTER THREE

"Roads, lanes, paths": Geoffrey Grigson, *Freedom of the Parish* (London, 1954).

"It is a great day for me, sir . . . I have established a right of way": Sir Arthur Conan Doyle, *The Hound of the Baskervilles* (London, 1902).

"but they don't want to be near the nasty niffs and noises": Ian Johnson, quoted in Audrey Gillan, "You don't get country folk moving to London and demanding that they stop the buses," *The Telegraph* (July 19, 1998), reprinted in *The Hedgerows Heaped with May.*

"In Britain, identifiably, there is a persistent rural-intellectual radicalism": Raymond Williams, *The Country and the City* (London, 1973).

"Is there no nook of English ground secure": William Wordsworth, "On the Projected Kendal and Windermere Railway" (1844).

"unfreedom of the villein or serf was never a generalized condition": Frances and Joseph Gies, *Life in a Medieval Village* (New York, 1989).

"One spot shall prove beloved over all": Rudyard Kipling, "Sussex" (1902).

"Laws for themselves and not for me": A.E. Housman, "The Laws of God, the Laws of Man," in *A Shropshire Lad* (Oxford, 1896).

CHAPTER FOUR

"Would you tell me, please, which way I ought to go from here?": Lewis Carroll, *Alice in Wonderland* (London, 1865).

"stock exchange, his reading-room, his club": Richard Jefferies, "The labourer's daily life," *Fraser's Magazine* (November 1874).

"nurseries of naughtiness": James Moore and Paul Nero, *Ye Olde Good Inn Guide: A Tudor Traveller's Guide to the Nation's Finest Taverns* (Stroud, 2013).

The writer A.A. Gill decries the Trust: A.A. Gill, *The Angry Island Hunting the English* (London, 2005).

"That in the beginning of June, 1741, he observed a Man": Bill of 1744 to Dissolve a Marriage, *Journals of the House of Lords*, Vol. 26.

"where a footpath diverged from the highroad": E.M. Forster, *A Room with a View* (London, 1908).

"Woods, where we hid from the wet": Alfred Lord Tennyson, "Marriage Morning," in *The Window* (London, 1871).

CHAPTER FIVE

"rides on his foot, slung over his knee": *Mary Gladstone (Mrs. Drew): Her Diaries and Letters*, edited by L. Masterman (London, 1930).

"Blisters? Simply make a lather of soap suds inside your socks and break a raw egg": Francis Galton, *The Art of Travel* (London, 1872).

"continuous zeal": in *A History of the County of Oxford*, Volume 10, *Banbury Hundred*, edited by Alan Crossley ([London], 1972).

"They are the only people in the world who think of jam and currants as thrilling": Bill Bryson, *Notes from a Small Island* (London, 1993).

"He halted again and bought from the old applewoman two Banbury cakes": James Joyce, *Ulysses* (Paris, 1922).

"The moodiness makes for lovely landscape painting": Lyall, *The Anglo Files*.

"He to whom the present is the only thing that is present": Oscar Wilde, "The Critic as Artist," in *Intentions* (London, 1891).

"You must come down for the weekend": *Dreaming of Toad Hall*, produced by Emily Williams, presented by John O'Farrell (BBC Radio 4, 2008).

"The Bluebell is the sweetest flower": Emily Brontë, "The Bluebell," in *Poems by Currer, Ellis, and Acton Bell* (1846).

"A couple of flitches of bacon are worth fifty thousand Methodist sermons": William Cobbett, *Cottage Economy* (1823).

"Under the soil the old fish to lie. Twenty years he lived, and then did die": John Timpson, *Timpson's England: A Look beyond the Obvious* (London, 1994).

CHAPTER SIX

"Two roads diverged in a yellow wood": Robert Frost, "The Road Not Taken," in *Mountain Interval* (New York, 1916).

"Much has been written of travel": Edward Thomas, *The Icknield Way* (London, 1913).

"The idea of a village, romantically dishevelled": Linda Proud, *Consider England* (London, 1994).

"And was Jerusalem builded here": William Blake, "And Did Those Feet in Ancient Time," in preface to *Milton a Poem* (London, 1811).

"the country house came to represent an ideal of English civilization": Roger Scruton, *England: An Elegy* (London, 2000).

"intersected, blast it, by a public footpath": E.M. Forster, "My Wood" (first published, 1926; reprinted in *Abinger Harvest*, London, 1936).

"paddocks and swimming pools and pheasant shoots": Gill, *The Angry Island*.

"brilliant at running a corner shop": Paul Theroux, *The Kingdom by the Sea: A Journey around the Coast of Great Britain* (London, 1983).

"The picture of the rural life of England must be wholly defective": William Howitt, *The Rural Life of England* (1838).

"We see death coming into our midst like black smoke": Jeuan Gethin, quoted in David Miles, *The Tribes of Britain* (London, 2005).

"Even when the sun is obscured and the light is cold": J.B. Priestley, *English Journey* (London, 1934).

"a huddle of warm-looking Jurassic stone houses, clustered amicably": Simon Winchester, *The Map That Changed the World: The Tale of William Smith and the Birth of a Science* (London, 2001).

"one of these enchanted little valleys, these misty cups of verdure and grey walls": Priestley, *English Journey*.

CHAPTER SEVEN

"compleatly fitted up and accomodated for the Entertainment of Gentlemen": in "History of the Bear Inn," www.hares-antiques.com.

"bitter Mohammedan gruel": Matthew Green, *The Lost World of the London Coffeehouse* (London, 2013), also at publicdomainreview.org/2013/08/07/the-lost-world-of-the-london-coffeehouse/.

"I am with Lord Bathurst, at my bower": Alexander Pope, letter to Martha Blount (October 1716); Pope, letter to Martha and Teresa Blount (October 1718); and Pope, letter to Robert Digby (1722), in *The Works of Alexander Pope: Correspondence* (London, 1886).

"Within a limited radius one encounters some remarkable diversion": Bill Bryson, *The English Landscape* (London, 2000).

"I must go down to the seas again, to the lonely sea and the sky": John Masefield, "Sea-Fever," in *Salt-Water Ballads* (London, 1902).

"It is the place where you eat, drink, commiserate, flirt, laugh": Jeremy Paxman, *The English* (London, 1998).

CHAPTER EIGHT

"Roused to still greater excitement, the mob was led up the hill": David Bick, *Old Leckhampton* (Cheltenham, 1994).

"biologically sustainable farming linked to conservation": The Prince's Highgrove garden is a mélange of organic utilitarianism and aesthetical delight. In his recently published *Highgrove: A Garden Celebrated* (London, 2014, with Bunny Guinness), the future king reflects that each part of his garden is a "separate painting and the result of ceaseless walking, ruminating and observing those moments of magic when the light becomes almost dreamlike in its illuminating intensity."

"Life is a game of two halves": Chris Hastings and Elizabeth Day, "Churches heed the prayers of football fans," *The Telegraph* (June 13, 2004).

"We are not helpless young ladies in these parts, nor yet timorous": Anthony Trollope, *The Last Chronicle of Barset*, Vol. 1 (London, 1867).

"A hole into which drunken and bleeding men were thrust": Charles
   Dickens, *Barnaby Rudge: A Tale of the Riots of Eighty*, serialized in
   Master Humphrey's Clock (1841).
"One need not be a mystic to accept that certain old paths are linear":
   Robert Macfarlane, *The Old Ways* (London, 2012).

CHAPTER NINE

"It kind of feels like losing a loved one": in Michael Powell, "Royal Navy's
   old workhorse makes her final voyage," *The News* (Portsmouth)
   (August 3, 2012).
"Inns of good dimension and repute": Albany Poyntz, quoted in Thomas
   Burke, *The English Inn* (London, 1930).
"France was a lady, Russia was a bear": Siegfried Sassoon, quoted in Frank
   Chapman, "War poet was tasty with bat," *Kent and Sussex Courier*
   (December 10, 2010).
"The half-smile is the fruit of your awareness that you are here": Thich
   Nhat Hanh, *The Long Road Turns to Joy: A Guide to Walking Meditation*
   (Berkeley, Calif., 1996).
"May the fumes suffocate Squire Trevor-Battye": Eleanor Farjeon, *Edward
   Thomas, the Last Four Years* (London, 1958).
"The peace I have dreamed about is here, a real thing": John Steinbeck, to
   Ero (March 30, 1959), in *Steinbeck, A Life in Letters*, edited by Elaine
   Steinbeck and Robert Wallsten (London, 1976).
"The other night I discovered": Steinbeck, to Elizabeth Otis (June 17, 1959),
   in Jackson J. Benson, *John Steinbeck, Writer: A Biography* (New York,
   1984).
"I read Prayers this morning at C. Cary Church": James Woodforde, *The
   Diary of a Country Parson, 1758–1802* (Oxford, 1935, reprinted Norwich,
   1999).
"Miss Mary Donne is a very genteel, pretty young Lady": *Ibid.*
"We had for Dinner to day one Fowl boiled and Piggs face": *Ibid.*
"Whilst I was preaching": *Ibid.*

CHAPTER TEN

"myth, legend, and the land of faeries": Susan Toth, *My Love Affair with
   England: A Traveler's Memoir* (New York, 1992).
"beyond them a far green country": J.R.R. Tolkien, *The Lord of the Rings:
   Return of the King* (London, 1955).
"To sail beyond the sunset, and the baths / Of all the western stars": Alfred
   Lord Tennyson, "Ulysses," in *Poems* (London, 1842).

"I turned flat west by a little chapelle": John Leland, *The Itinerary of John Leland in or about the Years 1535–1543* (London, 1907).

"At the very south ende of the chirch of South-Cadbyri": *Ibid.*

"Camelot is a noted place; it is a noble fortification of the Romans": William Stukeley, *Itinerarium Curiosum* (1776), quoted in Leslie Alcock, *By South Cadbury Is That Camelot: Excavations at Cadbury Castle 1966–70* (London, 1975).

"Cadbury Castle has few equals among British hillforts": Alcock, *By South Cadbury.*

"was the principal building — the feasting hall, in fact": *Ibid.*

"The figure of Arthur remains, as it always will, a symbol of British history": Michael Wood, *In Search of England* (London, 1999).

"Yesterday something wonderful. It was a golden day": John Steinbeck, letter to Ero and Chase Horton, May 1, 1959, in Appendix, John Steinbeck, *The Acts of King Arthur and His Noble Knights* (London, 1976).

"And did those feet in ancient time": Blake, in preface to *Milton a Poem.*

"It may seem peculiar but if I am wearing my farming cap I would certainly not like our badgers culled": John Kerton, Letter to the Editor, *This Is Dorset* (December 17, 2010).

CHAPTER ELEVEN

"little lines / Of sportive wood run wild": William Wordsworth, "Lines Composed a Few Miles above Tintern Abbey, on Revisiting the Banks of the Wye during a Tour, July 13, 1798," in *Lyrical Ballads* (London, 1798).

"We could never have loved the earth as well": George Eliot, *The Mill on the Floss* (London, 1860).

"stocked with thyme and parsley and sage": Flora Thompson, *Lark Rise to Candleford* (Oxford, 1939–43).

"as in a graven image": Edward Thomas, *The South Country* (London, 1906).

"hobbit of the garden; the sprite of the window box": Gill, *The Angry Island.*

"if the town were a woman": in Sunday Mercury, "Buzzing boutique hotel in Dorset is becoming a must-visit for foodies," *Birmingham Mail* (October 20, 2012).

"riotous expenses and unlawful games": S.H. Burton, *A West Country Anthology* (London, 1975).

"journeymen out for a holiday, a stray soldier or two": Thomas Hardy, *The Mayor of Casterbridge* (London, 1886).

"If all the world and love were young": Sir Walter Raleigh, "The Nymph's Reply to the Shepherd" (first published 1600).

"she battered a pheasant to death recently": in David Harrison, "RSPCA militants want to drop Queen over her support for hunting," *The Telegraph* (June 13, 2004).

"When the war times came we had Americans in Melbury Park": Diana Mitchell, "My Childhood Memories," The Francis Frith Collection, www.francisfrith.com.

"One of the benefits of colder weather is that it encourages men to cover up": in "Bad togs and Englishmen," *The Telegraph* (May 23, 2004).

"not at the Sow and Acorn, for she avoided inns": Thomas Hardy, *Tess of the D'Urbervilles* (London, 1891)

"Ding-dong, ding-dong, went the bells of the village church": Thompson, *Lark Rise to Candleford.*

"Every village has its idiosyncrasy": Hardy, *Tess of the D'Urbervilles.*

CHAPTER TWELVE

Thomas Hardy refers to such a Wessex character: Thomas Hardy, "The Withered Arm," in *Wessex Tales* (London, 1888).

"the most obscure edible object produced in Britain today": Adam Edwards, "Le knob est arrivé," *The Telegraph* (February 23, 2002).

"Beyond the Wild Wood is the wild world": Grahame, *The Wind in the Willows.*

"Neil Shepherd, 41, a crossword compiler": Richard Savill, "Gipsies victims of race crime," *The Telegraph* (June 12, 2004).

"It is normal practice in England not to answer anything directly": Idries Shah, *Adventures, Facts and Fantasy in Darkest England* (London, 1987).

AFTERWORD

"If we want the Golden Country to exist outside the imagination": Kim Taplin, *The English Path* (Woodbridge, UK, 1984).

"wisest philosopher or the most egregious of donkey": Robert Louis Stevenson, "Walking Tours," in *Cornhill Magazine,* 1876.

"Bilbo used to say there was only one Road": J.R.R. Tolkien, *The Lord of the Rings: The Fellowship of the Ring* (London, 1954).